PRAISE FOR ALL *H*ANDS *ON* *D*ECK

"Will Sofrin's thrilling account of the eventful, sometimes terrifying delivery of the tall ship that starred in Peter Weir's adaptation of Patrick O'Brian's *The Far Side of the World* is a must-read. Even if you haven't seen the movie or read O'Brian's novels, this is an adventure story of the highest order." —NATHANIEL PHILBRICK, author of the National Book Award-winning *In the Heart of the Sea* and *Travels with George*

"Lovers of the Aubrey-Maturin novels and the movie *Master and Commander: The Far Side of the World* will find his account a worthy addition to the salty O'Brian world we love. You don't want to miss it!" —DEAN KING, national bestselling author of *A Sea of Words*, *Patrick O'Brian: A Life Revealed*, and *Skeletons on the Zahara*

"While researching for paintings I have probably read hundreds of ships' logbooks from the glory days of the Royal Navy, just as Patrick O'Brian did, so I know what things looked like from the quarterdeck (there are very, very few surviving accounts from the crews). But with this book Will Sofrin gives us a great insight into the intense working life of the lower deck, now just as it was then, constantly battling the elements, gear failure, and sometimes each other." —GEOFF HUNT, marine artist, and illustrator of the Patrick O'Brian book covers

"*All Hands on Deck* is a fascinating read: a combination of a travelogue to distant lands, maritime history, and adventures and misadventures on the high seas. Through it all, author Will Sofrin is learning to live in tight and uncomfortable quarters on a tall ship alongside crewmembers of very divergent personalities. They ultimately form a team with the common goal of staying alive on an unforgiving and unpredictable ocean." —MICHAEL TOUGIAS, *New York Times* bestselling author of *Extreme Survival* and *A Storm Too Soon*

"A thrilling account. Readers needn't have ever set foot on a boat to enjoy this story." —TRACY EDWARDS, trailblazing round-the-world sailor

"Will Sofrin takes us on an unbelievable ride on the high seas . . . I have played pretend on the open ocean. Will Sofrin has lived the real experience and survived to tell the tale." —DAN SHOTZ, executive producer of the Emmy Award-winning Starz series *Black Sails*

"Sofrin spares little detail, making all the issues of sailing and shipbuilding much less intimidating through carefully rendered diagrams, with all parts of the ship's superstructure and complex rigging meticulously labeled. Fans of the movie and serious sailors will revel in Sofrin's tale." —BOOKLIST

"With a cast of shipmates on the replica tall ship, from bowsprit to capstan, a door is opened for the reader between a developed modern world on a well-traveled ocean route and long-gone days when it was first being sailed, written, and talked about. A lively blend of new and old adventure stories, this book bromantically and informatively bridges time on the timeless seas." —TANIA AEBI, bestselling author of *Maiden Voyage*, and the first American woman and the youngest person to sail around the world

"A tale worthy of Patrick O'Brian himself . . . *All Hands on Deck* is a vivid reminder not only of how far the sailing world has come, but also of how much we still share with the Jack Tars who came before us." —QUARTERDECK

"Sofrin's is a compelling account. Thanks to him, the experience of sailing an eighteenth-century Royal Navy frigate is now imaginable through the words on the page, and with a deep connection to the modern day, and through a writer to whom we can relate." —WOODENBOAT magazine

"Lucid, personal, funny, and instructive, it could be read next to *Two Years Before the Mast* with no apologies. Ships and times may have changed, but the sea and young souls drawn to the sea have changed but little. This story is a worthy tale of a young man and a ship and the sea. I enjoyed it immensely." —CAPTAIN DANIEL MORELAND

"With accomplished and insightful storytelling, Sofrin recounts an extraordinary, often hair-raising voyage, and in doing so reveals to readers the lives of the modern-day sailors of the big rigs." —JAMES L. NELSON, award-winning author of the Norsemen Saga and *Benedict Arnold's Navy*

"So you want to go to sea, do ya? Will Sofrin takes us aboard Rose as the vessel endures storms and near calamity. After a long delivery under the glare of Hollywood lights, Sofrin tells us what it was like to sail the seas on a tall ship. This intriguing tale will inspire you to head offshore." —GARY JOBSON, America's Cup Hall of Fame sailor

ALL HANDS ON DECK

A MODERN-DAY HIGH SEAS ADVENTURE *to the* FAR SIDE *of the* WORLD

WILL SOFRIN

ABRAMS PRESS, NEW YORK

ABRAMS The Art of Books
195 Broadway, New York, NY 10007
abramsbooks.com

For Alicia and Samantha

Contents

Technical Drawings and Tables

FOREWORD

by TOM ROTHMAN

Chairman and CEO of Sony Pictures Entertainment's Motion Picture Group

IN MY THIRTY-FIVE-PLUS-YEAR CAREER IN motion pictures, I have worked on more than four hundred films. I am often asked which is my favorite. My stock answer to that question is: "I love all my children." But that is not really true. A select few are the nearest and dearest to my heart, and *Master and Commander: The Far Side of the World* is perhaps the foremost of those. I first read and fell in love with the Patrick O'Brian books in the early 1990s when I worked at a small independent film company, the Samuel Goldwyn Company, for Sam Goldwyn, Jr., the son of the legendary co-founder of MGM, and a great film producer in his own right. Sam supported my dream to adapt O'Brian's works to the screen, and we optioned the rights, but it took more than a decade—and my becoming the co-chairman of the major film studio 20th Century Fox—before the realization of that dream became possible.

There were and are only a select few directors on earth with the skill and artistry to make a film as challenging as *Master and Commander*. I believed that Peter Weir, the filmmaker responsible for masterworks such as *Gallipoli*, *Dead Poets Society*, and *Witness*, was the singularly best man for the job. The only problem was, he didn't agree. At least not right away. Peter turned me down twice, but finally on my third approach he agreed to take command of the *Surprise* . . . provided. He would do it, provided he was supported in making a film of consummate accuracy as to life at sea in the British navy in the age of sail.

We have the ability in Hollywood to build almost any set and re-create almost any reality and could certainly have done so for a British man of war. But Peter wanted the real thing. Peter wanted the *Rose*, a real-life replica of an actual eighteenth-century Royal Navy tall ship, which he had visited and adored. And I wanted Peter. So, 20th Century Fox went into the boat business. We purchased the *Rose*. Ah, but our studio, the massive tank facility used for the filming of Jim Cameron's *Titanic*, was located in Baja, on the westernmost coast of Mexico. The *Rose* was in Newport, Rhode Island. Therein lies the tale.

Enter Will Sofrin, deckhand on the *Rose*. The distance between the two coasts, over two oceans, provides the map of the journey depicted in his book. It is complete with all the high seas drama one would hope for (and which kept us up at night in Los Angeles as we anxiously awaited word of survival and arrival and checked and rechecked our insurance policies). It is full of fascinating nuggets about O'Brian's books and the history of points along the way. But that is not what this book is *about*. Sofrin quotes O'Brian as saying that, for all their derring-do, "the essence of my books is about human relationships." So it is here. The real story of this book is the journey of a young man, who begins metaphorically at sea as much as literally so, along a path of self-discovery. Reflecting on a passed time in his life with the wisdom that comes with age, Sofrin reminds us all of the similar young times in our own lives when we looked to the horizon for answers, and sometimes found a friendly port and sometimes only empty sky. It is an entertaining passage and a profound one, because of the bonds we see formed and the growth we experience along the way.

Accordingly, this book put me in mind, on more than one occasion, of the line from the movie I still quote often to this day, which is very resonant for Sofrin's story. When things get hard at work or at home, I will say to my colleagues or family what Jack Aubrey says to the young midshipman as he picks him when he is ducking down in the face of incoming enemy fire: "We stand tall on the quarterdeck, son. *All of us.*"

*A*UTHOR'S NOTE

THIS IS A PERSONAL ACCOUNT of my experience sailing a ship called *Rose* more than six thousand miles from Newport, Rhode Island, to San Diego, California, in 2002. This was no ordinary mission, no pleasure cruise. We had to get out of Newport, down through the Atlantic and the Caribbean to the Panama Canal, then up the Pacific to California, because a production company was waiting to use *Rose* for the making of the film *Master and Commander: The Far Side of the World*. The clock was ticking, tens of millions of dollars on the line. We departed with a crew of thirty on a ship of questionable seaworthiness, came close to sinking, and could have died, all while trying to deliver a movie prop.

As a courtesy, the names and descriptions of some individuals have been changed. The experience I describe was on a replica of an eighteenth-century English Royal Navy frigate with accommodations for maritime regulations of the twenty-first century, and my descriptions of how we operated our ship are specific to how I was taught to do it on board for this journey. I say this because I know from experience that different boats may have varying methods or routines for accomplishing the same task. Much of the nomenclature used on a ship like *Rose* is archaic; even readers familiar with modern nautical terminology will encounter unfamiliar words. For this reason, I have developed and included technical drawings to help the reader visualize and understand much of the terminology specific to the operation of the ship. Additionally, the material in this book has been reviewed by many qualified professional sailors, historians, and subject-specific experts to ensure accuracy.

In his book *Mother Sea*, Elis Karlsson writes, "Nothing is impossible for God or for sailors." I believe that for one to be a great sailor requires more than the ability to set a sail, pull a rope, or steer a boat. A great sailor is willing to do anything and everything. They must learn how to be the navigator, mechanic, cook, plumber, carpenter, engineer, medic, teacher, and, most important, the ever-curious student. The best sailors I know have mastered the art of problem-solving under pressure. Because there's going to be pressure.

PROLOGUE

IT WAS THE SUMMER OF 1969; the familiar scents of fresh-cut timber once again overwhelmed the rural waterfront of the quaint fishing port of Lunenburg, Nova Scotia. Standing tall on the edge of town, facing out toward the mouth of the harbor, stood a large barnlike building. Inside, sawdust flew through the air, loud noises of machinery and pounding mallets rang out, and the laboring shipwrights worked to position the first enormous curved frame in its place on the ninety-five-foot-long Douglas fir keel. In a matter of weeks, fifty-five more rows of frames would follow, revealing the form of an eighteenth-century English frigate that would be called *Rose*.

At the same time, a new book written by an accomplished but relatively unknown author named Patrick O'Brian was being prepared for publication. O'Brian had made good on his contract to write and deliver *Master and Commander* on schedule. Remarkably, Macmillan, the UK publisher that had originally agreed to commission the book alongside American publisher J. B. Lippincott Company, rejected the manuscript after review. In the UK, the novel sat in limbo until William Collins picked it up.

In the years that followed, O'Brian continued writing. His small loyal readership grew in the UK, but his series didn't quite take off in America. J. B. Lippincott Company discontinued the books after the third installment, forcing fans to import their own copies for nearly a decade. Then, in 1989, W. W. Norton acquired the rights and reissued the books, and the series became a total phenomenon, taking off and selling millions of copies. All this set up the potential of a major Hollywood movie, for which they needed a ship . . .

STANDING RIGGING AND SAILS

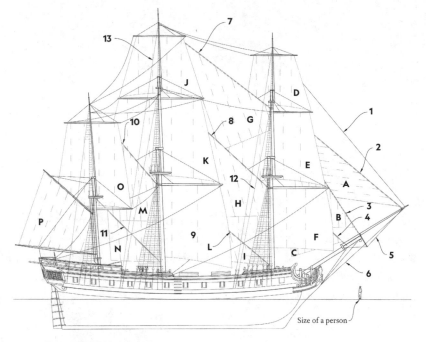

Size of a person

STANDING RIGGING

1 Fore t'gallant stay
2 Outer foretopmast stay
3 Inner foretopmast stay
4 Forestay
5 Martingale stay
6 Bobstay
7 Main t'gallant stay
8 Main topmast stay
9 Main stay
10 Mizzen topmast stay
11 Mizzen stay
12 Topmast backstay
13 T'gallant backstay

SAILS

A Flying jib
B Outer jib
C Inner jib
D Fore t'gallant
E Fore topsail
F Fores'l
G Main t'gallant staysail
H Main topmast staysail
I Main staysail
J Main t'gallant
K Main topsail
L Mainsail
M Mizzen topmast staysail
N Mizzen staysail
O Mizzen topsail
P Spanker

SPAR PLAN

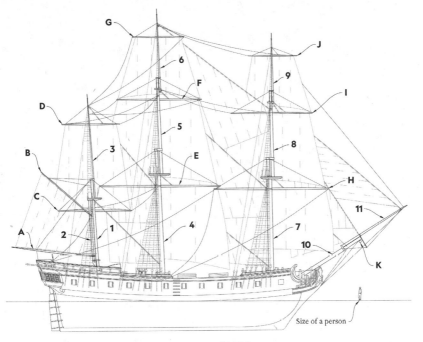

Size of a person

MASTS

1 Mizzenmast
2 Spencer mast
3 Mizzen topmast
4 Mainmast
5 Main topmast
6 Main topgallant mast
7 Foremast
8 Fore topmast
9 Fore topgallant mast
10 Bowsprit
11 Jibboom

SPARS

A Spanker boom
B Spanker gaff
C Crossjack yard
D Mizzen topsail yard
E Main yard
F Main topsail yard
G Main topgallant yard
H Fore yard
I Fore topsail yard
J Fore topgallant yard
K Spritsail yard

MAINMAST SECTION LOOKING AFT

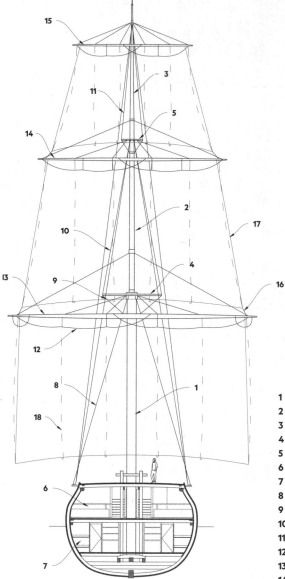

1   Mainmast
2   Topmast
3   T'gallant mast
4   Fighting top
5   Cross trees
6   Gun deck
7   Lower deck
8   Lower shrouds
9   Futtock shrouds
10 Topmast shrouds
11 T'gallant shrouds
12 Foot rope
13 Course yard
14 Topsail yard
15 Topgallant yard
16 Sheet
17 Outline of sail when set
18 Buntlines

INTERIOR PROFILE

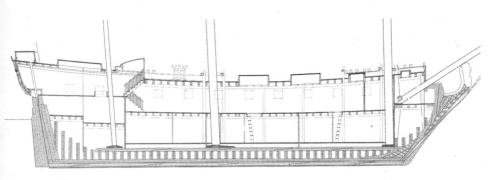

1	Fore peak	7	C-Compartment
2	Gun deck	8	B-Compartment
3	Great Cabin	9	A-Compartment
4	D-Compartment	10	Tank room
5	Engine room	11	Lower fore peak
6	Fuel tanks/chippy stores, dry stores		

CHARTED COURSE

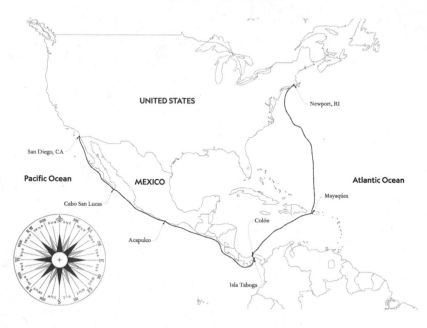

LEGS

1   Newport, Rhode Island, to Mayagüez, Puerto Rico
2   Mayagüez, Puerto Rico, to Colón, Panama
3   Colón, Panama, to Taboga, Panama
4   Isla Taboga, Panama, to Acapulco, Mexico
5   Acapulco, Mexico, to Cabo San Lucas, Mexico
6   Cabo San Lucas, Mexico, to San Diego, California

— *Chapter 1* —

*W*ELCOME HOME

THE SKY WAS GRAY, filled with cirrostratus clouds. It was near the end of October, and even though I was within a degree of latitude from Villefranche-sur-Mer, the warm, sunny climate of the South of France was now a distant memory swept rudely away by the cold winds of the oncoming New England winter. My reentry to the United States via Boston had not been all I had hoped. It started when the jet bridge wouldn't connect to my airplane, meaning my first whiff of America after a one-way flight out of heaven was of jet fuel fumes from the tarmac.

There was maybe a half hour of sunlight left when I finally cleared customs and had my bags in hand. It had been less than two months since 9/11, and the arrival area was no longer filled with family and friends waiting to greet returning loved ones with hugs and smiles. Only arriving travelers and security agents were allowed. It felt hostile, and I quickly got moving.

My stomach twisted as I began to regret my decision. I was already starting to realize how dreadfully wrong I was about what I thought I had been missing back in America; MTV, fast food, muscle cars, and *Sunday Night Football* felt less important after my time abroad. I had just seen a whole new world I hadn't known existed.

I quietly stood with Casey, my captain, near the airport's exit doors, waiting for Todd, our mate, to pick us up. The cold, dry air was like a wake-up call I couldn't silence. I was back in New England with no plan and no job. I didn't have a place to live or any idea what my next step in life would be. I was heading back to Newport at the worst time of year to look for work. Boats with positions had already started heading south for the winter, and their crew slots were already filled.

I had not planned for this moment or even considered what I might do after my time on *Onawa*, the boat I had been sailing in Europe. I could have blamed my lack of preparation on being distracted by 9/11 while in Europe, but that would have been a cop-out. The truth was, I was twenty-one years old, and up to that point, everything had always just worked out.

Casey kindly offered to let me stay at his house in exchange for some carpentry and maintenance services. This seemed like a good arrangement for me since I had spent almost all the money I had earned in Europe on fine dining and debauched late nights out in the bars. I probably still had a bit of back pay to come in, but I wasn't sure when that would settle up.

For those who haven't had the pleasure of visiting, Newport, Rhode Island, the southernmost of three towns on Aquidneck Island, is famous for its yachting history and decadent mansions. Like many cities in New England, it was founded by a group of English settlers fleeing religious persecution after some very public theological battles with the Puritan clergy of the Massachusetts Bay Colony. In 1663, it became one of the five rotating capitals of the newly minted Colony of Rhode Island and Providence Plantations, a decision made by the colony's experimentally minded founders to distribute power. Newport's reputation as a port began to take off in the mid-eighteenth century, when a group of immigrating Portuguese Jews seeking freedom of worship helped develop Newport as a shipping destination. The city became a hub for the trade of rum, silver, fish, whale-oil candles, horses, cheese, and many other goods. Newport, and the rest of Rhode Island, also became a central hub for the North American slave trade.

Newport continued to prosper through the eighteenth century as a prominent component of the triangular trade between Europe, Africa, and the Americas. Recognizing its importance, the British occupied Newport in 1776 until abandoning it in 1779. In 1780, under Admiral Charles de Ternay and Comte de Rochambeau, both the French army and navy used Newport as a base until marching to Yorktown in 1781 with George Washington. By that point, many of Newport's trading merchants had relocated their businesses to other ports and cities. With Newport no longer a significant trading port, its population and economy entered a steep decline.

In the early nineteenth century, Newport began to build a new identity as a vacation destination due to the charming quality of its architecture and the pleasant summer climate. It became the top destination for families like the Vanderbilts, the Astors, the Griswolds, and the Morgans, the American royalty of the country's Gilded Age. The influx of extreme wealth and ideal sailing conditions in Narragansett Bay helped transform Newport into a trendy yachting capital every summer. These families built famed mansions there (referred to as "cottages") that became exemplars of Gothic Revival, Beaux-Arts, and Shingle Style architecture. Bellevue Avenue, a once exclusive street where many of these mansions are located, is now filled with cars or buses loaded with tourists seeking a glimpse of late-nineteenth-century luxury.

Newport began a slow decline in status as America's premier summer resort following the implementation of a federal income tax in 1913 and then the Great Depression. Its reputation as a sailing destination, however, did not falter. Following World War I, Newport became the home of the famed America's Cup (until the Australians won it in 1983). When I washed ashore in 2001, it still held its status as the sailing capital of the United States.

⚙

As hesitant as I felt about my return to Newport, I was looking forward to catching up with my good friend Jared. We had met eighteen months prior, before my trip to Europe, when I was invited out for a sail on a boat. I did not know anyone other than the boat's owner, and I showed up early, eager to be punctual. But that didn't matter since our departure was delayed by an hour because some guy named Jared was late. One of the girls on the boat told me this was typical of Jared and not to get too upset, as he was well worth the wait. When he eventually showed up, he came wearing a smile bigger than Jack Nicholson's, holding a handle of Goslings rum in one hand and a big bag of sandwiches and several pounds of mac and cheese in the other.

Jared was five years older than me, medium height, sun-bleached hair, and had a wardrobe consisting of oversized collared shirts and khakis that should have long since been retired. He was a bit heavyset and mischievous and could charm any woman in any room. He was the kind of guy who could talk a cop out of writing a speeding ticket by offering to buy him a lap dance at the strip club just up the street. Jared's flexible morals were constantly adjusting depending on the urgency of the situation. He had moved to Newport for college with no plans to go anyplace else. Sailing, closing out the bar, and charming the skirts off the girls were his priorities. He hated being woken up by anyone for any reason; he slept with a knife and would threaten to stick you with it if you tried to interrupt his sleep.

Shortly after we met, Jared was evicted from his apartment. He immediately moved onto the sofa of a college ex, whom he introduced to me as Mrs. Robinson, a joke based on the film *The Graduate*. They had been broken up for years but had become great friends; Jared was an absolute master of making amends. One night I was waiting for him to meet me at Mrs. Robinson's apartment. She was home too, and while I waited, the drinks went down. Sure enough, one thing led to another. Looking back, I am sure Jared planned that all along. Now we could hang out whenever he wanted, and he could keep living on her sofa rent-free.

The arrangement worked well for quite some time, and when I returned from Europe, Jared and Mrs. Robinson were still living together. I thought the three of us would just resume hanging out while I figured out my next steps, but she made clear in an email exchange that while I was away she had moved on to a new relationship, and I should steer clear. Being the loyal friend he was, Jared welcomed me back to Newport by taking me out to nearly every bar in town, distracting me from my longing for romance and direction.

As entertaining as our debauchery was, and no matter how many shots we did, my inner monologue would eventually start whispering, *Hey, idiot, what's next? What do you do now?* I didn't have a plan. I had no aspirations, no goals. I didn't care about becoming rich or having any sort of long-term career. I also didn't have any bills, and my family was a two-hour drive away, which gave me the breathing room I needed to avoid their questions about what I was doing with my life.

While living at Casey's, my only obligation was to complete the worklist he scrawled for me each day. The work was easy, mostly just painting and minor woodworking projects like fixing doorjambs or repairing a rotten piece of exterior trim. It didn't take very long for Casey to see he needed to nudge me along, so I didn't overstay my welcome. One morning he told me that instead of working on the house, I would spend the day working on a ship called *Rose* docked just down the hill in the harbor. He told me to ask for Tony, the chief mate.

"They need some daywork, so I want you to go down and help." He left no room for questions. I was not happy about having to go, but I knew what I had to do.

Daywork is a term used in the yachting industry for temporary employment. You are paid by the day to augment the yacht's crew, sometimes for a particular task, like varnishing or detail cleaning the hull. It is prevalent especially during the spring and fall shoulder seasons, and in most cases, day workers are hired to help offset large workloads on the permanent yacht crew. Daywork usually comes with a meal, generally pays in cash, and sometimes results in a long-term position. *Rose* was a tall ship, and tall ships do not normally hire day workers, mainly because of their small operating budgets.

A tall ship is a large sailing vessel that is traditionally rigged, such as a schooner or a square-rigged ship. In the 1950s, as the age of sail was nearing its end, retired Englishman Bernard Morgan helped to create an international race to celebrate the importance of sail training on tall ships. Soon thereafter, the Sail Training International Race Committee was formed to organize what would become the first tall ship race in 1956. The race occurred between the United Kingdom and Portugal, with twenty participants. It was so successful that it became a biennial event. In 1972, the American Barclay Warburton III sailed his brigantine *Black Pearl* to Europe with his two sons and several friends to participate in the tall ship races from Cowes, England, to Malmö, Sweden. The experience inspired Warburton to champion the formation of the American Sail Training Association known today as Tall Ships America.

As I walked down the hill to *Rose*, I wondered if I was being bigheaded about the whole thing. I was not happy about having to go. I had just returned from the biggest global sailing event of the year. Better yet, I was one of the handful of sailors getting paid to be there. That job hadn't come easy—I had worked harder than I ever had at anything to beat out anyone who wanted the spot I got on *Onawa*. I should have listened to the older and more experienced sailors back in Europe who told me to look for a job on a boat going to the Caribbean. I thought about how Casey and Todd never stopped telling me how easy I had it on yachts and how hard their lives were when working on tall ships. Like older siblings trying to scare a younger brother, they told tales of weird people, slave-like working conditions, and little to no pay.

I saw *Rose* from a half mile away. She was a stark contrast to anything else in the harbor. It must have been indescribable to stand on a distant shore 250 years ago and witness a ship like that crossing over the horizon for the first time, not unlike watching a modern-day spaceship take flight. The mid-autumn air was cold, and the wind picked up as I neared the water, exacerbating its sting. I saw a cluster of men standing on deck just aft of the mainmast, talking and smoking cigarettes. They were dressed in layers of ratty, mismatched clothes. I felt like I was walking up to the front entrance of a hostel for vagabond hippies. The oldest of the group looked to be in his late fifties, and the youngest looked my age.

"I'm Will Sofrin," I shouted up. "Is Tony aboard?"

Chapter 2

THE HELLS ANGELS
OF THE SAILING WORLD

WAFTS OF ROTTING FISH BAIT and diesel fuel quickly replaced the pleasant smell of the crisp morning air. Standing alone, waiting at the bottom of the gangway on the nearly vacant dock, I watched the large, grimy commercial fishing boats on the next pier over preparing to disembark. They offered a brief distraction from the woeful thoughts I was having about my fading fortunes. Somehow, I had gone from drinking $300 bottles of Champagne on a beach in southern France to looking for daywork on a tall ship of questionable seaworthiness. I was not happy about being there, but I didn't feel like I had much of a choice.

I stared up at the unusual ship that I was preparing to board. *Rose* was massive, easily the largest boat in the harbor, and also one of the most run-down. If the harbor was a parking lot, she was a beat-up school bus, covered in primer, with a piece of rope tying the hood closed. Aging layers of paint were flaking off her pockmarked sides like the bark of a sycamore, accentuating the countless streaks of rust drizzling down her hull from the aging iron nails holding her together. The cluttered deck looked like the donation bin at a Salvation Army. There were piles of rope, scraps of metal, wooden spars, and three small boats.

Rose was 179 feet (54.6 meters) long, about the length of two NBA basketball courts. She was wide in the middle, with a 30.5-foot (9.3-meter) beam, and the top of her tallest mast was 130 feet (39.6 meters) above the water, as tall as a thirteen-story building. Her wooden planked hull was predominantly painted black, with yellow bands running along the entire length of the ship from bow to stern, punctuated by black gunports. This was the famous "Nelson Chequer," a color scheme traditionally attributed to Admiral Lord Nelson, which became popular in the Royal Navy and many other navies after the Battle of Trafalgar in 1805.

Rose at the dock in Newport

Rose was a "full-rigged ship," meaning she had three masts, each carrying square sails. Her rig was an intimidating matrix of rope, wires, and spars. Gazing up at the ship's masts, I tried to imagine what it would be like to climb up to the top of that rigging in the middle of the ocean. How would it feel to have the wind blowing against me with the ship charging through the rolling waves beneath her? Then I wondered what life must have been like on her namesake, HMS *Rose*. She would have had nearly two hundred men living and working on her at any given time. Life aboard the ship must have been terribly uncomfortable.

I could have walked onto any other boat and had a solid understanding of how to get her sailing, but not *Rose*. She was, by far, the most complex vessel I had ever set foot on. Sailing a ship like *Rose* required skills largely forgotten, made obsolete by numerous innovations in the intervening centuries. Back then, the crews needed to be able to maintain, repair, and replace any element of the ship no matter where they were in the world. If a mast broke, they would build a new one and rig it into place. If a sail wore through, they would sew a new one. Ships of her era did not have internal combustion engines, meaning sails and twenty-six-foot-long oars, called sweeps, were the only means of propulsion. There might only be a handful of captains today who can sail a ship like *Rose* in and out of a harbor without the assistance of an engine.

A loud, sharp voice shouting down at me broke my reveries: "Hey . . . Will . . . come on up!"

Above me was a fit man waving his hand, motioning for me to come on board. That was Tony, the chief mate, and second only to the captain on the ship. Tony was not what I expected. He had begun his maritime career as a steward working for Casey on the *Mystic Whaler*, a schooner based out of Mystic, Connecticut, and I was expecting leathery looks: dark tanned skin as thick as a saddle, long hair, beard, tattoos everywhere, and a weathered, raspy voice. You know, the Captain Jack Sparrow type. Instead, I saw a man who looked like a stunt double for Tom Cruise, but four inches taller. Tony had on clean, well-fitting blue jeans and a white T-shirt even though it was hovering just above 30° Fahrenheit (−1° Celsius). He was clean-shaven, with dark eyes and short jet-black hair parted on the side.

Tony looked me up and down while smiling and then chuckled as if laughing at a private joke. This left me feeling insecure, wondering exactly what Casey had told him about me. Maybe something along the lines of me being a pretty boy in need of some toughening up. I cautiously stepped onto the worn industrial gangway, which looked like a Cold War relic. I hadn't even reached the deck before Tony turned around and started walking aft toward the main companionway. I picked up my pace and chased after him.

He walked quickly, and I ducked down to avoid hitting my head on the low header of the companionway, following him down the stairs to the ship's interior. At the bottom of the first flight of stairs we passed the great cabin, the elegant space occupied by the ship's captain and the traditional site of formal entertaining on board. It was usually the one place of glamour and comfort on board a ship like *Rose*.

The door to the great cabin was open, and a beautiful morning light shone in through the long row of windows running across the stern of the ship—the only windows on the ship. There were the gunports, but for safety reasons they always remained closed, especially when the ship was underway. The cabin was painted white, with raised paneling accented with gold trim. A double-wide ladder stood in the middle of the cabin leading to the deck above. Behind the ladder, I saw a large oval dark wood dining table flanked by six upholstered brown leather chairs and a long upholstered settee that ran the width of the cabin, just under the windows.

Without stopping, Tony told me to feel free to look in but that it was off-limits to anyone other than the captain, the officers, and their invited guests. I got only a few seconds of gawking before we made a 180-degree turn, using the well-worn newel post to swing down the second flight of steps. We were now walking toward the ship's bow, and the air was heavy with the unpleasant smells of tar, mildew, and grease. Tony led me through a short, dark corridor, passing by the ship's galley and a small mess area consisting of three pine tables with benches. We continued through a small doorway, revealing a large common space running the length of the deck. We were walking on the gun deck, the mid-level deck of *Rose*'s three decks. It was where the ship's cannons were stored and, like a living room, it served as the hub for all common activity on board the ship.

The lack of windows or skylights meant the ship's interior had to be artificially illuminated with a mix of industrial fluorescent lights and randomly placed marine cage-light fixtures. I could easily see that *Rose* was the polar opposite of the pristinely manicured yacht I had spent the previous seven months restoring and living on in Europe. The interior was in a sad state of decay. The white paint of the overhead (what landlubbers would call the ceiling of a room); bulkheads (the interior walls on a boat); and the interior planking used to line the inside of the hull (confusingly called the ceiling) were covered in a tie-dye splatter of discoloration caused by the rusting iron fasteners used to hold the ship's timbers together. The sole—the interior flooring on a boat—and the treads on the stairs and ladders were ebony, probably the result of an applied oil finish that had darkened the wood over time in the absence of any natural light. At an absolute minimum, the interior was long overdue for a good sanding and a fresh coat of paint.

We continued making our way forward, weaving through an obstacle course of ladders and hatches that led to the weather deck above or the sleeping compartments below. To my left on the port side, we passed an extended elevated platform stacked high with a mess of sails and lines. To my right, on the starboard side, was a series of pine tables and benches akin to the ones I spotted in the mess area just forward of the galley. The tables were all lined up under the ship's gunports and stoutly built to support the weight and force of the ship's cannons.

We stopped forward near the bow just before a bulkhead with two doors on either side of a ladder leading up to a small closed hatch. Looking down by my feet, I could see a small grated hatch with light shining up through it. Tony pulled the grate up and moved it to the side, revealing a ladder leading down to a small compartment. When I got to the bottom, I found that there wasn't enough headroom to stand upright. We were so far forward in the ship that the narrowing curvature of the hull left me feeling claustrophobic. Looking around the crowded compartment, I saw two huge tanks and mechanical equipment I wasn't familiar with. Tony looked at me and said, "This is the tank compartment, and this is our watermaker. We need to rebuild it. Can you do that?"

A watermaker presses ocean water through a series of membranes to filter out the salt and marine life at a micron level, resulting in fresh water that may not taste very good but is safe to drink. Before the invention of watermakers, fresh water was a limited resource that could be reliably procured only on land and was carried aboard ships in casks called butts and stored in the hold. This was my first time seeing a watermaker. I assumed that it must be a rather large one, considering the size of the ship and the number of crew that might be on board. I'd heard of watermakers and how mechanically sensitive they could be. But my training and work exposure had been strictly focused on design, construction, and finishing, meaning that my knowledge of mechanical systems was limited. This was well above my pay grade.

"I can definitely take it apart," I said. "But I'm not so sure how well I can put it back together."

Tony ignored my circumspect reply and launched right into a speech about *Rose* and where she was headed. Twentieth Century Fox had recently purchased *Rose* to make a movie based on Patrick O'Brian's Aubrey-Maturin series of novels, with Peter Weir as the director. The title was still being worked out, and they had not yet cast the main characters. I had never heard of O'Brian but knew of Weir as I was a fan of some of the films he had directed—*Dead Poets Society*, *Fearless*, and *The Truman Show*.

Patrick O'Brian was a reclusive English author best known for his acclaimed twenty-book historical fiction series that took place during the Napoleonic Wars of the early nineteenth century. O'Brian began the series with the publication of *Master and Commander* in 1969 and was midway through the twenty-first novel in the series when he died on January 2, 2000, at the age of eighty-five. The books are centered on the friendship of characters Jack Aubrey, a captain in the Royal Navy, and Stephen Maturin, a physician, naturalist, and spy. The series was popular in England from the beginning but stopped being published in America after the first five books. Eventually, after being relaunched in America by publisher W. W. Norton, the series became a literary phenomenon, selling millions of copies and being translated into twenty-four languages.

In the early 1990s, Tom Rothman, responsible for movies such as *Much Ado About Nothing* and *The Madness of King George*, was president of worldwide production for the independent Samuel Goldwyn Company. On a rainy afternoon, while visiting his in-laws in Connecticut, Rothman's father-in-law gave him an old copy of *Master and Commander*. Rothman was immediately hooked, read the entirety of the series in print at the time, began thinking of making it into a film, and suggested the idea to his boss, Sam Goldwyn Jr., a producer and son of the film pioneer Samuel Goldwyn. Sam read the books too, and was equally a fan. He bought the film rights to *Master and Commander* from Patrick O'Brian and optioned the rights to the other novels in the series.

With the rights secured, Goldwyn had to figure out how to adapt the sprawling series into a film. Rothman flew to Australia to pitch Peter Weir the idea of making a film of O'Brian's books, but Weir passed because he didn't believe the series could be adapted to make a good movie. Years went by as scripts were written and rewritten, and the adaptation stayed in development, but the producers couldn't seem to figure it out. Rothman brought the project with him in 1994 to Fox Filmed Entertainment, where he founded and became the first president of Fox Searchlight Pictures. Persistent, Rothman pitched the film to Weir again. Weir again turned it down, saying he still believed the series could not be adapted.

More years went by, and not being one to give up, Rothman, now co-chairman of FFE, organized a third attempt to pitch the film to Weir. Knowing that the symbol of command was a sword, Rothman had the Fox prop department fabricate an English naval sword that he hid behind his chair. Rothman told me that midway through the meeting with the director, he pulled out the sword and presented it to Weir, saying, "Peter, all these projects are good, but what you really need to do is take command of the *Surprise*." The gesture intrigued Weir. As their conversation continued, Weir said that if he were to do it, he would not start the film as the series begins but instead open in the middle of a long voyage and then introduce the friendship of the main characters. Rothman said the idea sounded good and suggested Weir take some time to think about it.

Weir then went to England to visit HMS *Victory*, conducted research, and attended several boating festivals. At one point, someone suggested he go to Nova Scotia to attend a tall ship festival, and he did so in July 2000. Weir told me, "It was alive with people. It was early afternoon, and I hurried along the quay past the forest of masts to find *Rose*. There she sat, perfect." *Rose*'s captain, Richard Bailey, invited Weir on board, and he spent a large part of the day on the ship, which he learned was for sale for $1.5 million. There was no doubt in Weir's mind that he had found the *Surprise*.

Shortly thereafter, Weir returned to Los Angeles to say he would like to make a movie based on the tenth book in the series, *The Far Side of the World*, and that he felt it was in the film's best interest to buy *Rose*. By this point, the studio was successful enough to undertake such a daring project. Confident that Weir would deliver, Rothman made the risky and bold move to option the purchase of the ship, and Weir got to work on writing the script.

♚

As we stood in the bowels of the ship, Tony filled me in on the mission and projected timeline. *Rose* would be departing for California in three months. She would go through the Panama Canal and then onto the Galápagos to scout potential filming locations before docking in San Diego. He asked me if I would be interested in joining the crew for the passage and then staying on to make the movie.

I did not expect this pitch. I was still trying to process this alien ship and deciding if I could even figure out how to rebuild the watermaker. I had assumed that I'd be spending most of a single day on *Rose*, doing a bunch of dirty work that nobody else wanted to do. Instead, I had just been offered a paid crew position to sail from Newport to California to make a movie.

I must have looked stupid or even catatonic, managing only "That sounds cool."

"How about I take you on a slower and more detailed tour of the ship?" Tony said. "We can keep talking, and I can answer any questions you have." He grabbed the ladder and began climbing back up to the gun deck.

We spent the next hour walking through *Rose*, going over the mission and what my role would be as a deckhand and the ship's chippy, or carpenter. Along the way, I met Rich from Wisconsin, who dressed in all black and looked very much like the pencil-illustrated "Wanted" poster of the Unabomber, down to his glasses and mustache. He was tall, with receding blond hair, and had bony shoulders and a black wardrobe that emphasized his pale complexion. He was in his mid-thirties but looked older and seemed very insecure when Tony engaged him in conversation. Apparently, Rich had been volunteering on another ship; *Rose* was his first actual job on a boat. He was on janitor duty that morning, cleaning toilets.

We next ran into Russ. He was working at a bench in a small, dimly lit compartment called chippy stores, using a grinder to remove chunks of rust and corrosion from a pile of old iron fittings. He had medium-length brown hair, a burgeoning beer gut, a great big inviting smile, and a Texan drawl. He was also filthy. Tony told me that Russ was in his mid-thirties and had shown up one day walking the dock looking for work. Like Rich, this was his first job on a boat, a pattern I was beginning to find disturbing.

The last person we ran into was Shannon, the only woman on the ship at that point. She was from Massachusetts, tall and thin with long curly brown hair and vibrant eyes. She was wearing a pair of stained blue jeans and an old oversized sweatshirt. Shannon was articulate and polite and had a pleasant soft laugh. We ran into her while she was inspecting the bilge in the ship's engine room, a job that inevitably covered its occupant in nasty remnants of oil, grease, and fuel that had accumulated from the ship's engines and generators. Other than being content to climb around in a rank old bilge, Shannon seemed very normal, and that alone made me suspicious about her. Tony told me she was the senior deckhand and had already been on *Rose* for two seasons. Unlike Rich and Russ, Shannon knew her way around the ship and was an adept sailor.

After finishing the second and more detailed tour, Tony walked me back up to the weather deck, stopping at the top of the gangway. "So, what do you think? Are you in?" he asked.

"It's interesting," I answered unenthusiastically, frozen with indecision. I thought I was showing up to do some light daywork like sanding and painting, but here was the chief mate offering me a job to sail *Rose* thousands of miles, through two oceans, to California. Tony did not seem the least bit put off by my apathy and invited me down to the ship for dinner that night and then to join the crew to see the captain speak at the International Yacht Restoration School (IYRS). I knew IYRS well, having recently completed a two-year apprenticeship focused on wooden boat restoration.

Before walking too far, I turned back to admire *Rose* from a distance. I might have felt numb and confused about what was next for me in life, but I was suddenly enamored by the scale of her presence. With time on my hands, I took a long detour to stop at a local bookstore called the Armchair Sailor to explore O'Brian's books. A friend of a friend was working at the counter when I walked in. I told him about the offer I had just received, and he gave me a five-minute synopsis on the series. He recommended I jump ahead to the third book in the series, in which the ship HMS *Surprise* is first introduced. That way I could better understand the significance of the role *Rose* would play in the film. He handed me the book, said it was on him, and told me to get going.

Walking slowly back to Casey's house, I thought about how lucky I was to be living there rent-free. I was sure that him sending me down to the ship was his way of telling me I was at risk of overstaying my welcome. I needed to tread lightly because I would be opening a world of trouble if he suspected I thought this opportunity was beneath me. Casey was Mr. Tall Ship. His whole career had been built on sailing the world on schooners and square-riggers. When it came to seamanship, he knew more than anyone I knew, and he attributed it all to his time on tall ships.

I snuck back into the house, anxious to avoid questions. Luckily, my guest room was on the ground floor. Once I was in, I stayed quiet, reading O'Brian's *HMS Surprise* for a few hours until my stomach eventually got the better of me, sending me upstairs. Casey was sitting at the kitchen table reading *Surfer's Journal*. He looked up, and I knew what was coming.

"Soooo, how did it go?"

I'd spent enough time with Casey to know that when he knew more than he wanted to let on, he dragged out his vowels, raised his right eyebrow halfway up his forehead, and wore a devilish smile. He already knew I was offered a job. How clever of him to pawn me off onto Tony—it felt like a Don Vito Corleone kind of move.

I rolled my eyes and said, "He actually offered me a full-time job, but I'm not sure."

I was waiting for Casey to say, "What, are you stupid?" But he didn't do that. He just kept reading his magazine and said it sounded like something I should do. I shrugged and headed back down to my room to clean up before returning to the ship for dinner.

It was already nicer the second time, walking up the gangway as a guest, not needing to ask permission to board the ship. That was when I got my first tiny sense of belonging. Nobody was on deck, so I made my way aft toward the main companionway and proceeded below. The sound of the crew talking and laughing grew louder as I walked down the two flights of stairs, emerging on the starboard side of the gun deck.

It was pleasantly warm inside the ship, and instead of tar and mildew, delicious fragrances of cilantro, cumin, and chilies filled the air. A perk to working on a ship like this was the dedicated cook who served three hot, calorie-packed meals a day. I was curious what was being prepared but knew the rule: unless invited, nobody was allowed in the galley. Casey had warned me how tyrannical the ship's cook, Hunter, could be and to give him a wide berth.

I was warmly greeted by the small group of deckhands who were mingling while dinner was being prepared. There were six of them, including the three I had met earlier with Tony—the black-clad blond, Rich; the inexperienced Texan, Russ; and Shannon, the senior deckhand. Everyone was in a good mood, having just downed some cheap happy hour beers at a nearby bar. The new faces took turns introducing themselves. There was Vincent from Massachusetts, Jason from Oklahoma, and Marshall, who never did say where he came from.

Unfortunately, Vincent quickly commandeered the conversation like some overzealous frat recruiter. He came across as a real brute—thick, covered in streaks of grease, and smelling like a dirty locker room after a football game—and he was eager to tell me how hard the work was and how great he was at doing it. Rich and Jason tried to get a word in, but Vincent wouldn't share the floor. He was too busy bragging about taking only one shower a week to prepare for life at sea. I didn't understand and just stood there, hoping he would stop talking.

Fortunately, Tony showed up and saved us all by sending Vincent to inspect the dock lines before dinner. With Vincent gone, our conversation found balance. I learned that Jason was a Buddhist and had ridden a bicycle from Oklahoma to Newport. He was small, with short black hair, and wore a pair of sixties vintage rounded metal eyeglasses. He looked like he would be better suited to assisting a librarian than working on a tall ship; Tony hired him despite initially telling him there was no job available. Marshall was sporting a bleached-blond glam rocker hairstyle, making him look like a David Bowie impersonator, but without Bowie's stage presence. He was quick at redirecting the conversation whenever it seemed to be coming toward him.

Then Hunter called out that dinner was ready, and Richard Bailey, the captain and steward of *Rose*, appeared. I had heard much of him from Casey and Todd. He was a legend in the tall ship community, and without him we probably would not have had *Rose* to sail on. It was his love and appreciation of her that saved the derelict dockside attraction from being scrapped after suffering so much neglect and disrepair.

Captain Bailey had spent nearly three decades of his life giving everything he had to the ship when she was purchased for the filming of the movie. He was in his early fifties, balding, and nearly a foot shorter than me. What Captain Bailey lacked in height was easily made up for with his large personality and commanding presence. He introduced himself to me and seemed aware of my relationship with Casey and Todd, asking me polite questions about my time on *Onawa*. He spoke carefully, and I could tell he didn't like to waste time.

We sat at a dining table in the mess area, our group of nine able to fit at just one table. The meal consisted of chicken enchiladas, Spanish rice, refried beans, and a simple salad with creamy ranch dressing. I was told this was a crew favorite, and my taste buds agreed. The food was served buffet style, and while everyone filled their plates, Hunter headed up to the weather deck to smoke a cigarette and drink a beer in peace. He never ate his meals with the crew.

Following dinner, two of the hands cleaned the dishes and the galley while everyone else lounged. I walked around, taking in the feel of the ship once more. I enjoyed dinner, and I was mostly enjoying the company, but I was still not sold on joining this crew. I didn't get why they were all so enthusiastic. What was it about becoming a tall ship sailor that made it worth abandoning their old lives to sleep in a small bunk, do hard and dirty manual labor, and earn fifty cents an hour and all the salt water they could drink? I felt like I was surrounded by cultists trying to recruit me.

When the dishes were washed and the galley was clean, we departed for IYRS to hear Captain Bailey's opening introduction to the showing of the 1956 film *Moby Dick*, directed by John Huston. I spent much of the walk thinking about what I would need to do if I accepted the job. First on the list would be retrieving my boatbuilding tools and winter clothes, stored at my mother's house. I had been putting off going home since returning from Europe because I was dreading the obligation of having to listen to my mother's latest ramblings. I wouldn't be able to simply stop by to grab my tools because I was sure finding them would mean an entire day of rummaging through the jam-packed house.

My thoughts shifted back to where I was, on the cusp of a grand adventure, and feeling like one of the Goonies preparing to sail One-Eyed Willy's ship off into the sunset. The idea of sailing to California sounded romantic, but going to sea with these oddballs would mean putting my life in their hands. How well would I be able to sleep knowing one of them would be steering the ship? I then started mentally preparing for the onslaught of questions I thought I might get upon my arrival at IYRS. It would be my first time back since completing the program, and I would be showing up with the Hells Angels of the sailing world— the antithesis of everything that IYRS had spent two years training me to be.

Chapter 3

WHO ARE YOU? WHAT ARE YOU DOING? HOW ARE YOU GETTING THERE?

THE LIFE OF BUILDING BOATS or earning a living as a sailor was not something I was born into. My parents grew up in Connecticut and were high school sweethearts who continued their relationship through college. They dropped out of college and moved into a three-bedroom ranch-style house in a rural town in the northwestern corner of the state.

My father enrolled in a trade school to become certified in HVAC installation, and my mother became a teacher's aide. They married when they were twenty-two years old and had me two years later. I was the first of three kids, followed by my two sisters. Both of my parents eventually went back to school after the birth of my youngest sister. They worked during the day and took their classes at night, meaning everyone had to pitch in. Grandparents, aunts, uncles, and friends all helped my parents raise us as they worked hard to pay the bills and go to school. My dad pushed through and got his degree, while my mother dropped out because of a work injury.

Unfortunately, like some couples who meet and marry when they are very young, my parents grew apart instead of together. They divorced when I was thirteen. It was hard on me, and I did my best to navigate the new battlefield of my parents' post-divorce war. My dad quit drinking and became a completely different person, which was challenging for me to digest, especially after the divorce. I now know it was for the better, but at the time, it left me feeling like I had lost my hero. I didn't know who this clean-shaven, khaki-wearing, shirt-tucked-in professional person was. Where did the shredded Grateful Dead T-shirt, worn-out blue jeans, and Timberland work-boot guy go?

My mother remarried five months after the divorce was final, and we moved to my stepfather's house in West Hartford, a beautiful white-collar suburb filled with social clubs, golf courses, and private schools. It looked like the setting of a John Hughes movie. Many neighborhoods were made up of mansions and beautiful public parks and gardens. We lived in one of the less glamorous neighborhoods, in a split ranch house within walking distance of the public schools.

Life at home was almost always a challenge, as I learned how to navigate the emotional and financial roller coasters of my mother's second marriage. My mother and stepfather were devoted followers of an Indian guru named Sathya Sai Baba. Our house was filled with statues and pictures of Hindu gods and always smelled like incense. To them, the world was wrong, and they were enlightened. The hard truth was that our family was what was wrong; we were the Addams Family of the block.

One day my stepfather paid a dump truck to unload a full bucketload of a demolished brick building in our driveway. The pile was filled with brick, mortar, broken glass, wood, metal, and insulation. I was assigned to salvage the bricks from the rubble, chip off the mortar, transfer them to our backyard via wheelbarrow, and stack them into organized piles. These were to be used one day for building garden walls. My labor would be my contribution to offset the cost of my being added to the household's car insurance policy. The task took me almost an entire summer, so long that our neighbors filed numerous complaints with the town about the hazardous dump load of construction debris sitting in our driveway.

My stepfather's answer to the complaints was to purchase a few rolls of yellow police caution tape and wrap it around everything on our property, including our house. His stunt only drew more attention to the oddness of our household. My plate was full, and I mean that literally, as I tried to balance living with my nonconforming family while attempting to blend in at school and around town. I used food as a comfort during my parents' divorce, and I had become a chunky, overweight, glasses-wearing, Nirvana-worshipping, hormone-raging teenager who had nobody to talk to other than my sister Kate. Thank god for my sister Kate. We had fought incessantly before our parents' divorce but grew close in our new household.

At school, I learned how to know when to be quiet, blend in, and look the part so people would leave me alone. Life at home was more challenging, though, as I performed an Emmy-worthy act as a semi-complacent teenager around my mother and stepfather. I began sneaking out at night after everyone was asleep, riding my bicycle around town, smoking cigarettes, and hanging out with college kids I met at coffee shops. It was my way to cope and survive. I began drinking, too, often to the point of blacking out. One night at three o'clock, I remember waking up in the middle of a road next to my bicycle, not knowing how I had gotten there. One semester, I even tried to do an oral book report while high on acid. I kept pushing, looking for ways to escape.

Fortunately, through my missteps, I made great friends, and their families went above and beyond in giving me the love and support I so desperately needed. What got me on the right path was a class in school called ASK, short for Alternative Search for Knowledge. ASK was a double-period class held in a large basement classroom, and it was run by two teachers: Sol, an English teacher, and Cogan, a social studies teacher. It was the *Breakfast Club* of my high school, filled with a mismatch of troublemakers and oddballs.

Instead of standard core reading, I was able to read classic books I had always wanted to read or books on the *New York Times* bestseller list. We would watch the news, and I had to write a paper every day. ASK and the fellow students in the class became my escape from home, where I felt most comfortable being myself. The struggle to be me did not exist in that classroom. ASK provided the platform and confidence I needed to change everything in my life. I had a 1.2 GPA when I began and became an honors student by the end of my first semester. I learned how to be the driver of my life instead of the passenger.

When I was seventeen, my stepfather purchased a small sailboat that he kept moored in Jamestown, Rhode Island. The boat had been in a cradle in the woods for years when he bought it. We spent a few weekends painting and repairing it before launching it at a nearby marina. We had no idea what we were doing, but I loved every second of it. A year later, using the money I had saved from my job working as a barback at a Romano's Macaroni Grill, I bought a small fiberglass sailboat that had been wrecked in a hurricane. Employing trial and error as my guide, I worked on it for a year, buying a new mast and repairing the damaged fiberglass deckhouse.

Come senior year, I didn't have a clear vision for my life after graduation. Having no career goal or passion, I was encouraged by my parents to consider pursuing a trade instead of going to college. On a weekend trip to Newport, we discovered a new school called the International Yacht Restoration School.

IYRS was offering apprenticeships focused on wooden boat restoration. As I loved anything and everything about boats, I became obsessed with the idea of learning how to build them. I kept a journal of the work I was doing on my boat, which I presented at my interview with the IYRS program director when I applied to the program. There was one opening available when I interviewed. I accepted it on the spot.

At nineteen, I moved into an efficiency basement apartment with a single-burner stove and a bathroom without a door. Alone, in a new town where I knew nobody, I would be responsible for taking care of myself. I was suddenly thrust into a crash course of cooking, cleaning, doing laundry, and grocery shopping. Solo, without anyone to help, it was sink or swim.

IYRS is the Harvard of the boatbuilding world. The founding members of the IYRS board were mostly wealthy yacht owners with deep ties to the classic wooden yacht industry who leveraged their connections for the benefit of the school. IYRS placed enormous emphasis on perfection and beauty—the campus, the shop, the projects, all of it had to be impeccable. The work was both physically and mentally challenging, leaving me tired and sore at the end of most days. It was a two-year program without a summer break, with an apprenticeship curriculum that was structured to resemble the schedule of a professional boatbuilder.

Despite the heavy workload, I spent every moment I had outside of IYRS doing anything I could to make money to offset my living expenses. I initially got some help from my parents, but that quickly became sporadic. One of my favorite jobs was as a barback at the Black Pearl, a famous waterfront bar and restaurant located on Bannister's Wharf in downtown Newport. Working at the Pearl was like being part of a summer party that happened every night. Think *Weekend at Bernie's*, with all the clam chowder you could eat. Learning and working were meaningful, but I also had to make room for fun. For me, that meant taking advantage of living in Newport and sailing whenever possible.

My real breakthrough came when I started getting paid to sail. That happened one day when I was stuck in a traffic jam with Clark, the program director of IYRS. We had delivered the boat I had just restored to its new owner. I was told the buyer was a big deal—the restoration was a Father's Day gift for Estée Lauder's granddaughter's husband. I had no idea who Estée Lauder was. We delivered the boat to their house in the Hamptons, and I got to take the lucky man out for a shakedown sail. Due to summer traffic, the drive back to Newport took twice as long as it should have, giving me and Clark plenty of time for long, meandering conversations. Near the end, Clark suggested I go down to where America's Cup Charters (ACC) docked their fleet and ask if I could volunteer as a crew member for a sail. ACC has a fleet of former America's Cup 12-Meter yachts (the class used for the Cup from 1955 to 1987) available for cruising, racing, team-building corporate charters, and individual ticketed sunset sails most summer evenings. Clark told me to say he had sent me down.

I did as Clark said, and sure enough, Steve, the captain of *Nefertiti*, invited me out for a sunset sail that very night. Each boat had a captain, mate, and deckhand. From what I understood, Steve's mate, Adam, was very busy balancing his job as mate while completing his college degree. Steve's deckhand was a gorgeous, well-tanned French American girl named Marion. I got along quite well with Marion, and after two more sails, Steve offered to pay me as a fill-in crew member whenever I could fit it into my schedule. Word spread, and I became a regular fill-in on the other 12-Meters in the ACC fleet. This was mind-blowing. I had so admired the yachts from a distance, and now I was getting to sail them, and even better, I was getting paid for it.

It was fantastic spending that summer sailing, continuing to learn about building wooden boats and living in a town that was a constant revolving door of people looking to have fun. Summer soon ended, marking the beginning of my final year at IYRS. My apprenticeship would be over, and the school was pressuring me to decide what I would do with my new skill set. I loved building boats, but I loved sailing them more. I wanted to get hired on a boat full time and become a professional sailor.

It was around this time that I learned of a global sailing event planned for 2001 in England called the America's Cup Jubilee. That year marked the 150th anniversary of the first race known as the America's Cup, and the Jubilee was going to be the biggest international yachting event of the year. Past and present champions of America's Cup races would travel from around the world to participate in a star-studded regatta. Nothing like it had ever been done. I was laughed at many times when I made known my intentions of securing a paid spot on one of the boats going to the Jubilee. I had many obstacles, but the biggest was money; I could get there only if I were paid, since I was a very poor apprentice.

I let ignorance lead the way, and somehow after months of begging and pleading I secured a position as the deckhand on *Onawa*, the oldest sailing American 12-Meter yacht going to the event. *Onawa* was in the middle of an extensive restoration, and for the next five months, I worked tirelessly to complete my obligations at IYRS and *Onawa,* seven days a week. The work was hard, but the reward was great.

Casey, the captain of *Onawa,* had spent decades sailing the world on all sorts of ships and was something of a legend in the tall ship community. He was the kind of guy who could sail a 150-foot boat on and off a dock without an engine. Casey knew anything and everything there was when it came to boats, and he topped that all off with utter unflappability. Todd was the mate, and they had a long-standing relationship, having sailed together for years on several other yachts and a few tall ships. I would be their young, inexperienced, and lucky deckhand.

The Jubilee lived up to the hype. It was the Woodstock of sailing. After the Jubilee, we delivered *Onawa* to Southampton to be loaded back onto *Super Servant 3,* the transport ship that had brought *Onawa* to Europe. I managed to secure one of the limited spots on the ship for its passage from England to Italy through the Straits of Gibraltar. My spot gave me the time I needed to repair a bit of minor damage incurred during our racing in England and to prepare *Onawa* for the rest of the racing circuit in the Mediterranean.

The arrival of *Super Servant 3* in Italy was met with a grand celebration. There were many vessels on the transport ship, and a complement of crew ready to rejoin us as soon as the ship dropped anchor in Golfo Aranci off the coast of northern Sardinia. We unloaded *Onawa,* spent the night in Portisco, and the next day, we sailed to the Italian seaside resort Porto Cervo. The 9/11 terrorist attacks occurred only a few days after our arrival, and the tragedy made the future of our racing circuit uncertain.

Onawa's next destination port was Monaco, and with racing canceled in Porto Cervo, Casey decided we should leave early. We sailed north up the eastern coast of Sardinia, through the Strait of Bonifacio, stopping in the Port of Bastia, located on the northeastern coast of Corsica. The next leg of our passage took us northwest through the Ligurian Sea to Monaco. We managed to catch sight of the infamous Isola d'Elba (the place of Napoleon's first exile, in 1814) as we made our way north around the massif of Monte Stella.

The timing of our passage from Bastia meant we would sail through the night and arrive in Monaco at sunrise. This was the first time I'd ever sailed through the night. It was absolute magic; the glow of Monaco on the horizon before dawn made me feel as if I was sailing into the Emerald City in *The Wizard of Oz.* When we arrived in Monaco, Casey bestowed upon me a nice perk: his cabin, which was

Onawa docked stern-to in Monaco

the only single cabin on the boat. Both Todd and Casey had rented apartments in the remaining ports of our tour, making me the only paid member of the crew on *Onawa* at night. The cabin was tiny, just seventy-four by forty-two inches. Only enough room for a bunk and a tiny aisle a foot wide.

We raced out of Monaco for a week and then made our way westward toward Cannes and Saint-Tropez, the final port on the racing circuit. After Saint-Tropez, we sailed *Onawa* to Île de Porquerolles, a secluded island on the coast of the French Riviera. When the time came, we departed for Toulon, a large and vital French port, famous for its rich naval history. It was a foul contrast to all the other ports we had visited during our tour. When we arrived, Todd took one look around and decided he wanted to leave early.

Our last days in France were quiet as we prepared *Onawa* for her transatlantic shipment. With *Onawa* loaded on the ship, Casey and I spent our final night in Villefranche-sur-Mer enjoying one last dinner surrounded by breathtaking historical architecture and culture. I wanted to savor every last moment in France, but I could not shake the pressing thoughts of knowing I would be boarding a plane bound for America the next morning homeless, jobless, and broke.

— *Chapter 4* —

PLANET TALL SHIP

ROSE IS A REPLICA of an eighteenth-century British warship called HMS *Rose*. Since the prefix "HMS" means His (or Her) Majesty's Ship and may only be applied to a ship commissioned by the British Royal Navy, the contemporary *Rose* drops the "HMS" part.

The original HMS *Rose* was built at Blaydes Yard in Hull, England, in 1757 for the British Royal Navy and was defined as a full-rigged ship, a sailing vessel with a rig made up of three or more masts, all rigged to carry square sails. The Royal Navy further classified their ships using a ratings system based on the number of cannons they could carry, not including carriage or swivel guns and carronades. HMS *Rose* was a twenty-gun sixth-rate frigate.

A first-rate ship carried between one hundred and one hundred twenty guns; a second-rate ship carried ninety to ninety-eight guns; a third-rate ship carried sixty-four to eighty-four guns; a fourth-rate ship carried fifty to sixty guns; a fifth-rate ship carried twenty-eight to forty-four guns; and a sixth-rate ship carried twenty to twenty-eight guns. As a sixth-rate ship, HMS *Rose* was the smallest ship in the British ratings system to have been commanded by an officer holding the rank of post captain—a designation used to distinguish a more junior officer who simply used the courtesy title of captain when commanding a smaller vessel from an officer who was commissioned to command a rated vessel.

First-, second-, and third-rate ships were known as "ships of the line" and had multiple gun decks. Their purpose was to engage the enemy in a formation of two opposing columns of warships called "line of battle." The line with more firepower typically possessed the strategic advantage. The two-deck fourth- and fifth-rate ships lacked the firepower of the larger rated ships and were slower than the single-deck smaller rated ships. The single-deck fifth frigates and sixth-rated post-ships were designed for speed and maneuverability and had a wide range of assignments as the workhorses of the fleet. Ships of this size were not intended to be in the line of battle with the two- or three-decked ships of the line.

In 1968, historian John Millar set his heart on building a replica of HMS *Rose* because of her contributions to events leading up to the American Revolution and the establishment of the Continental Navy, the precursor to the United States Navy. After being launched, HMS *Rose* served in the Seven Years' War, from 1758 to 1762. She was briefly considered for service to Captain James Cook for his first exploration to the Pacific, but she lacked the holding space needed to store provisions for the circumnavigation. In 1768, HMS *Rose* was sent on patrol in the West Indies before being ordered back to England in 1771, but three years later she was sent to Newport, Rhode Island, where she successfully intercepted smugglers and caused massive disruption of trade for the thriving port. HMS *Rose* was then sent to New York, where she served in operations in the Hudson against American forces. She returned home in 1776, then sailed again for Savannah, Georgia, where she was scuttled in 1779 to create a blockade that limited French support to the Americans.

Millar contracted to have a replica of the original HMS *Rose* built at the Smith & Rhuland Shipyard in Lunenburg, Nova Scotia. The yard had an established reputation, having already built the replica *Bounty* in 1960 and the *Bluenose II* in 1963. The construction of *Rose* cost $300,000 (roughly $2.4 million in 2022) and was guided by original plans, the design services of naval architect Philip Bolger, and the experience of the shipwrights at Smith & Rhuland. The replica was constructed to the same profile and midsection as the original; however, the hull shape was modified below the waterline. Although the workmanship of her original construction had been professional, the choice of materials had been poor—too much maple, red oak, and other species of unseasoned wood, which compromised the long-term integrity of the hull.

In his book *30-Odd Boats*, Bolger describes design adjustments made to accommodate the financing requirements, such as the ship's ability to serve as a bar and restaurant when at the dock. To achieve this, interior deck placements were adjusted, and a covered deck was laid on top of the bulwarks so the replica could have a well-ventilated space with seven feet and six inches of headroom clearance. The deck structures were significantly different because a ship designed to the original standards would have been considered unsafe.

The goals of *Rose* were never fully realized. She was undercapitalized, and the expense of maintaining her versus her ability to generate revenue caused her to fall into a terrible state of disrepair. In 1984, an entrepreneur named Kaye Williams formed the HMS Rose Foundation, purchased the ship, and relocated her to Bridgeport, Connecticut. After an extensive rebuild, the United States Coast Guard inspected and certified the ship as America's only Class-A sailing school vessel. The mission developed by her foundation was to promote *Rose* as an educational platform offering a variety of sail training programs to the public.

Rose being rebuilt in the water in Captain's Cove in Bridgeport, Connecticut

I was desperately hungover the morning after the IYRS event. That night I had parted ways with the crew of *Rose* and met up with Jared to shoot pool, downing a half-dozen rounds of prairie fires, a shot of tequila with a heavy pour of Tabasco sauce mixed into it. I stayed in my bed longer than normal, hoping to avoid running into Casey. After hearing him walk out the front door, I crawled out from under my blanket and hobbled up to the kitchen for coffee.

Sitting there sobering up, I decided the best thing I could do would be to stop thinking about the pressing decision and instead focus on getting cleaned up and resuming work on a window repair in the house. Having made little headway by lunchtime, I decided to pay a visit to the home of "The Queen of Yachting," Elizabeth Meyer. She was the founder of IYRS and one of the partners of *Onawa*; it was Elizabeth who packed the spinnaker with me on the downwind legs when racing in England and France. She was revered for restoring the J-Class British yacht *Endeavour*, commissioned by Sir Thomas O. M. Sopwith to challenge for the America's Cup in 1934. She was not subtle and had strong opinions about most anything. I thought I would roll the dice and see what insight she might offer.

Elizabeth's home was next to her office, two historic Colonial buildings side by side. I stopped in the office, and her assistant, Marcia, greeted me from her desk on the first floor. Marcia knew who I was by this point and let me head up the steep antique steps to the second floor, where I found Elizabeth. After we hugged, I sat down and jumped right into my dilemma. Suddenly, she cut me off mid-sentence.

"Richard Bailey is just great, and you must go do this. I think you need this and should go away for a while. There is nothing here for you, and you are young, so you must go!" Then she looked back down at her computer and said, "I love you, darling, but you must now go because I need to finish this email, goodbye!" Her black-and-white reaction made me think I was probably making this decision into a bigger thing than it needed to be.

Back at Casey's house I worked for the rest of the day painting the back stairwell, even skipping lunch, which was not like me. I was having a hard time trying to wrap my brain around the idea of living and working as one of the crew on *Rose*. The tour of the ship and the introductions to the crew helped me build a solid picture of life on board. Like a band, tall ships have their own fans and followers, and I'd begun mentally labeling the ship and its groupies "Planet Tall Ship."

Planet Tall Ship was a smelly and dirty place filled with oddballs and weirdos. Members of Planet Tall Ship were okay with bathing occasionally or just not at all. They didn't mind smelling like fresh asphalt and mildew and certainly didn't care what anyone thought of them. The worse your wardrobe, the better you looked. The oddest members were the most popular members. Worn-through elbows or knees, and stains from tar and oil were badges of honor. They lived for cheap happy hour drinks because nearly everyone was broke. The pay was poor, if you were getting paid at all on Planet Tall Ship: working for free was not unusual. On

Planet Tall Ship, a two-hundred-year-old sea shanty was revered more than the latest hit single, and everyone believed that hard work should always be applied before smart work.

⚙

Later that evening at dinner, Casey asked me again if I was going to take the job.

"Dinner was fun, the food was good, but I don't know." I made sure to avoid direct eye contact.

Without skipping a beat, he looked straight at me like I was stupid. "Why don't you know? Put your jacket on and go down there and tell Tony you want to lay out on a yard."

I had no idea what that meant, but I knew I had no choice. I had been living under his roof for free, and the least I could do was show I did not intend to mooch off him forever.

I got up, cleaned my plate, and left. I had already planned to meet Jared after dinner, so I called him up and asked if he wanted to go to *Rose* with me. He had always made fun of me for my wooden boat fascination, so I was surprised when he said yes.

Jared's passion was for modern boats: he loved fiberglass and carbon fiber. His shining boat moment was when he acquired the first Olympic-class 49er, which he named *Bar Fly*. His unexpected interest in seeing *Rose* left me wondering if he was just bored out of his mind or actually thought it would be cool to walk around a full-size ship.

I skipped quickly down to the ship because it was cold. My wardrobe was limited to the bundle of clothes I brought to Europe for the warm, end-of-summer Mediterranean climate, not mid-fall in New England. My plan was simple: meet up with Jared, go to the boat to tell Tony I wanted to lay on a yard, do whatever that meant, and then go to the bar.

⚙

Having already been on the ship twice in the past twenty-four hours gave me the confidence to walk up the gangway without an invitation. I brought Jared up behind me and proceeded across the vacant deck to the main companionway and then down to the gun deck, where I hoped I would find Tony. Walking in unannounced, I saw a slightly different scene from the night before. Everyone was more spread out instead of all being clustered at one table. Russ and Marshall were sitting up forward at a table on the starboard side, watching a movie on the ship's small nineteen-inch TV. Tony was sitting alone eating dinner.

He saw me in an instant. "Hey, Will, how you doing?" he said while loading his fork up for his next bite.

"Hi, Tony, this is my friend Jared. Casey told me to come down here and tell you I want to lay on a yard . . ." I said, trailing off.

"Well let's go, then."

"No, don't get up! We don't need to go right now."

"No, let's go now."

"Can Jared come?" I asked.

Not looking back at us, Tony replied with a wholehearted "Sure." He led us aft and then up the main companionway doors to the weather deck.

We followed him to the starboard rail, stopping at the base of the mainmast shrouds. It was dark with only a couple of streetlamps illuminating the dock and the ship's deck.

We stopped at a metal bar lashed at shoulder height to the shrouds, the pieces of standing rigging used to prevent the masts from falling to the side. Hanging from this metal bar were a number of very heavily used canvas safety belts. Each had a twenty-four-inch section of three-strand line attached to the belt, with a large brass carabiner spliced onto the other end. Without saying anything and motioning as if we knew what we were about to do, Tony took three safety belts off the bar and handed one to each of us. I still had no clue what we were doing. I knew a yard was the horizontal spar that the tops of the square sails were attached to. I followed the lead of both Tony and Jared, latching the belt around my waist. I could see Jared was excited, and it was obvious we were going to climb the rig.

Tony said, "Don't fall, and follow me."

Taking a giant step, Tony got up onto the handrail, swung around so he was standing out over the water, and began climbing upward using the ratlines. Lashed across each shroud, with a vertical spacing of fifteen inches, the ratlines are nonstructural horizontal lines that create a rope ladder going up the rig to where the shroud reaches the top of each mast. The mainmast has three sections, and it's probably best to think of each section as a flight of stairs, except the top of the lowest section is fifty-four feet above the water, as tall as a five-story apartment building.

I made sure to follow Tony's footsteps exactly as we climbed the rig. I was grateful to be climbing under the cover of darkness, because I must have looked like a clumsy idiot. We were closing in on the top of that first flight and the bottom of the fighting top, a moderately sized platform with no rails or sides. The fighting tops existed only at the intersection of the first mast doublings, where the lower mast and the topmast overlapped. HMS *Surprise* would have used these platforms for marines to shoot small arms at an enemy ship.

Tony told us where to stop while he continued climbing, wedging himself under the fighting top just below a small hole near the mast called the lubber hole. Novice sailors tend to use the hole for getting on top of the fighting top, whereas the more experienced crew members take pride in pulling a Spider-Man and climbing out from under the fighting top using the futtock shrouds. This seemed insane to me, because the futtock shrouds were angled outboard from the bottom point where they connected to the mast up to where they met the fighting top. The angle was close to forty-five degrees, which meant you hung upside down when using them to climb up to the fighting top.

Like a teacher familiarizing his students, Tony began explaining how we would need to transition from the shrouds onto the yard. He then started climbing out on the yard, and I followed him. I first grabbed on to the jackstay, a metal bar mounted to the top of the yard running the length, used for attaching the top of a square sail to the yard. I pulled most of my weight onto the jackstay while stepping off the ratlines and putting one foot onto the footrope, a length of line used for standing on. The footrope hung below the yard and was secured at both ends. Relaxing my arms, I eased my weight, sinking down onto the footrope, leveling off so the yard was even with my waist.

The tension of a footrope can dramatically shift depending on where weight is applied. I had to be mindful of balancing my weight so my movements would be in sync with Tony's. He was standing on the same footrope, and any movement I made was felt by him. I also noticed the dramatic sway fore to aft; I could swing my feet in a large arc quite quickly. Tony told me to shuffle out toward the yardarm, the end of the yard, so Jared could lay onto the yard.

Using the footrope, the three of us shimmied our way out to the end of the sixty-foot-long yard until Tony stopped us just before reaching the yardarm. Without warning, he suddenly threw one of his legs over the yard and looked back at us while sitting on top. He was perfectly balanced with his arms folded. "This is laying out on a yard. What do you think?"

I had just climbed fifty feet above the deck and was standing on a rope at the end of a yard five stories above the water. I now understood what laying out on a yard meant, and I looked over at Jared, who was chuckling and had a smile from ear to ear while he gazed out over the tightly packed rooftops lining the harbor front.

"Now keep in mind we are up in this rig while being tied to a dock in flat water with a light breeze," Tony said. "Can you imagine how different it would be up here, furling a sail in a huge storm while sailing through the middle of the ocean? The ship is rolling and pitching, and the wind might be blowing thirty knots, maybe gusting up to forty or even fifty! But don't worry, running into bad weather is rarer these days because we have weather-forecasting technology."

We sat up there for ten minutes. That was all the time I needed, especially considering how cold it was, below freezing. Any metal I touched was ice cold and caused my exposed hands to cramp up in pain. Even the light breeze nipping at my skin started to feel like a slap from a thorny branch. We shimmied back to the mast and down the ratlines till we were standing on the deck again.

We took off our harnesses and thanked Tony for bringing us up on the rig. I looked at Jared with a smirk. "What did you think? Not so bad for a wooden boat?"

"That was freaking awesome!" He was looking up to where we had just climbed as if he was trying to see what it would be like to go higher. There were two more sections of higher masts.

Jared trotted ahead of me down the gangway to light up a cigarette on the dock. Tony started walking toward the main companionway, and I instinctively followed him. We got to the bottom of the first flight of steps when he stopped. "So, what did you think?"

I smiled. "Thank you, and thanks for letting Jared come up also. I'm sorry I interrupted your dinner."

Tony raised an eyebrow. "So, you gonna sign on?"

"I'm into this, but if you can offer Jared a spot also, then I will definitely sign on." I had not put any thought into the idea of Jared coming along, yet here I was, a cocky little prick negotiating a job for someone who may not even want it.

Tony looked at me for a second, not breaking eye contact. "Have Jared send me his CV, but yes."

"Then yes, I am in!" I said with excitement, instantly realizing I finally had a plan. I just needed to figure out how to convince Jared to come along.

"Great, can you drop off your CV tomorrow? I need it as a formality. You can just handwrite it on some lined paper." He smiled and continued down the

steps to finish his dinner. I made my way back onto the deck and then down the
gangway to meet back up with Jared.

After a brisk five-minute walk, Jared and I arrived at the Pelham, a Newport
staple. Lining up at the bar, I ordered the first round of beers and prairie fires,
while Jared started lining up the balls at the pool table.

"Okay, so what did you think? That wasn't so bad, was it? Maybe wooden
boats aren't all terrible?" I looked at the table while taking my shot.

"Actually, it was pretty fucking cool. I think you should do it. I mean, no
rent, water view, a full-time cook, and a ticket to go make a movie in California?
Sign me up!"

I was shocked. Jared had spent the past two years teasing me about my affinity
for wooden boats. I was certain he was either messing with me or was jealous of
the opportunity. This was the moment I needed to make my pitch.

"Really? So, wooden boats are okay now? How about this: I will definitely
sign up if you come along too?"

"Sure, just got to figure out what to do with the dog, and of course I will need
to find someone to rent my room. I actually got fired today, and what the fuck
else am I going to do? It's winter here," he said as he sank the eight ball.

Chapter 5

RICHARD RUSS

IT IS FASCINATING HOW PATRICK O'BRIAN, being a man of neither the sea nor the military, was capable of constructing the complex world of Jack Aubrey and Stephen Maturin. Like an artist does with strokes of paint, O'Brian employs both incisive and arcane language to create the many colorful and elaborate scenes that he uses as the stage for his main characters. Aubrey is a large man, slightly overweight, who enjoys food, wine, and the company of women. When at sea, he is the embodiment of the many natural qualities that make a great leader—he's bold, inspirational, calculating, fair. However, when he's on land, Aubrey is gullible and makes poor financial decisions and social faux pas. He's out of his element. Maturin is his opposite, a small, thin man who loves culture and nature and possesses a strong desire for scientific discovery. He lives a double life as a physician and a spy. He endures a strained relationship with his romantic interest, nurses an addiction to laudanum, and, despite his many years of service at sea, fails to retain even the most basic fundamentals of seamanship. Through the series both men share a love of music, survive battles, explore the world, and, in one form or another, save the other from disaster or death.

Like his characters, O'Brian's own life was fascinating and filled with tragedy and triumphs. So, who was Patrick O'Brian? To start, his real name was Richard Patrick Russ, but his family called him Pat. He was born on December 12, 1914, in Buckinghamshire, England. The second youngest of nine children, he was plagued in his youth with health issues, including asthma and bronchitis, and his mother died of tuberculosis in March 1918. Four years later, Pat's governess married his father, a doctor and unsuccessful inventor. Growing up, Pat found solace in reading, and at the age of fourteen, he began writing. In October 1930, his first book, *Caesar: The Life Story of a Panda Leopard*, was published by G. P. Putnam's Sons.

Pat continued to write and publish stories through his teens, and in 1934, at age nineteen, his second book, *Beasts Royal*, was published.

Pat aspired to join the military but was rejected from the Royal Navy, so he joined the Royal Air Force as a pilot officer. Unfortunately, he didn't meet the cut and his commission was terminated. Pat moved to London to continue writing, and in 1936 he married Elizabeth Jones, a Welshwoman four years his senior. On February 2, 1937, his son, Richard Francis Tudor, was born. Needing to support a family, Pat worked as a tour guide while continuing to write, and in 1938, Oxford University Press published his third book, *Hussein: An Entertainment*. On February 8, 1939, Pat's daughter, Jane Elizabeth Campaspe Tudor, was born. Unfortunately, she suffered from spina bifida and lived only to the age of three. Soon fissures in the marriage grew, and in 1940, Pat abruptly left his family and moved to London.

By this point, World War II was underway and Pat's lingering health issues prevented him from joining the fight on the battlefield. Instead, he made his contribution to the war effort by becoming an ambulance driver in London, and there he met fellow ambulance driver Countess Mary Tolstoy, the wife of an exiled Russian count, during the Blitz. Suffering from unhappy marriages, the two fell in love and moved in together in 1941. Because of their linguistic capabilities, both Pat and Mary were recruited into intelligence work.

In November 1942, Mary's divorce was finalized. Six months later, Pat's wife, Elizabeth, filed for divorce. Though bitter, she allowed Pat to continue his relationship with their son, Richard. On June 25, 1945, Pat's divorce was finalized, and he married Mary ten days later. Then, on July 20, Pat officially changed his, Mary's, and Richard's surname to O'Brian and his first name to Patrick. Richard Patrick Russ had become Patrick O'Brian.

Following the war, the O'Brians left London and moved to a simple cottage with no running water or electricity in Cwm Croesor, Wales. The O'Brians helped their landlords work the land and care for the livestock, which provided them access to vegetables and milk, which supplemented the meat and fish hunted by Patrick. The winter of 1946–47 was unusually harsh, and the couple solidified their acceptance into the community by working together with the other villagers to survive the bitter cold. In 1948, they moved into a larger cottage and Patrick's son, Richard, soon moved in with Patrick and Mary, who took on his education. For income, Patrick converted books to braille, and continued to write; *A Book of Voyages* was published in 1947, *The Last Pool* three years later.

Seeking change, in 1949, the O'Brians moved, without Richard, to Collioure, France, on the Mediterranean very close to the border with Spain. Their tiny third-floor apartment was simple, with no electricity or running water. The O'Brians made a great effort to become part of their new community and master the local Catalan language. Despite their plans, financial issues soon plagued them. A policy put in place by England restricted the export of a payment from O'Brian's publisher, and the couple ran out of money in the winter of 1950. Word of their situation spread, and their new community sent gifts of food and wine, which helped them survive the winter. Spring came, and like in Wales, the O'Brians labored with their new community, helping to harvest grapes for making wine. O'Brian learned and appreciated the importance of the traditions within the Catalan culture, continuing to participate in the *vendange*—grape harvest—for many years.

The O'Brians' lives continued to thrive in Collioure. In the summers of 1953 and 1954, Pablo Picasso spent time in the seaside town. O'Brian enjoyed and respected the artist but resented the added media and tourism his presence attracted. Seeking seclusion, O'Brian bought a piece of land on a hillside overlooking the bay. He developed the land, terracing it with dynamite. A writing hut was built and soon a little house on top. In his first decade of living in Collioure, O'Brian wrote a number of short stories and novels, including 1952's *Three Bear Witness* (published in America under the title *Testimonies*), 1953's *The Frozen Flame* (*The Catalans* in America), 1954's *The Road to Samarcand*, 1956's *The Golden Ocean*, 1959's *Unknown Shore*, and 1962's *Richard Temple*. And to supplement his income, O'Brian began translating the works of other writers too.

Starting in 1960, the O'Brians began spending a fair amount of time in London, but a growing strain with Patrick's son, Richard, reached its breaking point, the last time they spoke was during the summer of 1964. Moving on, Patrick and Mary continued to expand their home and cultivate their land while O'Brian solidified his reputation translating books.

In 1966, C. S. Forester, the author of the Horatio Hornblower series, died. Sensing an opportunity, Robert White Hill, editor in chief of the Philadelphia-based publisher J. B. Lippincott Company, contacted O'Brian with the idea of his taking a stab at writing a maritime novel geared toward adults (*The Golden Ocean* and *Unknown Shore* were more for younger readers). Accepting the offer and being a student of history, O'Brian decided to write a book based on Scotsman Thomas Cochrane, 10th Earl of Dundonald. Cochrane was so successful as a captain that the French called him Le Loup des Mers, or the Sea Wolf. In 1801, outnumbered in men by six to one, Cochrane, as commander of the fourteen-gun sloop HMS *Speedy*, captured the much larger thirty-two-gun Spanish frigate *El Gamo*.

O'Brian's novel *Master and Commander*, featuring Captain Jack Aubrey and his friend Stephen Maturin, was reasonably well received, so he set to work on a sequel, *Post Captain*, which he delivered to his literary agent in the summer of 1971. The book held its own in England but was weakly received in America. Still, O'Brian continued to write, pleasantly consumed by the world he was building for Aubrey and Maturin. He delivered the manuscript for the third installment of the series, *HMS Surprise*, in September 1972. Unfortunately, tepid sales and the departure of O'Brian's in-house advocates meant this would be the last book to be published by Lippincott. The lack of American audience must have stung a bit, but in England, O'Brian's fan base was building.

The next book in the series would have to wait, though, because Bill Targ, a senior editor at Putnam, presented a sizable offer to O'Brian to write a biography of Pablo Picasso. The research required provided an opportunity for the O'Brians to travel to Spain, other areas of France, the Soviet Union, and the United States. O'Brian delivered a long—225,000 words—manuscript in 1975 and the book, *Pablo Ruiz Picasso: A Biography*, was published by Putnam in 1976.

With the Picasso biography behind him, O'Brian headed back out to sea. In 1976, he delivered the completed manuscript for *The Mauritius Command* to his editor, and the book hit the shelves in 1977 to rave reviews. In America, the small publishing house Briarcliff Manor offered to publish the book, and it did well enough to require a second printing. In the same year, O'Brian delivered the manuscript for the fifth book of the series, *Desolation Island*.

On October 22, 1977, the O'Brians were in a car accident after leaving a wedding, putting Patrick in the hospital for a month and Mary for two. The recovery would be long for both, especially for Mary, who had lost a lung and had her legs crushed. Despite the hard recovery, O'Brian had found his stride and in the next ten years wrote eight more installments for his series. O'Brian's fans grew in England, but in America, Briarcliff Manor dropped the books after *Desolation Island*. With the 1980s came routine, as O'Brian found balance in writing and working his land. The decade closed out with good news: O'Brian's agent had reached an agreement with W. W. Norton to publish the series in the United States.

In 1990, O'Brian completed *The Nutmeg of Consolation*, the fourteenth book in the Aubrey-Maturin series. Back in America, in October 1990, a poor review in the *New York Times* of *The Letter of Marque* made O'Brian's future look bleak despite the hard efforts being made by his editor at Norton, Starling Lawrence. Fortunately, in January 1991, the tide turned following a rave review on the cover of the *New York Times Book Review*. Under the headline "An Author I'd Walk the Plank For," Richard Snow, the editor of *American Heritage* magazine, sang the praises of *The Letter of Marque* and the Aubrey-Maturin series in general. "The best historical novels ever written," Snow called them, and ended his piece by writing, "On every page Mr. O'Brian reminds us with subtle artistry of the most important of all historical lessons: that times change but people don't, that the griefs and follies and victories of the men and women who were here before us are in fact the maps of our own lives."

The review seemed to unlock the American audience for O'Brian—his read-ers grew into the hundreds of thousands, then into millions. Edging toward his late seventies, O'Brian continued to write, and his well-deserved financial windfall and notoriety provided access to private clubs as well as to the company of scholars and celebrities. Book sales were on fire, and at the request of Norton, the O'Bri-ans visited America in the fall of 1993 for a tour to promote the latest book, *The Wine-Dark Sea*. O'Brian was then seventy-nine years old, and his private nature made him cantan-kerous when it came to interviews with journalists—talking about his private life was off-limits. *The Commodore* was published in 1994, the same year O'Brian suffered a fall that crushed two vertebrae and eliminated his ability to work his own land.

The O'Brians were per-suaded to return to America in the spring of 1995 to promote *The Commodore*. One of their stops was a special press event in New York City on April 14, 1995. W. W. Norton had chartered *Rose*, and a private reception to celebrate O'Brian was hosted in the ship's

Patrick O'Brian standing in front of *Rose* in New York City

great cabin. Among the attendees were fans, including journalist Walter Cronkite. The guests enjoyed an authentic meal prepared from the recipes published by Anne Chotzinoff Grossman and Lisa Grossman Thomas in their book *Lobscouse & Spotted Dog: Which It's a Gastronomic Companion to the Aubrey/Maturin Novels*. At one point, O'Brian fired an actual cannon, and while enjoying a drink with Captain Bailey, he commented on similarities between *Rose* and HMS *Surprise*.

Back at home in Collioure, O'Brian continued to write and, in the winter of 1996, delivered his eighteenth installment of the series, *The Yellow Admiral*. Mary died in the spring of 1998, the same year *The Hundred Days* was published. O'Brian continued to write and published his next book, *Blue at the Mizzen*, in the fall of 1999. On January 2, 2000, O'Brian died at the Fitzwilliam Hotel in Dublin, Ireland.

❀

It's impossible to ignore the multitude of experiences and passions O'Brian shared with his characters, especially Stephen Maturin. As an ambulance driver during the London Blitz, O'Brian was surrounded by exploding bombs as he gathered the wounded. As the ship's surgeon, Stephen is surrounded by exploding weapons while attending to the wounded or dying. O'Brian did intelligence work for the British government during World War II. Stephen's role expands as he becomes an invaluable spy for the Royal Admiralty. O'Brian's daughter died from an incurable birth defect, whereas Stephen's daughter fully recovers from her birth ailment. The connection between the two runs so deep that Stephen's wife is killed in the novel that was published in the year that O'Brian's wife, Mary, died.

Beyond incorporating himself into his fiction, O'Brian took liberty to introduce fiction into his reality. In *Patrick O'Brian: A Life Revealed*, author Dean King describes an incident where Pat, as a new father in his mid-twenties, was working as a tour guide. He took a particular interest in two young women who were sisters and, in an attempt to impress them, embellished his past. King writes, "He told them that he was Irish, and . . . that he had been an RAF pilot until an accident with a propeller had sent him to the hospital, where, he said, the doctors had put a steel plate in his head." As the years passed, O'Brian continued to command and modify his personal narrative. An example of this can be found in the compilation *Patrick O'Brian: Critical Essays and a Bibliography*, where he writes what seem to be less than accurate tales of sailing as a youth.

Why O'Brian chose to say he was from Ireland or embellish elements of his childhood may forever remain an enigma. Ultimately, he was an extremely intelligent man who led a complex and interesting life. It seems O'Brian used his power as the author to give Stephen the better version of a life O'Brian may have wished for himself. When I asked Peter Weir about how he chose to write the characters of Jack and Stephen for *Master and Commander: The Far Side of the World*, he said, "Making a film of a book can be compared to composing music for an opera, from a libretto. It's a complete transmutation. Casting is a major factor in this change—the actor is a fusion of their own persona with that of the character they play. Of course, the reader of a book imagines their own Jack and Stephen. Some can accept the screen characters, some cannot. It's like a portrait of a notable person—one might say, 'But it doesn't look anything like him!' Another replies, 'True, but the painter has caught the spirit of the man.'"

To me, it appears O'Brian the author fused himself to his character much as Weir describes the fusion of the actor to the character.

Chapter 6

FIRST DAY OF WORK

I SHOWED UP TO THE SHIP on Thursday, November 1, at 7:30 a.m., for my first day of work. I had with me a duffel bag slung over my shoulder containing everything I would take with me to California. I had delayed starting work by a week so I could retrieve my tools and winter clothes from storage. On *Rose*, I would have only a twelve-inch section of a closet rod and a small storage cubby measuring eighteen inches wide, twenty-four inches long, and eighteen inches deep to store my gear. Anything else would have to fit with me in my bunk, which was only thirty inches wide, seventy-eight inches long, and sixteen inches high. I had seen that the work environment was harsh, and I knew anything I brought on the ship would likely be damaged or destroyed by the end of our mission.

My European sailing tour had taught me how to pack lightly. On *Onawa*, I had to be able to fit all my possessions into a duffel bag that wasn't much larger than an airplane carry-on. I had proved I could live for months with next to nothing, but I had sailed in Europe for a season of warm weather and mostly calm conditions; my experience on *Rose* would be very different. I was going to need an arsenal of gear and clothing to survive both the frigidness of the North Atlantic Ocean in January and the relentless humidity and heat of Central America near the equator.

Casey gave me a list of must-haves for the trip: an eight-inch marlinspike with a sheath and lanyard; a knife with a sheath and lanyard; a foul-weather jacket and bibs; a winter jacket; one pair of sea boots; one pair of sneakers; one pair of leather gloves; long underwear; one sweatshirt; two pairs of pants; four pairs of socks; Teva sandals with a toe divider; underwear; T-shirts; three pairs of shorts; a sleeping bag, sheets, and a pillow; and personal products like toothpaste, soap, and razors.

The first items on the list—a knife and marlinspike—had to be with me at all times. They were essential tools for helping me when working in the rigging, for tasks like opening shackles and cutting rope. My knife and spike had to be attached to a lanyard that was attached to a sheath strapped to my body, because dropping a knife or a spike from a hundred feet up in the air could kill a person standing below. The sheaths had to fully enclose the knife and spike so they would not rub against any of the rigging when climbing.

I got a big leg up in the weapons department from one of Casey's former shipmates, Captain Dave. Dave kindly bestowed upon me his knife belt from when he had sailed on *Rose* to Europe in 1996. I soon realized that Dave's belt was excessive compared to the gear of my other shipmates because of its multitude of tools. It was a heavy, worn-down two-inch leather tool belt meant only for strapping tools to my body, not for holding my pants up. I felt a little ridiculous wearing the belt, like it was the tall ship version of Batman's utility belt.

I added order to my belt by assigning individual names to each tool on the belt. I got this idea from a summer I spent painting houses in high school. We had a bunch of ladders of varying lengths, and each ladder was named after a famous porn star. Everyone got a good laugh, and nobody ever got a ladder request wrong. I thought it would only be fitting to carry on the tradition and spent a few hours doing the necessary research to come up with names for my ten-inch marlinspike, seven-inch marlinspike, eight-inch blade knife, Maglite flashlight, and Leatherman.

Dave's belt freed me up to focus on other needs. I had a bunch of grungy clothing left over from my time at IYRS, most of it already covered in oily stains, dried-up paint, and hardened epoxy. I decided to bring my fancy foul-weather gear despite knowing the risk of ruining the expensive garments in exchange for the benefit of the comfort they would provide. Many of my shipmates opted for the less expensive rubber gear, which was colder and stiffer in winter climates and much hotter and heavier in the tropical climates.

I also brought with me a camera, a couple of magazines, and a copy of *Master and Commander*. Casey told me to plan on having little free time for rest and relaxation while underway. I had learned from my time on *Onawa* that I didn't actually need much to live and that living where I worked meant I would want to be off the ship any chance I had. When those moments came in Europe, I got off the boat and explored the ports we visited.

Most of the crew on HMS *Surprise* had but few possessions. Pay was low and space limited. Most hands would have had only clothing, bedding, and a knife. Those in a better financial position might have also owned books, and handy objects. Items like clothing, bedding, tobacco, and other items could be purchased against their wages through the ship's purser, but at a highly marked-up price. An alternative to the purser would be the onboard auctions for the possessions of a dead sailor.

Despite being hired as a deckhand/ship's carpenter, I would be paid the same as the deckhands with no special skills or experience. Before becoming an asset of 20th Century Fox, *Rose* belonged to a 501(c)(3) nonprofit corporation. Under that ownership, deckhand positions could be a mix of volunteers or paid crew. For being unconditionally available to work twenty-four hours a day, seven days a week, the compensation for a paid deckhand position was around $95 per week *before* taxes, with no benefits, a bunk on the ship, and three hot meals a day turned out by the ship's cook. There was no overtime pay or bonus structure. My understanding was the only changes in terms of service and compensation under the new ownership was there would be no volunteers and all deckhand positions would be paid $190 per week. Double the pay but still well below minimum wage.

Knowing how little I would be getting paid helped me to better understand why nearly everyone on the ship was dressed in filthy, stained clothes that you wouldn't want to use as rags. This absurdly low pay rate meant I would need to get even better when it came to how I spent my money. Fortunately for me, having just completed a period in life called "miserably poor apprentice," I was an expert at knowing how to stretch a dollar. I convinced myself the low pay would not be a problem because of the number of days we would be at sea. I wouldn't be able to spend money when the ship was underway, and I had absolutely no expenses because living on board meant I wouldn't pay rent or buy groceries. All the money I earned I was free to spend on libations.

My position as a deckhand was comparable to that of an ordinary seaman in the early nineteenth century. On HMS *Surprise*, an ordinary seaman would have been paid 25 shillings 6 pence per month, an amount equivalent to less than $22 per week in 2001. Standards of living were different then, and the perks of a job in the Royal Navy included a guaranteed wage, a place to sleep, food, and a daily ration of rum. There was also the allure of a windfall of prize money, the financial award paid to the crew of a vessel responsible for the successful capture of enemy vessels or cargo and salvage during times of war. The distribution of prize money was outlined in the Convoys and Cruizers Act of 1708. Under the act, the distribution of the proceeds of a prize, less costs as settled in prize court, was divided into eighths, heavily favoring senior officers. Prior to 1808, the captain received three-eighths (of which one-third went to the commanding flag officer the captain operated under), one-eighth was shared by all the lieutenants, one-eighth went to the warrant officers, one-eighth to the petty officers, and the remaining two-eighths were split among the rest of the crew.

In some cases, men flocked to join the Royal Navy because of famed tales of large prizes taken, such as the Acapulco galleon *Nuestra Señora de Covadonga*, captured in 1773 by the sixty-gun ship *Centurion*. Upon their return to England, each member of the *Centurion* crew received (at the least) an amount equal to twenty years' pay. The lure of prize money plays a repeated role in the Aubrey-Maturin series, starting with the first book, *Master and Commander*. Outmanned and outgunned, Aubrey captures the larger Spanish thirty-two-gun xebec-frigate *Cacafuego* but is denied the reward of promotion and prize money by his superior because Aubrey had an affair with his admiral's wife. Still, fame of Aubrey's accomplishments spread as is shown in *Post Captain*, when Admiral Haddock says of Aubrey, "Lucky Jack Aubrey, they called him. He must have cleared a pretty penny—a most elegant penny indeed. And he it was who took the *Cacafuego*!" On *Rose* I wouldn't have the opportunity for prize money.

That first day was a crash course on becoming acquainted with my new life on *Rose*. I learned quickly that nearly everything revolved around working hard and long hours. Deckhands did almost every job on the ship to keep her operational. We cleaned, fixed, maintained, and then sailed, all in that order. Captain Bailey had told me the ratio of sailing to work was something like ten hours of work for every one hour of actual sailing.

Work started promptly after breakfast. The day began and ended with a muster at the capstan on the weather deck, a formal meeting of the ship's crew where work assignments were handed out for the day and the officers made the crew aware of any new information. On *Rose*, work assignments were called "work-party," a term meaning a coordination of labor for maintenance. I got the sense I was being treated differently than the other hands because I was the new resident chippy. My work assignments were specific to maintaining the integrity of anything related to wood. That could mean replacing structural framing, repairing sections of the deck, building new spars for the rig, or simply fixing the captain's chair.

Jared and Will on the gun deck

Following the employee welcome tour, I was directed to familiarize myself with the ship's woodworking tools. This assignment sent me down to chippy stores, a small compartment located in the bowels of the ship on the port side of the lower deck, immediately forward of the engine room. The space was cramped and narrow, with a small alleyway on one side and a workbench covered in dried paint spills on the other. It was dark and poorly ventilated, smelling of grease and paint thinner. Above and below the bench were open shelves packed tight with plastic milk crates full of old tools, paint, adhesives, and what looked like a collection of junk.

Alone, I stood there for a minute and leaned on the workbench while looking up at the ship's deck beams over my head. I felt like I was starting life over again, and I wondered how I had ended up back at square one. It reminded me of the first night I spent in my basement efficiency apartment when I moved to Newport to start my apprenticeship at IYRS. After a couple of minutes of self-loathing, I ended my pity party and got to work assessing the inventory of the tools. Most of them were in very poor condition, as if someone had already thrown them in the trash once.

At 10:00 a.m., Captain Bailey came looking for me to tell me we would soon be moving the ship to American Shipyard to be hauled out to install new engines and that a fair amount of underbody work would need to be performed to ensure a safer passage. He also said I would spend the next few days doing typical deckhand work with the other deckhands to familiarize myself with the ship's rig. However, once in the yard, I would be pulled off to focus on a structural deck repair up around the foremast.

Captain Bailey then slapped me on my back. "Go find Carrie and shadow her for the day so she can show you the ropes on how to be a deckhand. I hope you are ready to get dirty. Do you know what tar varnishing is?"

I did not. I would soon learn.

⚓

Carrie was new too, having joined the ship in between the days of my being hired and starting work. She was like a real-life Pippi Longstocking, at five feet six inches tall, with pigtails and an infectious smile that was always accompanied by her jovial laugh. Carrie was very chatty, and I soon learned that she could easily outdrink any of the men on board, except for the ship's cook, Hunter.

She grew up in New Hampshire and went to college at Lewis & Clark in Portland, Oregon. After college, she did the ski bum thing for a while, and more recently, she had sailed another tall ship called the *Tole Mour* across the Pacific from Hawaii to Seattle. Carrie loved the tall ship lifestyle but carried herself differently than the other Planet Tall Ship junkies, making her very pleasant to be around. She was clearly a natural leader and had a real Bob Ross kind of way about her when she was teaching.

Knowing *Rose* was so different from any boat I had been on before, I asked Carrie to teach me as if I knew nothing about boats. We started by climbing around the rig together so she could show me how to safely maneuver myself up and down the rigging. The rig was the biggest jungle gym I had ever climbed. It was an overwhelming array of twenty-two spars controlled and held in place by hundreds of lines running in every direction. She suggested I prioritize memorizing the names and associated functions of the many elements of the rig as soon as possible because my comprehension would be crucial for safely executing sail evolutions when at sea.

DECK ARRANGEMENT

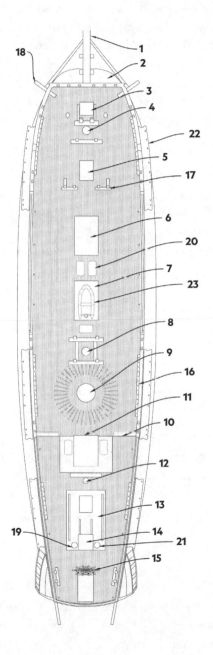

1. Bowsprit
2. Monkey deck
3. Forepeak hatch
4. Foremast
5. Bell hatch
6. Forward main hatch
7. Aft main hatch
8. Mainmast
9. Capstan
10. Break of quarter deck
11. Main companionway
12. Mizzenmast
13. Aft deckhouse
14. Aft companionway
15. Helm
16. Pinrail
17. Bits
18. Cat head
19. Compass
20. Life raft
21. Engine controls
22. Channels
23. Inflatable dinghy

The weather deck was the topmost deck and served as the roof of the ship's interior, meaning it mostly kept the rain and waves on the outside. Much of the perimeter was lined with pinrails, to which most of the running rigging was secured. Inboard, on both sides, there were long alleyways running the length of the ship that remained clear of obstructions so the crew could move along the deck without interference. Forward, secured on the port side, was the ship's longboat, appropriately named *Thorne*. A longboat is a small boat powered by oars or sails, used for transporting people or supplies when the ship is not at a dock.

Centered on the deck, moving from the bow to the stern, was the forepeak hatch, followed by the foremast; the ship's bell (I was warned that only a person with a death wish would dare ring the bell); two large cargo hatches, which were rarely opened, making them ideal platforms for stowing the ship's two inflatable dinghies with outboard engines; the mainmast; then the ship's capstan. A capstan is a large, permanently mounted, manually powered machine oriented on a vertical axle, used for lifting heavy loads such as the anchor or a mast. Aft of the capstan were two steps that led up to the quarterdeck, also where the main companionway hatch was located, then the mizzenmast, the aft deckhouse, and, finally, the ship's helm. Forward of the helm was a ladder leading down to the great cabin from the quarterdeck so the officers could have direct access to the deck from the great cabin. The quarterdeck was reserved for the officers and was where the navigating and ship handling decisions were managed and delegated. Deckhands were allowed on the quarterdeck only when steering the ship, being directed by an officer, or working the mizzenmast.

From the deck, and using her finger like a cursor, Carrie took me on a visual tour of the rig, focusing on elements as if we were building it from scratch, starting with the ship's masts, the vertical spars rising up from the deck. The masts were assembled in sections. In ascending order, they were the lower mast, the topmast, and the topgallant (more commonly referred to by the contraction "t'gallant") mast. On *Rose*, the three lower masts and bowsprit were made of steel, and the remaining spars were made of wood. The foremast and mainmast had three vertical sections, but the mizzenmast had only two. The joining of each mast section was an overlap referred to as the doubling; the lower doubling at the base of the ship's three topmasts was where the fighting tops were located. The bowsprit was like a mast except it projected forward of the bow and was tilted thirty-two degrees above a horizontal plane. Extending forward from the bowsprit was a spar called the jibboom, with the outermost point, the tip, being forty feet above the surface of the water.

The square sails were set from and controlled by horizontal spars known as yards—what Jared and I had laid out on. The name of each yard was prefaced by the name of its corresponding mast. For example, on the mainmast, the name of each yard in ascending order was main yard, main topsail yard, and main t'gallant yard. Like the masts, the name assignments helped the crew understand the relative assignment to the orders given when setting, striking, and trimming sails. There were exceptions; the lowest yard on the mizzenmast was called the crossjack yard, and the yard on the bowsprit was called the spritsail yard.

Carrie then rolled into breaking down the two types of rigging. Standing rigging was used to hold a rig upright and prevented the masts from toppling over. The predominant elements of standing rigging were stays (providing fore-to-aft support along the centerline axis of the ship) and shrouds (side-to-side). "Running rigging" was a broad term used to distinguish any line that in some form connected to the rig, was not fixed on both ends, and was used for the setting and striking of sails, as well as controlling their shape (trimming).

After lunch, Carrie helped me get set up for tar varnishing the rig. This was a typical work assignment for deckhands that was never ending because the miles of fixed lines and wires on the ship needed constant maintenance to protect them from the decay caused by the sun, wind, and salt air. "The best way for you to get comfortable is to get up as high as you can comfortably climb and start crawling around while looking for areas of the rigging needing maintenance," she told me.

On *Rose*, steel wire was used for the standing rigging instead of the traditional natural fiber lines that would have been used on HMS *Surprise* in the early nineteenth century. Steel is stronger and much more durable, but it is not impervious to the elements of the ocean environment. Salt water corrodes the steel wire as it splashes and sprays onto it, and when the water evaporates, it leaves behind the salt.

Originally devised to protect natural hemp fibers from the harsh maritime environment, the process of tar varnishing was adapted to protect modern steel rigging from corrosion. The steel rigging was prepared first by filling the channels in between the wire strands to reduce cavities that could become pits of corrosion, a process called worming. Next, a layer of burlap was tightly wrapped around the wire, a process called parceling, followed by the slathering of a thick coating of tar varnish, a concoction of pine tar, linseed oil, and turpentine, to fill any voids.

Tar varnish has a feel and viscosity similar to molasses, and it sticks to anything it touches. The application must be done carefully, because no drops can be spilled, especially when applying while aloft in the rig. Spilled drops can make a mess of the deck, or, even worse, fall on an unsuspecting person standing below. A well-known rule on the ship was that a case of beer was owed to the crew by any person who spilled or dropped anything from aloft.

To apply the tar varnish, one dons a white cotton sock on one hand and, using an old dish soap bottle as a dispenser, squirts a large glob of the tar varnish into the palm of the sock-covered hand. Then, grip the rigging with the tar-covered sock and stroke with some force to ensure the area has been well coated and all fibers are saturated. I quickly learned tar varnish permanently stains clothing, and the hand doing the work will smell like a newly paved road for some time.

The last step is the serving. Serving is the process of tightly winding seine twine around the parceling in a direction perpendicular to the length of the wire. When completed, this step gets yet another heavy layer of tar varnish. By the time I started work on *Rose*, all her rigging had already been wormed, parceled, and served. Because of the harshness of the environment, servicing the rig was a never-ending process, always underway and constantly being redone. It was a tradition of hard work, going back centuries, that would never go away as long as there was wind, salt water, and sun.

We spent the entire afternoon up in the rigging looking for areas needing repair and applying tar. Come the end of the workday, with the sun low on the horizon and frost forming on the rigging, Carrie patted me on the back. "Great job today," she said, smiling. "There's thirty miles of rigging, so if you ever need something to do, go put a sock on your hand and grab a bottle of tar!"

Chapter 7

JONNY TWO-TIMES

MY FIRST DAY OF WORK on *Rose* felt like an eternity. It had been only a month since my last day of work on *Onawa*, and I had grown soft, enjoying the reprieve from a schedule and accountability. We worked until 5:00 p.m. and then had an hour of free time before dinner. Not wanting to waste a minute, I rushed to pick a bunk in my new home so I could take a short nap before dinner. I was lucky when it came to picking my bunk because most of the ship's crew had not yet arrived and more than half of the bunks were available for the taking. The living accommodations were co-ed because that was how it had always worked on *Rose*. There was no privacy. We all slept and got dressed in the same space, meaning decency and courtesy were expected.

There were three sleeping compartments for the deckhands located below the gun deck, which also meant my bunk would be below the waterline. Starting forward and moving aft there was A-Compartment, B-Compartment, and C-Compartment. The ship's fuel tanks were located in between chippy stores and the galley dry stores, immediately aft of C-Compartment. The engine room was then located aft of the fuel tanks. Aft of the engine room was D-Compartment, the sleeping compartment for the officers and ABs, short for able-bodied seaman, the lowest Coast Guard–certified position on the ship. They were the lead deckhands for each watch group and were paid $20 more per week than the deckhands.

The other deckhands who had already been living on the ship were settled up in A-Compartment. B-Compartment was being used for short-term storage, which left C-Compartment as my only option. C-Compartment was completely empty when I first set foot in it, giving me pick of the litter, and I claimed a middle bunk on the starboard side of the compartment.

INTERIOR DECK ARRANGEMENT

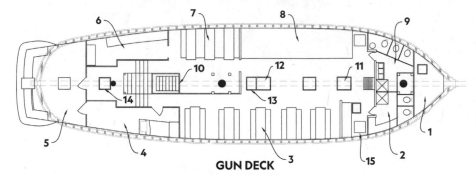

GUN DECK

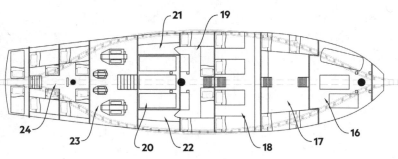

LOWER DECK

1	Forepeak	**13**	Hatch entrance to C-Compartment
2	Women's head	**14**	Hatch entrance to officers' quarters
3	Starboard dining/common area	**15**	Hatch entrance to tank compartment
4	Captain's quarters	**16**	Tank compartment
5	Great cabin	**17**	A-Compartment
6	Galley	**18**	B-Compartment
7	Port dining area	**19**	C-Compartment
8	Sail loft	**20**	Fuel tanks
9	Men's head	**21**	Chippy stores
10	Entrance to engine room	**22**	Dry stores
11	Hatch entrance to A-Compartment	**23**	Engine room
12	Hatch entrance to B-Compartment	**24**	Officers' quarters

C-Compartment felt like a tall sardine can filled with coffins stacked three high with no portholes or ventilation ducts. The sole was painted a traditional shade of gray typically applied in bilges or mechanical spaces on all types of vessels. All the other surfaces were painted white. The bunks were small and tight, with just enough room to roll on my side. Each bunk had a thin vinyl-covered mattress, a reading light, and a privacy curtain. The compartment had a sweaty, musty odor, like my grandmother's damp basement. It made me think of the hundreds of bodies that had slept in the bunk long before me.

I knew my luck of not sharing the sleeping compartment with others would be short-lived. Tony was aggressively building the crew, and soon the compartment would be filled with his new hires. Jared had selected a bunk in C-Compartment but had not yet spent a night on the ship despite having worked for a week. He was not obligated to because we were in daywork mode and night watches would not begin until we were ready to depart for California. Eventually he would need to move on board, but for the time being he was enjoying every cent he paid in rent at his apartment, especially because Mrs. Robinson refused to let him out of their lease because she was angry he was leaving to sail with me.

Lying in my bunk after the hard day's work was absolute heaven. It was noticeably different from how the crew would have slept on HMS *Surprise*. Whereas *Rose* had two subdecks below the weather deck, HMS *Surprise* had three. Her crew benefitted from not having to sleep between the guns like the crew of a ship of the line. Instead, the men slept on the lower deck, below the upper deck, where the twenty-four thirty-two-pounder carronades were housed, and above the main hold, where various supplies were stored. The drawback to having the additional subdeck on HMS *Surprise* meant the lower deck had a maximum of four feet six inches of headroom between the deck beams and less at each beam.

Unlike *Rose*, the crew of HMS *Surprise* slept on hammocks because a hammock took up little space, was easy to store, and helped to absorb the rolling and crashing a ship could experience while underway. Credit for the adoption of hammocks on boats has been given to Christopher Columbus, who observed them in use by Indigenous people in the New World. For the crew, the Royal Navy allotted six feet of length with a minimum of one foot two inches' width per man. Besides the limited headroom and lack of ventilation and light, the crew also had to work around the rows of tables lining the perimeter of the deck with sea chests used for seating.

Every inch counted when considering that the typical company for a ship like HMS *Surprise* would have been around two hundred men, of whom 150 would have slept in approximately 1,750 square feet (162.6 square meters) of space on the lower deck between the standing officers' cabins aft and the storerooms forward. Fortunately, the ship's crew was often divided in two watches, meaning only seventy-five men on average would have shared the small, dark, and unventilated space for sleeping when the ship was underway. Accurately captured by O'Brian in *Master and Commander*, Jack Aubrey expresses his frustration with the tight accommodations: "He was still red in the face as he went down into the boat after the midshipman. 'Do they really imagine I shall leave an able-bodied man on shore if I can cram him aboard?' he said to himself. 'Of course, their precious three watches will have to go. And even so, fourteen inches will be hard to find.'"

⚙

I fell asleep as soon as my head hit the pillow. I had not even been in the compartment for more than ten minutes when I was suddenly startled awake by the overzealous voice of a new shipmate.

"Hi, I'm *Blythe*!" It was almost as if she knew I had just fallen asleep and wanted to prank me by screaming into my ear. Startled, I rolled over, looked out of my bunk, and there, staring back at me, was the face of a very chipper young woman looking to be in her early twenties, medium build, dirty-blond hair, and wearing an out-of-place vintage ski hat. In addition to the hat, she had a really big smile and a lot more enthusiasm than I had available at the moment.

Not moving, I responded with a meager "I'm Will."

"Are any of these bunks taken?"

"No, I don't think so, you can pick any one you want, they're all yours."

Blythe proceeded to set herself up in a bunk adjacent to mine and told me her story as she unpacked her belongings. She had been working on a schooner out of Camden, Maine. The season was over, and Tony called her because of a résumé she submitted to *Rose* after graduating from college earlier in the year. She was looking forward to cutting her teeth on a ship with square sails. Her preppiness made it clear that she was not from Planet Tall Ship. Blythe surprised her family with the decision to make a career out of sailing instead of using her new college degree. Nobody else in her family sailed for a living.

Like her name, Blythe radiated familiarity and good spirit. It took only a few minutes for me to realize that despite the boisterous interruption of my well-earned sleep, it was going to be great having her join C-Compartment.

⚙

By the end of my first week on the ship, we had a second mate, a third mate, and a boatswain, and half of our deckhand slots had been filled. Andy, our second mate, had sailed previously on *Rose* when Casey was the chief mate. He had a long, scraggly beard, could talk longer than anyone about absolutely anything, and had a real skill for coming up with laborious and tedious work. Andy was the perfect embodiment of tall ship culture. After graduating from college with a degree in sculpture, he became a city bus driver in Aspen. Seeing an issue of *Yankee* magazine, he traveled to Maine to join a fleet of schooners, launching his career as a professional sailor. Christina, our third mate, was Tony's girlfriend, but their romantic relationship was not why she got the job. Christina had plenty of experience, having also previously crewed on *Rose*, and had most recently been working as the captain of a river dory on the Potomac when Captain Bailey offered her the job. She was strong for her small build and, like a loyal mother hen, loved everyone on the ship. Christina had long brown hair, an infectious smile, and a will like steel.

The ship finally had a boatswain by the name of Kerns. A boatswain (or bosun) is the officer of the rig, and on *Rose*, he was responsible for overseeing the maintenance and upkeep of all aspects of the ship's rigging. Kerns was a giant at six feet six inches tall, had long blond hair, a beard, and looked like he had just come off the set of *Braveheart*. Kerns loved to roll drum cigarettes all day and had a hard demeanor. He marched to his own beat and had a short temper when it came to having to teach the same task twice.

One day after clearing my plate following lunch, I headed up to deck to enjoy a bit of downtime before the afternoon work session started. The air outside was unusually warm. Looking around, I realized everyone else also had the same plan to bask in the warm sunlight for a few minutes before trudging back to work. It was a good day because both the workload and the weather were cooperating.

I was looking to the south out over the harbor when I heard a chuckle. I flipped around and saw a few of the other hands talking to someone on the dock and motioning for him to come aboard. I couldn't place the voice, but I knew it.

I winced while trying to remember how. He was on deck, but I still couldn't see him because of a group of three hands crowded at the top of the gangway.

Someone moved, and I saw who it was. His curly blond hair, blue eyes, and gaping grin were unmistakable. It was Jonny Two-Times. I charged at him with all my strength and speed. I needed only a few steps to get my weight behind my speed, undecided whether to punch him in the cheek or just tackle him. I roared, "Jonny Two-Times!" as I closed the distance between us. He saw me and gritted his teeth.

"One-Eyed Willy!"

☸

The night after accepting the job on *Rose*, Jared and I were at a bar called the International Yacht and Athletic Club. The IYAC is the end-all be-all sailor bar in Newport. It's small inside but has large windows facing Thames Street to help bring in a lot of light to counterbalance the dark navy-blue walls filled with pictures of racing sailboats and half hulls. There is a jukebox and pool table on one side, a bar on the other. In the summer, the IYAC overflows with sailors smoking cigarettes on the sidewalks outside. Then there are the sailor groupies hanging off the hotshot racing sailors. That's the fun part, the real deal mixed in with the wannabes.

The bar was much more intimate that time of year since most sailors had long since left Newport for warmer waters. Still, it filled up on the weekends with locals and the few remaining transient sailors who were either working on a refit or just coming back from a delivery. We were probably four hours into the night and god knows how many drinks when we met Jon. He caught our attention because he had a wad of two-dollar bills he was using to tip the bartender.

Jon was having one last blast before sailing south on a delivery, and as it turned out Tony was going to be skippering it down. I assumed this was something Tony had previously committed to, explaining why he would be taking a short leave from *Rose* and would therefore not be on the ship during my first couple of weeks.

Jon made a polished first impression, like he had walked off the set of *The Great Gatsby*. He had both the looks and sophisticated charm of Shakespeare's Mercutio, five feet ten inches, lean, with blond curly hair, glasses, and sharply dressed. His sense of humor was explosive, and I was immediately curious and envious of his unwavering confidence. We hit it off right away. Jon had graduated from Colby and worked as an architect in Boston for a year. He then decided to take a sabbatical to do some sailing and was staying with some Colby friends who lived in Newport and had recently founded a new beer company called Newport Storm.

We learned Jon would be joining *Rose* as a deckhand when he returned from his delivery with Tony. Somewhere in the middle of this, maybe four or five Dark and Stormys into it, we came up with a spectacular plan to play a prank on the crew of the ship by staging a fistfight the moment we first saw each other on the ship. None of the others had met Jon or knew he had been hired, and nobody knew we now knew each other. The stage was set for "Jonny Two-Times" and "One-Eyed Willy" to do battle.

⚙

I took Jon down good, but kind of pulled back as I was about to hit him since I did not really want to hurt him. The moment was like a flash.

There were gasps and looks of total confusion. None of that mattered, though, because I did not realize the captain's Jack Russell terrier, Jackal, had keenly picked up on what was about to happen. Jackal may have been small, but he was fierce. The moment I started sprinting, Jackal took off. He ran toward Jon also, not to greet him, but to attack. I felt Jackal bite me as soon as I hit Jon, and he kept nipping at us again and again until we curled up, shrieking like teenage girls who had spotted a shark in the water.

Lying on the deck, kind of laughing, I looked around and saw our other shipmates confused and in a state of disarray. I smirked and looked at Jon. "Welcome aboard."

Someone else shouted for Jackal to get back, and we stood up, laughing. The tension was immediately eased. Jon and I congratulated each other on remembering to pull off the prank. I had forgotten our plan until I heard his voice as he walked up the gangway.

After the dust settled, I invited Jon to grab a bunk in C-Compartment. There was no hesitation in his acceptance. I was feeling less out of my element and developing a growing confidence that more like-minded individuals like Jon and Blythe would be joining the crew as we got closer to our departure.

— *Chapter 8* —

PREPARATION

PETER WEIR WAS FIRST INTRODUCED to the world of Patrick O'Brian in the early 1990s, when a friend saw that he was reading a book by Alexander Kent and said, "If you like that, you should read O'Brian." When Weir was finishing up *The Truman Show* for Paramount, the studio asked if they could give him a gift. He asked for the entire Aubrey-Maturin series, first edition in hardcover. Weir told me, "One day the gift arrived all wrapped up, there were nineteen books at the time." He finished his work on the film and then read all the books.

In 2001, now having committed to bringing O'Brian's work to the screen, Weir brought his skeptical team of shipwrights to Newport to assess *Rose*, and their general reaction dampened his enthusiasm. He said, "From a distance, the *Rose* looked pretty good." The issues came into focus the closer they got. With Weir was Bill Leonard, who led the construction of the *Endeavour* replica, and two other Perth shipwrights, Nick Truelove and Igor Bjorksten. According to Weir, Leonard cast a cold blanket over what he saw, saying it was not a great reconstruction, but that it could be improved. At the time Weir found her, *Rose* was the only frigate actively sailing in the world. Understanding the task that lay before them, Weir's team began developing a plan for getting *Rose* to California so they could transform her into HMS *Surprise*. Leonard's schedule limited his involvement to consulting from Australia after the initial inspection, while Truelove and Bjorksten were able to work on location through the preproduction preparation and were cast as seamen for the film.

❁

On November 14, we moved *Rose* to American Shipyard (now known as Newport Shipyard) to haul her out of the water for the planned major refit before departure.

A refit means to repair, fix, restore, and/or renovate. The main priorities of this refit were replacing the engines, some structural deck work, recaulking the bottom as necessary, and adding a layer of copper plating up near the bow below the waterline.

This was exciting because it was the first time the ship had left the dock since I joined. The move was a short pleasure cruise, not more than ten minutes, less than half a mile as the crow flies. I was eager to see how the evolutions of commands and coordination would be executed on a ship like *Rose*. It was the largest vessel I had crewed on, and much of what I knew did not apply.

I was assigned to the helm and quickly learned the helmsman does not think, just follows the orders by the commanding officer. Captains don't drive ships; instead, they act like the conductor of a large symphony by choreographing the entire process. Captain Bailey stood at the engine controls and directed my steering of the ship's wheel as he throttled the engines. His commands were calculated and instinctual.

We motored over to a floating dock on the north side of the yard to break down the engine room and remove the old engines. This took several days. Then, with the engines out and the assistance of two tugboats, we moved the ship over to the marine railway, a traditional method for hauling a ship out of the water. The railway was literally an oversize cradle that slid out of the water on a sloped rail like a train. There was a cable system connected to a machine room. The cable was eased out, allowing the cradle to slide down the rail into the water. The cradle had staging rails on either side rising high above the water to serve as anchor points for securing the vessel's dock lines.

We approached the rail slowly while coordinating with the tugs via handheld VHF radios. *Rose* moved ever so slowly over the cradle, and when within reach, heaving lines were sent over to the shipyard crew waiting on the staging platforms on both the port and starboard sides of the ship. Captain Bailey showed his expertise as he coordinated the collaborative effort to position the ship into the cradle without the use of engines. He did everything perfectly.

With our lines secured, the ship was now under the control of the shipyard crew. The cradle began to slowly move forward along the rail. There was a soft thud followed by a hard feeling as we moved up the ramp; that was the moment the ship stopped floating and all of her weight had been transferred to the cart as it moved forward, rising up out of the water. The process from start to finish took thirty minutes.

Being hauled out and so high up out of the water meant the weather deck at midship was thirty feet above the hard—what the ground is called in a shipyard—so the yard crew set up a scaffolding staircase to be used as our means for getting on and off the ship. We continued to live on the ship during the extensive and rapid refit. A shipyard is a dirty industrial space filled with terrible chemical smells and noisy heavy machinery. Typically, the crews of yachts move into hotels or temporary housing when their boats are hauled for yard work. Not so on Planet Tall Ship.

Rose hauled out at the shipyard

Living on *Rose* hauled out at a shipyard in southern New England at the start of winter was terribly uncomfortable for many reasons but mostly because of the frigid northerly winds that blew hard against the ship's hull and rigging. When in the water, a boat can absorb the forces of wind by rocking. Being so high in the air added a substantial amount of wind resistance, and *Rose* would vibrate and rattle in unsettling ways as the strong, cold wind blew.

Plans for the refit were so extensive and costly that the production company sent a representative to ensure there was a legitimate reason for all the work being performed. Enter Rick Hicks.

Rick owned a company called Big Screen Marine, a marine service business that worked exclusively with the film industry. He was Hollywood's fixer when it came to anything related to watercraft used in film production. He had worked on many movies, including *Interview with the Vampire*, *Waterworld*, and *The Perfect Storm*. Rick blended in well with everyone on board—ironic, because he himself was such an unusual character. He was originally from a small town in Maine called China, but he talked like he grew up behind a dumpster in South Boston. He was in his mid-forties, lived in Los Angeles, and always looked like he had come from some hard-core biker bar with his "skull rag" covering his bald head.

We had less than two months to complete the massive worklist Captain Bailey and the officers had put together to prepare the ship for our blue-water adventure to the far side of the world. The long worklist had to be broken up and delegated to the shipyard, a shipwright named Leon Poindexter, and the ship's crew. The shipyard was responsible for repowering the ship with two brand-new, massive Caterpillar 3406 diesel engines, rebuilding the bilge pump manifold, and installing two giant rubber fuel bladders to extend the ship's range.

Leon was a sawdust-covered man who looked like he had been on the sea for decades. He had a ponytail, always wore a black classic Greek fisherman's cap, and drove the same old-lady kind of car my deaf grandmother used to drive. Leon had worked on *Rose* for decades, he knew her inside and out, and most importantly, he always got the job done. Leon was responsible for managing and coordinating the shipwright work, including rebuilding some of the ship's structural elements below the weather deck and overseeing the copper plating being added below the waterline up near the bow. At the same time, he was working with Peter Weir's team and would fly out to California to work with the art department at Fox Studios once we got underway.

Nearly everything else on the worklist was assigned to the crew. The list included items like rebuilding all the ship's blocks (the nautical term used for a pulley), repairing and sealing the spars, preparing safety gear, and rigging up all the sails. Much of the work involved heavy lifting or working with rusty metal and grime.

The worst job I heard of was the repair of the old steel freshwater tank. Poor Jared spent a week inside grinding out the rust. The baffles—long metal plates that attached to the inside to prevent fluid surging—made it nearly impossible for a big guy like him to get into a comfortable position for more than a few minutes without having to shift his weight. One day Jared was in the back of the tank when the ship lost power, plunging him into darkness. He froze up, not knowing what to do or how to get out. He said he was terrified. I felt sick just hearing him describe being stuck in that small, dark, rust-filled maze, in a contorted position, with no light to help guide him out.

The scope of chippy work was extensive, so a few additional shipwrights were hired to help with the worklist. Todd from *Onawa* was hired to help me rebuild the mast partners at the foremast. Mast partners are the structural components of the deck framing that provide the lateral support needed to prevent the mast from moving out of place where it enters the deck. The task required that we tear up a section of the deck surrounding the mast to gain access to the framing elements beneath. The project took two weeks, so we built a makeshift tent of tarps around the base of the mast to prevent the cold winter weather from penetrating our ship's interior for the duration of the project.

Other than working on the mast partners, I spent a good amount of my time applying new copper plates to the hull below the waterline near the bow. This project meant lathering a thick layer of tar to the hull, before covering it with a series of two-foot-by-four-foot copper plates, then fastening them to the planks with copper nails. It was known that *Rose* leaked very badly up near her bow, and the hope was to use the copper sheathing in combination with the tar to help mitigate the amount of seawater that would come in when the ship was underway.

The Royal Navy began applying copper plating to ships in the mid-eighteenth century to prevent *Teredo navalis*, commonly called the naval shipworm, from burrowing into the ships' planking, which destroyed the integrity of the hull. An additional benefit of the copper sheathing was that it helped to combat the growth of weeds and barnacles on the hull, which limited the maximum speed a ship could achieve. The universal practice took some time to adopt, since it had drawbacks, such as the high expense and the limited understanding of galvanic corrosion, an electrochemical process in which two dissimilar metals, such as iron and copper, are immersed in an electrolyte such as seawater. The copper sheathing caused significant corrosion where it came into physical contact with iron elements such as the bolts in the ship's keel as well as the gudgeons and pintles of the rudder, the metallic fittings used to connect the rudder to the hull. After decades of experimentation, this issue was solved in 1783, when bolts began being forged from a newly created metal alloy made from copper and zinc.

B-Compartment was cleared out so those of us living in C-Compartment could move forward because the massive new fuel bladders took up so much space. Jonny Two-Times, Blythe (the boisterous vintage-ski-hat wearer), Jared, and I had become a sort of clique and were happy to take over the starboard section of B-Compartment. I thought our new living situation was the best on the ship next to Captain Bailey's private cabin. Whereas the other living compartments were arranged so the bunks were exposed to a central passageway, ours were hidden around a corner, providing us with some much wanted separation from the die-hard Planet Tall Ship crew members living in A-Compartment and D-Compartment.

We offered our new ship's medical officer, Erinn, one of the bunks in our section. Erinn was a recent graduate of the United States Merchant Marine Academy. She outranked most of the crew on the ship but bunked with us because the ship's medical officer was a deckhand position on *Rose.* Erinn had a light complexion and long brown hair, wore oversize clothes, and was initially very reserved, with a calculated sense of humor. However, after a few nights at the bars, we all learned Erinn had a wild and fun side.

Erinn's best friend from the academy was Michael Gordon, who went by GT. He was hired on to be the ship's engineer, an officer's position, meaning he got to bunk with the other officers in D-Compartment. GT was clean-cut with short dark hair parted to the side, skinny but muscular, built like a Broad-

Starboard side of B-Compartment: Jon, Jared, Erinn, Blythe, Will

way dancer. He put a lot of effort into contributing to anything that needed to get done.

I felt bad for GT, because he had shown up in the middle of a refit that was well underway, and I appreciated how hard it must have been for him to have been thrown into such a large and complex undertaking. Fortunately, GT had Rick and his experience to help with the coordination and management of the yard crew. Unfortunately, GT had Vincent, "the brute," assigned as an assistant. It got so bad that GT had to bar him from the engine room because he was terrible at following directions. In addition to the engines, GT was also responsible for anything mechanical on the ship, and, like my grandfather's recliner, everything was well worn in. GT always had to rush to fix the next broken thing.

The smorgasbord of personalities on the ship continued to expand as we rolled into December. There was Scott, who could be mum as an oyster, with a scraggily demeanor that complemented his hand-tossed greasy hair and beard. He came with experience, having sailed on the three-masted schooner *Denis Sullivan*, and knew a good amount about rigging. There was Aaron, who hailed from New York City and most recently had been working for the Winter Olympics in Salt Lake City. Tony tracked him down and persuaded him to leave Utah to join the ship. There was Alex, a famous *Rose* alumnus who sailed on the ship as a teenager when it went to Europe in 1996. Alex finished college early so he could make the passage with us. Then there was Peggy, who was a real enigma. She had red hair, a medium build, and always wore a blank stare when anyone spoke to her. She was like the squirrel who eats out of a bird feeder, and I had no idea why she joined the ship. I don't believe she had any previous experience.

We were also joined by April and Dwight, a romantically involved couple who set themselves up on the port side of B-Compartment. I was less than thrilled because they were devout Planet Tall Shippers who seemed to worship the smell of tar so much that when they bathed, and I don't recall it happening often, they used a soap intentionally scented to smell like tar. With their presence, B-Compartment took on the smell of a seasoned mechanic's shop. April had short blond hair and was kind of punkish. She may have been more progressive than Dwight, but in all honesty, I kept my distance because it was obvious our personalities were not compatible.

Dwight rubbed me the wrong way from the beginning. He came off as a know-it-all, had short, scruffy brown hair, a thick handlebar mustache, and wore a lot of Carhartt clothing. Dwight appeared to resist modern amenities, and if he had his way, everyone on the ship would have been living in the same squalid conditions that the crew of HMS *Surprise* endured. He geeked out real hard when it came to anything having to do with rigging. Like a sommelier at a fine restaurant, he could waste hours telling you about hemp rope, rope splices, wire splices, seizings, knots, hitches, snatch blocks, belaying pins, deadeyes, grommets, beckets, boltropes, bumpkins, jiggers, oakum, saddles, snotters, flemish eyes, lashings, parcellings, or baggy wrinkle. His knowledge was impressive, but I thought it was impractical. Dwight was unwilling to consider progressive rigging technology, especially if the suggestions came from an individual without a tall ship pedigree.

Our crew was closing in on Tony's target of thirty members. We had all our officers, and more deckhands were on their way to the ship. We had become a real melting pot of characters, which resulted in the formation of small subgroups. There were the cult-type sailors who embraced Planet Tall Ship, idolizing their glorified version of an archaic sailing lifestyle. Then there were the rebels, the group of sailors who, like me, were mostly newer to the scene, more inclined to enjoy the benefits of a modern sailing lifestyle and willing to consider newer methods and techniques instead of accepting the old way as the only way. Lastly, there were the floaters, the few random sailors who were trying to find the best of both worlds.

Subgroup divisions were not limited to deckhands; even the officers were divided. Tony, our chief mate, was a rebel. Andy, our second mate, was a Planet Tall Shipper. Christina, our third mate, was a floater. I came to believe Captain Bailey was the leader of the rebels, basing my claim on his hatred for sea shanties. One day Vincent played some shanties on a boom box in one of the living compartments, and Captain Bailey came flying down, screaming at the top of his lungs for him to "Turn that goddamn shit off now!" He bashed in the boom box with a crowbar. Captain Bailey was henceforth dubbed the "Anti-Shanty Captain."

❂

Despite the growing crew, time was working against us. The prevailing conditions of the North Atlantic Ocean would become only more hostile as the winter wore on. We were still weeks away from leaving Newport, and we could not afford any setbacks or holdups. Missing our window could mean potentially delaying our departure until spring.

As our target deadline for completion of the refit closed in, Tony called a special motivational muster, kicking it off by complimenting us on our progress and thanking everyone for all the extra time we had put in. He then got to the point: "We need to extend our workdays even more. People are going to need to start working late if we are going to make our deadline."

He then shifted gears. "We are all in this together, and we all need to help one another in getting the job done. Job assignments should never be passed down. I am willing to do any job on the ship, but I am the chief mate, and with that comes responsibilities sometimes requiring me to delegate jobs. However, no person will be asked to work late if I am not working also, and if this happens, I will always work as late as anyone still working."

This blew my mind as I was more used to being told what to do, and in that moment, he inspired me to work harder. Shit rolls downhill, and most people are happy to pass it on to the next person down the line. Not Tony.

The work did get harder and longer. The sun set around 4:30 p.m., meaning we were in the dark long before our workday was over. Dinner service was frequently delayed because of the work we were trying to pack in. With Jared and Jon, I occasionally started skipping dinner so we could finish work and blow off steam at a bar when we were done. Tempers were getting short, and the officers were trying to motivate us by buying fresh donuts for breakfast or having a cold case of beer ready for everyone at the end of a particularly long workday.

Christmas came and went. We launched the ship without any problems. The new engines fired up as planned. That put a smile on everyone's face, drumming up some much-needed confidence that our hard work was paying off. There still was plenty of rigging work happening, and we had begun bending on sails, attaching the sails to the spars, so they were ready for use. We were now in January and nearly ready to depart for California. It was hard work, requiring lots of hands. Usually, Captain Bailey kept me exempt from the typical deckhand tasks so I could stay on track with my chippy projects, but even I was rallied to help bend the sails on.

I remember the night we bent on the mizzen and main topsails. I wished I had a camera, but I don't think I would have been able to operate it due to the freezing weather. It was dark, and the shipyard was quiet because the yard workers had long since gone home for the evening, enjoying the warmth of their homes, maybe eating dinner with their families or watching TV. Not us—we were heading into our twelfth hour of work for the day when it began snowing.

There was something about being aloft at night that felt so wrong. It was so cold, but I couldn't wear gloves because I needed the dexterity of my fingers to tie the knots. We were fifty feet up in the rig, and the snow combined with the occasional gust of wind made it hard to stay nimble. I found myself constantly smacking my hands on the yard to feel the sting and keep blood flowing in my fingertips.

Pain aside, there was something special about looking forward and seeing my shipmates aloft on the mainmast doing the same. I thought it was both terrible and beautiful to be up there, looking down at the snow falling on our ship. The stillness of the shipyard magnified the sound of the snow as it hit the hanging sails, with a sort of rat-tat-tat like the sound of a drum brush during a soft extended solo.

In that peaceful moment, Jon first dropped his Annie Lennox call on us all. He was up on the mainmast, and out of nowhere came a very loud "Do-be-do-be-do-do-do (oh)!" The line is the chorus of Lennox's song "No More 'I Love You's.'" It was then awkwardly followed by his loud chuckling laugh, a pause, and then he did it again: "Do-be-do-be-do-do-do (oh)!"

Jon had sung the song a few random times over the past couple of months, and we all knew what came next. Without any coordination, I, along with the other hands up on both masts, wholeheartedly and at the top of our lungs sang out, "Ah-ah!"

From that moment onward, "Do-be-do-be-do-do-do (oh!)," became our war cry. If you were walking on the dock or at a bar or going to the bathroom or climbing the rig, you knew if someone sang, "Do-be-do-be-do-do-do (oh!)," you would be obligated to return it with "Ah-ah!"

☸

With a week to go before departure, the officers announced a plan to host a costume party on the ship. It was to be a grand send-off, a chance to celebrate all the hard work we had done to prepare *Rose* for the passage. The ship would cover all expenses and we were each allowed to invite one guest to the party. The timing was serendipitous because I had the sense that morale was sinking and something needed to happen to pull everyone together.

Personally, I felt good and was having plenty of fun with Jared and Jon. We were always cracking jokes and trying to rally the rest of the crew to join us. Differences between the rebels and Planet Tall Ship were left on *Rose* when we all went to a bar after work. A bunch of us would pile into a few cars to cruise the Newport bar scene, hoping to catch the end of a happy hour or a weeknight drink special. On Sundays we would all go to the Pelham for the $3 draft beers and to see a band called the Booze Brothers play raunchy covers of famous songs. The mix of locals and a dozen tall ship sailors made quite an interesting crowd.

The farewell party was a great success. Having the added company of guests and significant others on board helped to diversify the crowd just enough to make it interesting. The costumes were better than expected, and nearly all were of a nautical theme except for Jon, who was dressed up like Hugh Hefner, and Todd, who dressed as a reggae rock star with a dreadlock wig and all. Blythe made her own mermaid costume, and Tony was Popeye. I was lazy, donning my red foul-weather bibs and calling myself an offshore sailor.

Tony dressed as Popeye at our farewell party. Jon is standing behind him, and Blythe is holding his left shoulder.

The party ran its course, and by its end many of us were looking to keep the momentum going by taking it out to the bars. Like shepherds trying to herd a litter of kittens, Jon, Jared, and I somehow managed to persuade half the crew to join us for more drinks at the Star Bar, a popular watering hole for local college students and the cleaner, preppier young locals. The vibe was modern and fresh, with three billiard tables, a bar running the length of the establishment, a smattering of cocktail tables, and a row of tall windows overlooking the harbor.

We scattered on arrival, some rushing to the bar and others taking over the pool tables. I grabbed a drink and got into a conversation with Tony, Jared, Jon, and Christina. While talking, I caught sight of a girl I knew talking to a guy in a corduroy blazer. Driven by my own insecurities, I made the mistake of pointing her out to Tony while griping how she acted as if she was just meeting me for the first time every time I saw her. Glances were made over in her direction as I whined.

"Hey, do you mind if I go say hi to her?" Tony asked.

Not waiting for my answer, and still dressed up like Popeye, Tony the sailor-man walked over and stepped in between her and the guy, cutting him off, and said, "Hi, I'm Tony!"

You could immediately see the confusion on her face. Enraged, the guy grabbed Tony's arm and turned him around, saying, "What the fuck, dude!"

Tony quickly put his arms up like he was being held up at a robbery and with a big goofy smile on his face said, "I'm sorry, man, I didn't realize you were talking to her."

Calmly, Tony then turned around and began walking back toward us. We all sighed in relief while laughing and telling Tony we thought he was going to start a huge fight. Then, not saying a word, Tony turned around and walked back over to the same girl and guy and did the exact same thing again, stepping in between them, cutting the guy off, and saying, "Hi, I'm Tony!"

And just like the first time, the guy grabbed Tony and swung him around, but this time Tony used the inertia to load up a clenched fist, ready with a Mike Tyson–esque punch, sending the guy flying back in the air!

A woman screamed, pint glasses and bottles were suddenly shattered, and two other completely random fights broke out in the bar. We found ourselves standing in the middle of a full-on bar brawl. Out of the corner of my eye, I saw the bouncers tossing their stools to the side as they grabbed people to heave them out of the bar. I was thirty feet from the door and managed to keep myself in a clear space with nobody around me. In a matter of minutes, half the people were thrown out of the bar and anyone left seemed utterly confused.

It was over just as fast as it had started. After catching their breath, the bouncers walked over to Tony and told him he had to leave and that he was out for the night. Tony shrugged his shoulders, said he was sorry, and walked out without looking back.

Christina smiled at us and said, "Good night." She then went running after him.

Sailors have always had a reputation for being troublemakers when ashore. When at sea, sailors live by a rigid schedule and must abide by a strict code of good conduct. Patrick O'Brian's sense of humor shines when depicting the mayhem of time spent onshore. Even Jack Aubrey sometimes has trouble moderating his indulgences when onshore, despite his maturing career, getting married, and having children. O'Brian paints a sorry picture in *The Mauritius Command*, when, having only just arrived in Cape Town, before breakfast, Stephen is greeted by a very hungover Jack: "Captain Aubrey had the yellow, puffy look of one who has drunk far too much—so much indeed that his twenty-mile ride back had not worked it off."

I felt terrible the next morning, much more hungover than I had been in a very long time—as yellow and puffy as Jack. I drank way too much, and my body had every intention of punishing me for my poor decisions. It was Sunday, our one guaranteed day of rest. Hunter had Sundays off when we were at the dock, leaving us to feed ourselves; it was the only day we were allowed to go into the galley to help ourselves to the food in the fridge so long as we cleaned up our mess. Hunter made it easy by making sure to save leftovers from the week for us. It was around 6:30 a.m., and I thought the best thing I could do for myself was to eat leftover enchiladas from Friday night's dinner.

I was in the galley stuffing my face when Captain Bailey came walking in. He stared me down, scanning me from head to toe and shaking his head from side to side.

I looked over at him. "What?"

Captain Bailey walked slowly past me toward the refrigerator. "How was your night?"

"Just fine, how was yours?" I asked, not really caring about his answer.

"It was fine, kind of quiet after you all left." He trailed off while gazing into the refrigerator. He then looked back at me with one eyebrow raised. "You sure it was just fine?"

I had just stuffed my mouth full of cold enchilada and replied, "Of courth, jutht fiiiiine."

Then Captain Bailey slammed the refrigerator door, swung around, and poked me hard, right in the chest, with his left index finger. "Oh really? Then can you tell me why there were two police officers here at three a.m. this morning with David Kilroy?"

I must have looked like a deer in headlights, with my mouth still full of food. I shook my head while looking at him, being sure to not break eye contact. "No."

Captain Bailey cocked his head to the right while looking right into my eyes. "Will, do you know who David Kilroy is?"

I did not.

"I'm surprised you don't, because he is a pretty important man in Newport. He owns a number of popular bars. I think you know some of them: the Pelham, the Landing, THE STAR BAR!"

I panicked. "It wasn't his fault!"

Captain Bailey looked up as if he was trying to figure out what kind of hell to bring down on me. Then, he seemed to lose his balance and fell over. I sprinted to stop him from falling. He was not falling; he was just laughing so hard that he collapsed.

"Holy shit, Wilbur, you idiot. Tony got back last night and told us all about the whole thing. You should have seen your face just now!"

Goddamnit, he really got me there, that bastard. I was all kinds of hungover and now I was going to have to listen to him tell everyone ten times over about this prank he pulled on me. All I could think was, *Game on, old man. Game on!*

Chapter 9

*U*NDERWAY

SO LONG, NEWPORT! We were officially off the dock on Thursday, January 10, at 1315, with all hands on deck. We had been ready to go for nearly a week, but ominous weather forecasts kept us tied to the dock. Ultimately, the patience of the production company had grown exhausted waiting out Captain Bailey's weather concerns, and they gave the order to go. Maybe the higher-ups calling the shots believed in dies infaustus (unlucky day), an age-old sailors' superstition believing it bad luck to begin a voyage on a Friday.

When it came time to get underway, the air temperature was a balmy 46° Fahrenheit (7.8° Celsius), and the wind, coming from the west, was blowing hard against our beam, pinning the ship against the dock. Susan Genett, the marine weather forecaster, told Captain Bailey that if we were not able to depart from Newport in the weather window, *Rose* would likely be impacted by multiple snowstorms in port. Coastal ocean-effect snow holds a high moisture content; it's heavy snow. The intricate workings of a three-masted, square-rigged ship require a lot of real-time vigilance and maintenance to remain efficient for sail operation after enduring a heavy snow. Delaying the departure of the ship until spring could have caused significant production issues for the film.

Waiting for the wind to die down was not an option, so reinforcements in the form of two tugboats were summoned to help pull the ship away from the dock. I found myself looking from side to side, asking if this was one of those moments in which the gods were doing anything they could to send a message telling us not to leave.

The tugboats sent massively thick towlines over to *Rose*. The lines were wet and heavy, each one as thick as my arm, able to withstand pulling hundreds of tons of weight without snapping. When loaded up, if such a line snapped, it would have enough speed and load to cut a person in half. With the towlines secured, the tugs throttled down their engines and headed away from the dock, straight into the wind, pulling us off the dock. Once we were clear, Captain Bailey was able to use our engines to maneuver the ship out of the harbor.

❀

We were given our watch assignments two days before our departure. The organization of the crew may be one of the most important elements to the success of any ship. The modern structure of a ship's crew is the direct result of hundreds of years of global maritime experience and culture. The roles of a crew are assigned and serve many purposes beyond recognition and seniority. Your life is always at a heightened risk of danger when at sea. It is your shipmates who are on watch while you are asleep, keeping you safe and alive, and they put the same level of trust in you when you stand watch while they sleep.

A ship has one captain. Then as rank descends, the number of individuals may increase relative to the needs of the vessel. A modern destroyer—the most comparable equivalent to a nineteenth-century frigate—relies on a crew of two to three hundred members. For our mission, we would be departing with a thirty-member crew. HMS *Surprise* would have had anywhere between 180 to 250 men on board. It made me shudder to imagine how terribly uncomfortable it would have been to live on a ship of similar size with two hundred more men, especially when considering there was no plumbing, electricity, or refrigeration. The harsh living and working conditions meant that a good percentage of the lower-ranking members of the crew were often impressed men. When Tony was working to round out our crew, he had to convince prospective members of the appeal of the adventure. The Royal Navy could use impressment—forcibly recruiting men into service using a variety of methods, some violent.

The final members of our crew had arrived the day before, and there were some last-minute shake-ups as well as some exciting additions. Our boatswain, Kerns, was fired by Tony for disobeying Captain Bailey's order to not leave the ship after watch routine was initiated. How unfortunate for him. He had been with us for two months, putting in the time and doing the laborsome work we all did to prepare the ship for passage. He would now miss the glorious part of the job, the reason we all signed up: the sailing.

Dwight was promoted to replace Kerns as boatswain. Dwight's incredible knowledge of the ship's rig qualified him for the position, but that didn't make up for his lack of leadership skills. Dwight knew only one way: the hard way. He was a proud pilgrim from Planet Tall Ship, and for lower-ranking members of the crew, that often meant being subjected to his stories of how someone did something the wrong way and how they should have known better. It was easier to dismiss him before this promotion, but as boatswain, he was outranked only by Captain Bailey and the mates. The rest of the crew would have to obey his orders.

Todd joined the ship for the passage. I found this surprising, as he had recently become engaged when we were in Sardinia on *Onawa*. At the time he had declared he was eager to live his married life onshore. So much for that. Todd was a tough mate on *Onawa*, but our dynamic had shifted to one of mutual respect. I came to realize that our time together in Europe was the reason we worked so well together on *Rose* leading up to our departure. Todd would be chippy number one, and I would be chippy number two.

The remaining deckhand slots were finally filled. One was Captain Bailey's sixteen-year-old cousin from Pennsylvania, Mandrew. Mandrew was tall and skinny, with bright blond hair. He was very quiet and a very picky eater. His real name was Andrew, but Jon started calling him Mandrew, and it was so fitting that not even being related to the captain could free him from his newfound nickname. I thought the idea of his sailing to California with us was crazy. Not crazy in the kind of way of "what are his parents thinking?," just more along the lines of "how could he be expected to go back to high school after sailing to California with us?"

Two other youngins, Charlie and Tom, were among the latecomers. I think Tom got the job as a favor to his uncle, a project manager at the shipyard. He was two years younger than me and was one of the most genuine, kind people I had ever met. Tom was very good-looking, the kind of person who stops a room when he enters. He was a big soccer player in high school and college but dropped out of school and joined the ship to figure out his next step since pro soccer was not on the table for him.

"Charlie-cakes," as Rick called Charlie, was from Cape Cod and was only a year or so out of high school. From what I heard, his parents knew Captain Bailey and they thought it might be good for him to get a bit of real-world experience. I sensed that being on the ship was not his choice.

An unexpected but welcomed addition was a blast from my past, Marion from the 12-Meter *Nefertiti*. Tony had asked me if I knew her and what I thought of her. I told him the truth, that I thought she would be a great contribution to the crew. She had recently graduated from Brown, was a musician, and could speak a few languages. I always looked forward to sailing with her but had not seen her since before leaving for Europe on *Onawa*. She was average in height, petitely built, and had shoulder-length, reddish-brown hair streaked with sun-bleached strands of blond. I wondered why she had applied to sail on *Rose*; I never would have thought her to be the type to join a tall ship. I had a crush on her, so I was very excited to have her join the ship. We had one more bunk in our section of B-Compartment, so I offered it to her when she arrived, and she accepted.

Rick Hicks would also be sailing with us because of his extensive marine systems and diesel engine experience. Having a guy like Rick on board would ensure better on-the-spot problem-solving. GT, though knowledgeable and hardworking, lacked Rick's practical experience. Rick was in a gray zone because he represented the ship's owner, meaning he was above the law and could pretty much do whatever he wanted. He was not Captain Bailey's boss, but Captain Bailey could not tell Rick what to do.

As an amusing side note, Rick did not want to sleep in the officers' quarters or the lower living compartments with the rest of us deckhands, so he had us custom-build him a cabin on the port side of the gun deck just forward of the galley breakfast tables. His makeshift cabin, a design of his own, ended up being something absurd. It was straightforward, just a few plywood sheets screwed to a couple of two-by-fours with a bamboo roller shade as a door partitioning his cabin from the rest of the gun deck. I thought the makeshift cabin looked like a poorly planned fort, but hey, I did as I was told and quietly thought, *Better him than me*.

With the use of satellite phone technology, Rick's wife would provide shore-side support by sending daily email updates of our progress to the family members of our crew. The satellite phone would also help *Rose* stay in communication and receive current weather updates. The only contact the crew of HMS *Surprise* would have had was the exchange of handwritten letters with other boats when at sea or when reaching a port.

Our ship would now be operating on a 24/7 schedule whether at sea or at port, meaning a portion of the crew would always be awake and working, to ensure the safe operation of the ship. When sailing out into the ocean, there is no natural end of a day; every day is continuous. We couldn't just anchor for the night in the middle of the ocean. Everyone on the ship was either working or on standby, ready to be called to action at a moment's notice, even if sleeping.

Frigates of the early nineteenth century mostly operated on a two-watch system named for the larboard, the left side of the ship when facing the bow; and starboard, the right side of the ship when facing the bow. (The term "larboard" was replaced by "port" in the nineteenth century.) *Rose* operated on a three-watch system: A-Watch, B-Watch, and C-Watch. Our watches rotated operational responsibility using a schedule established by the chief mate. Each watch was made up of a ship's mate, an able-bodied seaman (AB), and five or six deckhands. The position of AB on *Rose* was equivalent to that of a midshipman on a frigate in the early nineteenth century, a crew member in training to become a commissioned officer.

When underway, deckhands on *Rose* stood eight hours of watch for every twenty-four-hour period. Watch was broken up into two separate four-hour shifts and that four-hour watch block was further broken up into one-hour segments at designated watch positions. The typical watch positions were helmsman, steering the ship; bow-watch, looking out on the horizon for marine traffic, obstructions, or weather; boat check, checking bilges, living compartments, and the engine room; standby, performing tasks as needed, possibly requiring muscle (such as adjusting sails) or menial labor; dish duty, washing dishes and cleaning the galley after every meal; and soles and bowls, responsible for daytime cleaning of the common spaces, including the ship's heads and soles.

I was put on A-Watch, led by Tony. I assumed Tony assigned me to his watch because of my connection to Casey. I had recently learned that I was the newest member of a small, unofficial club of sailors called "Casey's Boys." I was sure that other than getting me out of his house, Casey set me up on this job as some sort of initiation into manhood. Carrie, our Pippi Longstocking look-alike, was listed as our AB, sharing responsibilities with Shannon, also an AB, the quiet senior deckhand I'd met in the ship's engine room. Rounding out A-Watch was black-clad Rich, Texan Russ, and Captain Bailey's cousin Mandrew.

B-Watch was run by Andy, Aaron was the AB, and the deckhands were Marshall, Scott, Peggy, Blythe, Jon, and Marion. C-Watch was run by Christina. Her AB was Alex, and the deckhands were Jason, Erinn, Jared, April, Charlie, Tom, and Todd.

A-Watch was assigned to the 8–12 block, meaning we stood watch from 0800 to 1200 (8:00 a.m. to 12:00 p.m.) and again from 2000 to 0000 (8:00 p.m. to midnight). We were responsible for the safe handling of the ship during our daytime watch and would partake in work-party when on standby while on watch between 0800 and 1200. We were also assigned to the second four-hour work-party block after coming off watch. The first daytime work-party block was from 0800 to 1200; the second was from 1200 to 1600. There was no work-party scheduled from 1600 to 0800 the following day. Meals were served on a fixed schedule; the oncoming watch ate first, followed by the off-going and off-watch crew. If I wanted to eat dinner, I needed to be awake and ready to stand watch thirty minutes before it started. Otherwise, I would have to plan on eating a PB&J sandwich on watch, plus dealing with the wrath of Hunter for missing a meal.

As we motored out of Narragansett Bay, heading southwest toward Long Island, the officers jumped into safety drills. We were a new crew, and the officers had a lot of ground to cover with us regarding SOPs (standard operating procedures). Many of us had not yet set a single sail on the ship. There was going to be a lot of learning by doing, with an intense amount of lessons and drills. Almost anything related to sail handling on a big ship required coordinating many crew members, and coordinating any large group of people in a new environment is challenging even in the best of circumstances.

It took just over two hours to conduct a fire drill, a man-overboard drill, and the abandon-ship drill. The man-overboard drill was a challenge. It involved dropping a coconut in the water and retrieving it. Captain Bailey pointed out that the human head was close to the size of a coconut, and so a floating coconut accurately represented how hard it was to keep visual track of a person in the water as the ship turned back to retrieve them.

We then had a brief lesson on sail handling before setting the main staysail, fore staysail, foretop staysail, mizzen staysail, and the spanker. A staysail can be a triangular or quadrilateral-shaped fore and aft sail with the luff—leading edge—hanked onto a stay; this kind of sail can be used for all points of sailing. The staysails had only four lines of running rigging for the triangular sails, and six lines for the quadrilateral sails. The spanker was rigged like no sail because the luff was bent onto the spencer mast and gaff, and the gaff remained hoisted at all times. When set, lines called brails were released, allowing the sail to be stretched taut to the aft end of the boom by means of the clew outhaul.

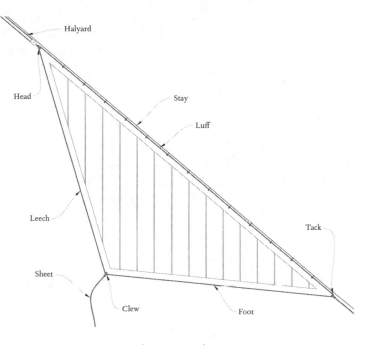

The main staysail

Setting the staysails was relatively easy. The bottom corner of a staysail, called the tack, prevents the bottom of the sail from moving up. The halyard, a rope used for pulling the top of the sail up to draw the luff taut, is attached to the top corner of the sail, called the head. Each staysail had a port and starboard sheet for trimming the clew, the lower corner of the sail. To understand this, imagine a triangular flag is hoisted up a flagpole. The luff would be the side of the flag against the pole. The clew would be the free corner of the flag flapping in the wind. The sheet, attached to the clew, pulls the corner of the flag away from the pole, stretching the flag out and preventing it from flapping in the wind. That is the point at which the flag has caught and harnessed the wind just like a sail.

C-Watch stood the first full watch, starting at 1615. Dinner would be ready by 1730, and I had some time to kill before standing my first watch underway. It didn't take long to tell who the green crew members were because nearly all of them opted to stay up on deck for the rest of the afternoon, whereas the seasoned crew members not on watch headed below to warm up and rest. I couldn't help but question Hunter's decision to serve split pea soup for lunch right before departing. Maybe it was because he knew it came up just as easy as it went down. Luckily for me, I love split pea soup and I have never been seasick.

Jon was as excited as Clark Griswold from the National Lampoon's Vacation films, with his video camera in hand the whole time. We each took turns holding it and recording obnoxious *Entertainment Tonight*–style interviews as the ship passed between Block Island and Montauk. Jon was a real natural when it came to engaging whomever he was filming. Mandrew told me he dreaded the regularly unscripted Jon and Will Show, and at the same time he never wanted to miss out when we were together. I think our demand for attention was why Jon, Jared, and I were assigned to separate watches.

⚙

The North Atlantic in the middle of January can be a challenge no matter what vessel you are on. Some would say that leaving from Newport in January was as smart as having a picnic on Normandy Beach on D-Day. Granted, it could have been worse. Hurricane season had ended two months prior, and the eighteenth-century design of *Rose* made sailing her in rough weather particularly uncomfortable. Modern vessels like fishing boats, ferries, and tankers are all operated from some sort of enclosed bridge, protected from the wind and the weather. The crew on those vessels operate from inside looking out. We didn't get to enjoy that kind of luxury. The ship's wheel and anything having to do with operating *Rose* was out in the open, exposed to the elements.

I did have some experience sailing in the winter when frostbiting twenty-two-foot-long sailboats with Jared. "Frostbiting" is a term applied to sailboat racing during winter months in cold climates. A benefit of frostbiting was the beer was always chilled. Mind you, it was a painfully cold way to pass the time. I did appreciate that my days of frostbiting helped me to be better prepared for what undergarments to wear when sailing at night in the North Atlantic Ocean in January. I wore a layer of long underwear under my pants and sweatshirt, as well as wool ski socks. Next came my yachty Henri-Lloyd bibs, a foul-weather jacket, a nice oversize ski hat, leather sea boots, and some faux lambskin–lined leather gloves. I must have looked like quite the fool when I came up onto deck in all that gear, and it felt hot as hell . . . for two minutes.

A cold and bundled-up crew muster

I could see Montauk Point Lighthouse ten miles off our starboard quarter when I took the deck for my first watch. That fading beacon would be our last sighting of land until Puerto Rico, some 1,700 miles away. The air temperature was hovering just above the freezing point, and the wind was coming from the west-northwest at less than ten knots. Up to this point I was accustomed to reporting wind speed in nautical miles per hour, but like nearly everything else on *Rose*, things were done differently. Wind speed was called out using the archaic Beaufort Wind Scale (BWS).

The BWS scale was named after Rear Admiral Francis Beaufort, a British Royal Navy officer who developed the scale in 1805 to standardize weather observations. The BWS was adopted by the Royal Navy in the 1830s. It was originally based on how the weather conditions affected the amount of sail a frigate should carry. Less wind means flying every sail you've got. As the wind gets stronger, you put less up until you are literally sailing with just your spars; that is when you pray. Wind speed was eventually added to the scale, and in 1916, the description of sails was replaced by descriptions of the state of the sea, because ships with engines outnumbered sailing vessels.

Watch started ten minutes before the top of the hour with a muster at the capstan led by Tony. The sun had set hours earlier, so the sky was dark but clear other than the faint glow of land light hovering above Long Island on our starboard beam. It took only a minute for my eyes to adjust to the darkness on deck. Christina briefed Tony prior to our muster. He then told us of the anticipated weather conditions, observations of marine traffic relative to our position on the water, and the state of the ship. Fortunately for us, we were motoring with our lower staysails and spanker set, with no change in weather expected.

Despite all of the below-the-waterline work completed in the shipyard before our departure, we were told to stay very aware of the developing situation in our forepeak, as it was already taking on enough water to merit having the pumps run continuously. The forepeak was the most forward subdeck compartment mostly used for storage of extra rope and rigging supplies. That amount of leaking gave me a very uneasy feeling, as we had just started out and the conditions were, in my opinion, moderate. I had never been on a boat that leaked as badly as *Rose*.

Tony directed Carrie to assign us all to our watch positions. I was assigned to the helm for the first hour of watch. Deckhands, not officers or the captain, steered the ship. The wheel was sixty inches in diameter with spokes. The helmsman always stood facing forward, typically on the port side of the wheel because the officer on watch stood on the starboard side just forward of the helm. In tough conditions, a second helmsman would stand on the starboard side of the wheel to help because of the need for more muscle. There was a narrow section of open deck less than three feet wide between the wheel and the aft bulkhead of the great cabin deckhouse.

I had been looking forward to steering the ship underway as we headed for a destination beyond the horizon. Fortunately for me, Casey had made a point to spend a good amount of time working with me on my helmsmanship one night when sailing north through the Ligurian Sea on *Onawa*. Because there was no binnacle light, I could not see the compass, so sailing the boat had to be done by sense of touch. He sat next to me, coaching me on how to feel the boat power up when sailed properly. I remember a tense few hours with a lot of "What the hell are you doing?" I spent much of the time with my eyes closed, devoting my focus to how the wind felt on my face. Trying to steer with my eyes open was actually a hindrance. I eventually got the feel for it, and after that night, he made sure I was at the helm as much as possible to ensure I would continue improving my skills as a helmsman.

After the first hour of watch, I was put on idle position with Russ and Mandrew. That meant sitting on the step at the break of the quarterdeck, crouched low near the rail so we could stay shielded from the wind. Shannon was on helm, Carrie was on boat-check, Rich was on bow-watch. Mandrew was quiet and might have dozed off for a second or two. I couldn't blame him. His friends back home probably spent the night watching TV, playing video games, and talking about the next school dance. Mandrew had come out of his shell since joining and was much more talkative. I learned that he was from a part of Pennsylvania known as the Lehigh Valley and grew up in a bustling small town surrounded by cornfields. He was a sophomore in high school, the oldest of three boys; his mother was a schoolteacher, and his father owned an adhesives business. Mandrew's parents had a hard work ethic, and his summers on Cape Cod were a balance of playing on the beach and helping his mom clean rental properties.

On HMS *Surprise*, Mandrew would have been considered one of the ship's boys, a position available to young men in their teens or even younger. It was common for a ship to have a number of boys on board, and many were recruited through the Marine Society, an institution formed to help supply young recruits to the Royal Navy. Some served as idlers or powder monkeys, responsible for transporting gunpowder from the ship's magazine to the artillery. Others were officers' servants, a forerunner to becoming a midshipman, an officer candidate position. From there, the track could continue to lieutenant and then master and commander of a sloop before reaching post captain. In the film *Master and Commander: The Far Side of the World*, it is noticeable how young some of the boys are on the ship. At thirteen years old, midshipman Lord Blakeney—based on a character from O'Brian's books—suffers the loss of an arm and near the end of the film is given command of HMS *Surprise* during an encounter. I couldn't imagine being handed that responsibility in the middle of a battle at the age of thirteen.

My third hour of watch was spent on boat-check. I welcomed the opportunity to stay below, enjoying the warmth of the ship's interior. Boat-check was probably the easiest watch position. It required constantly inspecting every compartment of the ship, looking for anything out of the ordinary, like a fire, a high level of water, or an injured shipmate. At night, people were asleep, so I needed to be quiet and use a flashlight when conducting my inspections. When inspecting the engine room, I had to record the engine and generator temperatures and conduct visual inspections, making sure no fluids were leaking. The one part about boat-check

I did not like was having to inspect the forepeak because it was accessible only through a small hatch on the weather deck up at the bow.

I was assigned to standby again for the last hour of watch. At this point, it was 2300, and the excitement and adrenaline from our departure had long since worn off. I was exhausted, and the bite of the cold and damp air only accentuated my growing irritability. I spent the hour torturing myself by thinking of how warm and cozy my bunk would feel. The last ten minutes of watch felt like an eternity. The feeling of time dragging out only became worse when the relieving watch, B-Watch, gathered at the capstan five minutes before the change of the watch to discuss the present conditions and assign watch positions. Andy went on and on, talking about god knew what for a good ten minutes after our watch was supposed to be over. Andy didn't seem to care that he stole those ten precious minutes of sleep from me. That bastard!

Chapter 10

SETTING THE SAILS

OUR SECOND DAY AT SEA was busy, with much of our time spent learning the evolutions for setting and trimming the square sails. I slept well through the night. The interior of the ship was warm, and the never-ending pitching and rolling motions of the ship helped rock me to sleep. I was in a deep sleep, having an unusually intense dream about flying around the world on a commercial jet, when Jared woke me up with a gentle knock on my bunk. Most dreams tend to occur during REM sleep and can become more vivid when factors such as stress, fragmented sleep, and sleep deprivation are introduced.

"Wakey, wakey . . . It's pretty damp up on deck. It is 45° Fahrenheit (7.2° Celsius), there is some light rain, and the wind is supposed to build, maybe up to fifty knots by the end of your watch."

"Go away," I whined, as I mourned for more sleep.

"You've got five minutes to get up on deck." He laughed and left as quietly as he came.

I lay there docile in my bunk until the actual overpowering smell of bacon motivated me to accept it was time to wake up. I never liked bacon when I was a kid but developed an addiction to it during our time in the yard on *Rose*. The heavy workload helped me burn through many calories, and I craved anything edible. Lying in my bunk, I made plans to eat piles of bacon, a half-dozen eggs, and four heavily buttered pieces of toast. Breakfast is always glorious, but even more so at sea. O'Brian touches on this early in the first book in the series, with Jack saying to Stephen (who has just bonked his head on a low beam), "What would you like for breakfast? I smelt the gunroom's bacon on deck and I thought it the finest smell I had ever smelt in my life—Araby left at the post. What do you say to bacon and eggs, and then perhaps a beefsteak to follow? And coffee?"

I hopped out of my bunk, threw on my gear, and headed up to the gun deck, skipping brushing my teeth so I could linger for a few extra minutes and enjoy a cup of coffee while standing in line for my bacon. The conversation happening at the breakfast table was mostly about the sightings of marine life through the night. Being offshore and with no artificial light, it was easier to notice the biolu-minescence from millions of dinoflagellates, single-celled organisms that light up the water when agitated. The most vivid light shows occurred in the stern wake of the ship and up where the bow pierced the surface of the water. The constant rise and fall of the ship as she pushed forward through the sea created visible waves of light spreading twenty feet to the sides and dissipating fifty yards behind the stern. The best feature of the light show was when dolphins came rushing up to swim with the bow waves, further producing vibrant tubes of lights as they swam back and forth, playing with the ship's cutwater (the leading edge of the ship's stem).

I learned we were ninety miles east of Cape May, New Jersey, and expected to enter the Gulf Stream sometime midmorning. At present, the recorded water temperature was 46° Fahrenheit (7.8° Celsius) and would be somewhere in the mid-seventies on the following day. I was advised to still bundle up but that in only a matter of hours, the air would become so warm and humid that I would no longer need the multiple layers of gear I was wearing to stay warm.

The Gulf Stream is a warm-water oceanic current that behaves much like a river moving through the North Atlantic Ocean. It originates in the Gulf of Mexico and moves north as it follows the Eastern Seaboard of the United States, then meanders east across the Atlantic to Europe. Like a river, it can have spin-off eddies that have quite an impact on the marine life and air temperature surrounding it. The Gulf Stream varies in width, between thirty and eighty miles wide as it runs up the eastern American seaboard, usually widening farther north.

Claim to the first recorded observation of the Gulf Stream goes to the pilot of a ship under the command of Spanish explorer Ponce de León in 1513. Ben-jamin Franklin gets the credit though for naming and developing the first map of the Gulf Stream, having done so with the help of his cousin Timothy Folger, a merchant captain and a former Nantucket whaler. At the time, Franklin was deputy postmaster general and was trying to understand why British mail ships took much longer than other westbound merchant vessels. Folger assumed cap-tains of the mail ships did not have any knowledge about the prevailing warm currents they were sailing against. Franklin made prints of the Gulf Stream to share with British mariners to improve the speed of their passages. Eventually,

Franklin stopped sharing the map with the British because of the outbreak of the American Revolution and instead began sharing it with the French to help them in their efforts to send supplies and weapons to the American Colonies.

⚙

After a quick feeding, I headed up to the capstan for our pre-watch muster before relieving C-Watch at 0800. Tony was quick when it came to bringing us up to speed on the most current weather forecast. The wind was light, and the sky was overcast with periods of rain. GT would be alternately shutting down the new engines for required servicing, and we would be busy adjusting the sails to compensate. The forecast called for the wind to build to thirty-five to forty knots (gale conditions) by midafternoon. Those of us on standby would be working with Carrie and Shannon aloft to learn how to reef the square sails.

A square sail is a four-sided trapezoid-shaped sail with the top attached to a yard. It could have up to eleven individual working lines used to set, strike, or trim the sail. I had never set a square sail and felt inadequate because my work as a chippy up to our departure had kept me mostly on deck. I was eager to experience the open sea aloft in the rigging.

Reefing, meanwhile, is the act of rolling up and securing a portion of the sail in order to reduce the amount of canvas exposed to the wind. At a certain point on any boat, too much sail area can be dangerous. Having too much sail area set in stormy conditions can overpower a vessel, limiting the ability to steer and operate the vessel safely. In strong winds, less sail area can lower the risk of damage to the sails, rigging, and vessel while improving its overall stability and performance. Casey always said, "If you are thinking of reefing, then you should already be reefed."

Just putting the reefs in the fore and main topsails took two hours. It could have gone much faster, but Shannon wanted to make sure we all understood what we were doing and why we were doing it. We had seventeen sails in total; eight square sails, eight staysails, one spanker, and about thirty miles of rope to set and operate the sails. Setting sails was no easy feat, and the process could take hours, depending on the circumstances, as there were only thirty of us on board, whereas HMS *Surprise* had a two-hundred-man crew.

We were relieved by B-Watch at 1200 and given thirty minutes to eat lunch before setting the square sails. As predicted, we had entered the Gulf Stream, and the air temperature quickly warmed up. I used the break to remove some

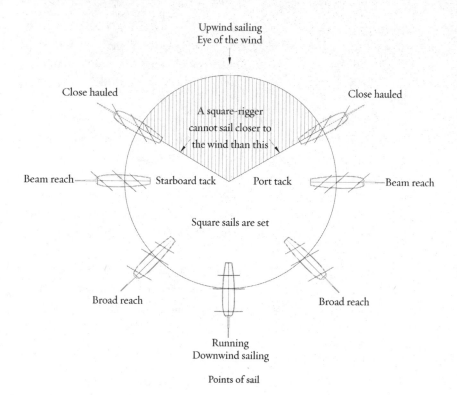

Points of sail

layers and returned to deck wearing only underwear and a T-shirt under my foul-weather gear. With the entire crew present, Tony began the muster by reviewing communication on deck. The first rule was not to talk, but listen for the orders as they were called out. All hands were expected to promptly shout back those orders to both show and acknowledge that everyone had heard the order. We were directed to stay on task until our job was completed before assisting others because leaving your job unfinished could result in two jobs not being done.

Then, switching gears, we talked about sailing fundamentals: to set sail means to stretch the sails out so they may catch the wind, thus driving the boat forward; to strike or take sail means to take down, stow, or to put away; to trim a sail means to adjust the angle of the sail relative to the wind; to sail upwind means to have the bow of the vessel generally pointed toward the source of the wind. A sailboat cannot sail directly into the wind, so a vessel must turn its bow toward, through, and past the eye of the wind—this is called tacking. To sail downwind means the bow of the vessel is pointed away from the source direction of the wind. The downwind maneuver for crossing the stern of a square-rigged vessel through the eye of the wind is called wearing; changing the direction of the wind from one side of the hull to the other is a maneuver called jibing on modern sailing vessels.

At 1300, Tony called for "Hands Aloft." We were divided into two groups, one going aloft, the other staying on deck. I was assigned to the group staying on deck. Disappointed, I watched my shipmates don their safety harnesses and swing out to the outboard weather shrouds of the foremast to begin their ascent. Once all hands were in place, the order was given to release the gaskets—lengths of rope used to secure a stowed sail to the yard—and unhook the bowlines. When all was done, Shannon shouted down to the deck, "Loose and in its gear." That meant the sail was free to be set.

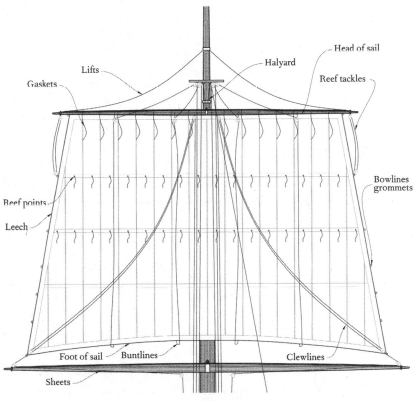

The main topsail

Shannon shuffled back toward the mast but stayed up at the topsail while everyone else climbed down to the fores'l yard. It should be noted here that some sails can have name variations. We called the lowest square sail on the foremast the fores'l. The same sail could have also been called the foresail or fore course. Contractions like fores'l were more common during the age of sail—other examples included "forecastle" to "fo'csle" or "boatswain" to "bos'n" or "bosun." The contraction presents a more accurate phonetic spelling of the word.

While the hands in the rigging prepared the sails, those of us on deck prepared the lines that would be used for setting the sails. The reef tackle and buntlines were removed from their belaying pins so they too could run free while the clewline was taken down to a single turn on the belaying pin to control the release. Dwight was running the deck and called out the orders starting with "Sheet home the fore topsail!"

"Sheet home the fore topsail!" We all shouted the command back as we began hauling the sheets in.

As we heaved away, the clewlines and reef tackles were eased out with a bit of tension being applied to ensure control was maintained throughout the process. Unlike the sheets, the clewlines, buntlines, and reef tackles were left loose.

"Hold well on the port and starboard topsail sheets!" Dwight next shouted, "Hands to man the topsail halyard!" The halyard raises the topsail yard. When not in use, the topsail yard is lowered to just above the doubling of the masts. I and all the other hands on deck formed a line with the halyard in hand, waiting for Dwight's command to begin hauling.

Dwight shouted, "Haul away!" And we began heaving the halyard with every ounce of strength in a synchronized rhythm, shouting the chant *"Two-six-pull!"* There are varying views of how this chant came to be. One theory is that it is an old British Royal Navy command used after firing a cannon.

"Well the topsail halyard!" shouted Dwight when the yard reached the desired height.

We all then dug our feet into the deck, holding the weight and load of the yard and sail while Dwight tied a stopper knot to the halyard to prevent it from running out, which would send the yard crashing down out of control, loaded and with the force of the wind-filled sail. With the yard hoisted and the sail set, we lined up to man the braces. Braces are the lines used to rotate a yard around the mast for trimming the square sails. Finally, the order "Coil and hang!" was given, and all lines were coiled and hung on their corresponding belaying pins.

It was a hard workout, taking more than an hour to set the fore topsail, fores'l, and main topsail.

Looking forward from the quarterdeck with square sails set

At 1400, the engines were shut down, and we were fully powered by sail for the first time. As predicted, the wind built to forty knots coming out of the northwest. The rolling waves had continued to build, exceeding fifteen feet in height. Standing midship looking aft, again and again, I watched the horizon come into view before briefly vanishing as our bow fell off the back of the waves and we sank to the bottom of the troughs before being lifted back up and thrust forward by the next wave. The rapidly evolving surface of the water looked like a violent mountain range made from jagged peaks of a vibrant emerald marble covered in streaks of animated white veins bursting into the mist-filled air.

Having harnessed the force of the wind, with occasional bouts of spray flying across the deck, *Rose* found her groove as she blasted along like a freight train cutting through the frothy sea. I loved being out in the open ocean and the feeling of nature driving us to our destination. The rush of adrenaline was intoxicating, and for the first time, I understood why the members of Planet Tall Ship loved *Rose* so much. Standing there on deck, I kept thinking that this was the real stuff, like surfing a wave at Mavericks or helicopter skiing in the French Alps during avalanche season.

In the early morning of our third day at sea, around 0500, the main engines would not start because they were hydrolocked. We had shut down the engines the day before because we were in ideal conditions to sail the ship, and unexpectedly, the engines became filled with salt water due to an unforeseen error in the engineering of the exhaust system. I wondered how that happened considering the amount of effort that had gone into overhauling the ship before our departure and installing twin brand-spanking-new diesel Caterpillar 3406s.

Hydrostatic lock, also known as hydrolock, is when a fluid has entered the engine and its presence prevents the pistons from reaching the top of their stroke. As a result, the engine cannot complete its cycle, resulting in an engine that will not work. A diesel fuel engine is different from a gasoline fuel engine in that it does not require an ignition system to ignite the fuel, as the high compression generated by the pistons causes enough heat to reach the ignition point of diesel fuel. Air is compressible, but water is not. Our engines could no longer turn over because the seawater had filled the space in the cylinder that was supposed to be filled with air.

The ship had two exhaust ports located just forward of the mizzenmast, above the waterline, one on starboard and the other on port. The problem with the location of the exhaust ports was that, when sailing, the ship heeled over, and water (through fluid mechanics) would force its way up the exhaust hose. That had been a problem on the ship before the repowering. To mediate this, an elevated loop in the exhaust was placed well above the waterline, and during the repowering, the loop was raised even higher, but apparently still not high enough. There were baffles in the system, but they were engineered to restrict the flow of air, not water. The backflow of seawater was not a problem when the engines were running because the pressure of the exhaust provided enough force to prevent the water from getting in. With the engines off, there was no pressure to prevent the seawater from bypassing the baffles.

This problem fell to GT and Rick to fix. The new engines required specialized tooling and an intense amount of time, two things that were in short supply. You can't call in a mechanic when at sea. A ship's crew needs to be able to make all necessary repairs or you may not make it back to port. The water needed to be removed, and the process of removing the water could be time-consuming and damaging. I intentionally sat next to the engine room door when eating breakfast so I could try to hear a bit of what was happening. All I heard was a lot of "fucks" coming from the engine room. Rick and GT were working on the situation, and the tension among the officers was palpable. GT explained to me that the normal approach to a situation like this would be to individually remove the headcovers from each cylinder and use a shop vacuum to suck out the salt water, then reassemble the cylinder head. That could take all day for both engines.

Instead, Rick pulled a rabbit out of his hat when he came up with a shortcut solution for getting the engines up and running again. On a gas engine, they could have just pulled the plugs and cranked over the engine to remove the water. Rick said, "It was either pull the injectors to extract the water or pull the cylinder heads. We did not have the tools to pull injectors, which is why I came up with that scenario." For our engines, Rick adjusted the exhaust valves at the rocker arms to allow the valves to never seat so they could roll the engines and not build compression. They didn't turn the engines to start, but turned them so the pistons would press the water out of the opened valves. They did this again and again, slowly but effectively squeezing the water out. It took a lot of careful effort, but they were able to get the first engine started after an hour of using this method to purge the water. Within a few hours, both engines were operational. They had pulled a successful Hail Mary and had gotten the engines back online five hours after the hydrolock was discovered. They still had plenty of work to do, spending the rest of the day working into the night cycling the engines on and off, performing five oil changes per engine to make sure all the water was out.

While working on this, GT and Rick also developed a fail-safe to prevent the engines from hydrolocking again for the rest of our journey. If an engine was shut down for any reason, a drain plug in the corresponding muffler system was pulled. This way if the seawater backflowed again before it could reach the engine, it would drain out of the muffler plug hole directly into the bilge instead of flooding the engine. The drain plug would be put back in place prior to the start-up of said engine.

The issues with the engines had overwhelmed the mood on the ship. The officers were tense, and we spent much of the day crawling around the ship ensuring we would be prepared for our next bout of rough weather, which was expected the following day. I didn't think much of it, having just sailed through the gale. Boy was I wrong.

Chapter 11

*T*HE ONLY WAY OUT
IS THROUGH

EVERY TIME THE SHIP LAUNCHED off a wave and came thundering down like an elephant trying to fly, I experienced a bizarre floating feeling. These zero-G moments usually ended with a hard-pounding smack when all five hundred tons of *Rose* hit the bottom of a wave trough. It was pitch-black because the lights were off in our sleeping compartment, and the combination of darkness and unpredictable jerking motions made me feel like I was trapped in a coffin being thrown down a flight of stairs again and again. I was sure I had spent more energy trying to sleep in my bunk for the previous five hours than I would have if I had just stayed up on deck in my foul-weather gear.

I had finished standing watch at midnight and headed straight to my bunk to get some much-needed sleep. We were experiencing near gale conditions, with wind speeds reaching thirty-five knots. I didn't think much of it. But while I tried to sleep, the weather quickly went from bad to dreadful. Trying to rest was impossible. The already-turbulent motions of the ship became jarring and violent, and the typical disturbing groans of the ship that I had only recently gotten accustomed to turned into eardrum-bursting screams as the waves and the wind twisted and racked the hull.

On top of the pounding, there was the whole invasive-water situation. Streams of salt water were coming in from everywhere, feeding a growing river of water running through the bilge, under the bottom of our floorboards. The pumps had been running constantly since we left Newport, and now they were struggling to keep up with the leaks, which were made worse by the pounding waves of the sea. There was a growing volume of water splashing around below our bunks. Waves soon formed inside our sleeping quarters, rolling from one side of the compartment to the other, soaking bunks and gear. Being sprayed with filthy bilgewater, in addition to being tossed around in my bunk, made for a torturous combination I'll never forget.

I had all I could take by 0600 and decided to head up to the deck. I dressed quickly and carefully scaled the ladder up to the gun deck, first stopping in the men's head to take a leak before facing the weather. Relieving myself on a sailboat while underway is a skill I have honed quite well. I know how to wedge myself hard into a corner so I can focus my aim and not splatter piss everywhere. Half of the guys sat when peeing, but I was not a fan of a bowl of piss splashing at my underside when the ship fell out from a wave. I wondered what the strategy was for the women on board.

I brushed my teeth and made my way aft toward the galley, sprinting and stopping to use the movement of the ship to my advantage. It felt like being in a pinball machine, bouncing from one hard surface to the next. I found the best way to move was to keep my knees limber and jump with the ship. If I timed it right, I could jump straight up and land a few feet ahead of where I was before jumping. The tricky part was anticipating the ship's up and down movements. Being below deck made it impossible to predict exactly when the ship would fall out from under me.

Passing by the galley, I decided to skip my morning cup of joe and climbed the two flights of stairs before pausing at the main companionway door to see what sort of hell I was about to step out into. I saw nothing through the windows but darkness and the wind whipping the spray off the glass the very second it landed. The weather had moved past dreadful to annihilatingly terrible. I planned to get up on deck, grab a harness, clip into a jackline, and wedge myself somewhere out of the way from the crew on watch. A jackline is a line that runs the length of the ship's deck, attached at both ends near the bow and the stern. It works like the metal pole you hold when riding a city bus. The idea is to use the lanyard on your safety harness to clip into the jackline so that you can move around on the deck, knowing you won't be washed overboard by a wave or a sudden drop of the ship.

The intensity of the wind blowing against the door made pushing it open a lot harder than I had anticipated. The wind had picked up while I tried to sleep, and we were now experiencing sustained wind speeds of sixty knots, with gusts exceeding seventy knots. According to the Beaufort Wind Scale, winds greater than sixty-four knots are classified as hurricane conditions. To understand what this felt like, imagine it is nighttime and you are riding in a car with no headlights while speeding down the roughest dirt road at seventy-five miles per hour (one hundred twenty kilometers per hour). In the darkness, you try to open your car door and climb onto the roof. Now imagine standing on top of that car while it is moving that fast and not knowing if it will suddenly take a turn, drop down a hill, or hit the brakes.

It was just after 0600 when I pushed the door against the ferocious wind and stepped out onto the deck, being careful not to let the door slam shut and shatter the glass. Crouching low, I grabbed the capstan while using my other arm to shield my face from the stinging rain and sleet. I got my bearings, pulled my hood down as far as possible, turned my back to the wind, and crab-walked up the tilted deck to the windward rail. The conditions were terrifying but also oddly exciting. My eyes adjusted to the sky, which was growing brighter as dawn approached, and, like a curtain that had been pulled open, the full fury of the sea came into view.

The waves had also built through the night and were now up to twenty to thirty feet; the tops of the rails were only eleven feet above the waterline at midship. Visibility was intermittent because of the squall lines we were moving through. We had three staysails set, with the engines revved up to just enough revolutions per minute (RPMs) to maintain a moderate headway. The goal was to maintain enough speed for the rudder to effectively steer the ship, but not so much that we smashed the hull into the oncoming waves. Earlier that morning, C-Watch had to reduce the engine's RPMs to help diminish the ship's rocking motion.

Earlier, at 0545, the great cabin had morphed into a WWF wrestling ring. The main table jumped off its mounts, smashing around the cabin until it could be turned upside down and secured by the officers. They lashed the table to the ladder leading up to the quarterdeck and tethered the six upholstered chairs in a row, running the cabin's width along the aft settee. Anything else that could move was set down low and wedged in place.

The weather conditions deteriorated as the morning went on. We had departed Newport in the wake of a cold frontal passage, of which the parent storm center merged with a polar low over the Canadian Maritimes, providing a five-hundred- to one-thousand-mile sea fetch over the western Atlantic. Fetch is the distance wind can blow on the surface of water without obstruction; the greater the distance, the larger the wave. The sea became more chaotic, like soapy water churning in a washing machine.

By 0705, the ladder leading up to the quarterdeck from the great cabin broke free and fell; the great cabin had been absolutely trashed. Electrical fires and shorts began breaking out in the lower forward living compartments caused by the waterfalls of salt water overtaking the interior of our ship. As a result, we had to go "black-ship" in the living compartments, a term meaning we had to turn off all electrical circuits. Orders were issued that nobody was to sleep in the living compartments; we could only go down to change clothes or retrieve items. Killing electrical circuits and forbidding sleeping in the living compartments was not good. I didn't think anyone could have slept in this weather until I saw Shannon and Carrie sleeping on the sole in front of the great cabin. I later learned that a handful of my shipmates, including some of the more experienced ones, were convinced our ship was going to sink and they had made peace with their god.

The great cabin during the storm

The ship's motions had become so violent that Alex, the famous *Rose* alumnus, hurt his back from landing on the edge of a table after being launched into the air when the ship fell out from a wave. More and more off-watch crew members were emerging onto the weather deck, and it became obvious who was doing well and who was not. The rule was that if you were going to get sick, it needed to be up on deck and not in the living compartments or into a toilet bowl. A few people spent some time sitting on the leeward rail, barfing. I was not one of them.

A-Watch took the deck at 0800, and I took the first shift at the helm. The wave heights were holding at twenty-five to thirty feet. The sustained wind speed was peaking around fifty knots, with periods exceeding sixty-five knots and higher in the squalls. Steering the ship in this weather was challenging due to the tremendous loads on the rudder. We needed two people on the wheel at all times. As the primary helmsman, I stood on the port side of the wheel, calling for help when I felt I might be overpowered. Carrie stood on the starboard side, stepping in as needed. Trying to steer the ship in a straight line was like trying to drive a school bus through an obstacle course on a frozen lake. I used every muscle I had to hold our course for that hour and was able to hold the wheel on my own for only maybe twenty minutes. There were a few moments when we needed three on the wheel, meaning Tony had to jump in as well. I felt like I had done five hundred push-ups and run ten miles by the end of my shift.

There was not much to do after my stint at the helm, which left me mostly sitting at the quarter rail on standby. At this point, nearly everyone was on deck. Not many people wanted to stay below since Russ had lost his balance while using the head and ripped the toilet bowl right off its mounts. Our head used a vacuum flush system, and the severed bowl prevented the system from sealing itself. The vacuum pump had to be turned off so it did not burn itself out struggling to make an impossible vacuum. Gravity was now the only thing that could empty the bowls.

To make matters worse, the violent motions of the ship shook the contents of the black tank (excrement storage), resulting in the release of horridly foul-smelling gas every time someone opened the head valve to drain the bowl. The gun deck was the only place we could seek refuge from the weather, and it was also where we had to eat. Sleeping and eating in a swampy space that smells like human waste is uniquely terrible.

I was assigned to boat-check at 1000. Waves were breaking over the fore-deck, so it was deemed too dangerous for anyone to stand anywhere forward of the mainmast on the weather deck. Still, boat-check had to go up to the bow and climb down into the forepeak to make sure the pumps were working. Getting to the forepeak required a strategically timed assault to absorb the occasional waves breaking over the deck. Once on the bow, I lifted the hatch carefully so neither waves nor wind could possibly catch it, either ripping it off or shattering it. A loss of the hatch would create an opportunity for water to flood the interior of the ship from the deck, potentially overwhelming the pumps and sinking the ship. I waited for the perfect moment, lifted the hatch, scurried into the small thirty-by-thirty-inch opening, and closed the hatch behind me.

Now I had a front-row seat to all the violence our five-hundred-ton ship was charging through. There was no electricity; the only source of light was my trusty Maglite. The darkness, mixed with the slamming motion of the ship, was compounded by the deafening blows of the bow hitting never-ending walls of water. Moving as fast as possible, I climbed down the first ladder, holding on tight because every impact felt like a grenade going off. I waited for the right moment, jumped off the ladder, lifted the small grated hatch beneath me, and climbed down into the lowest section of the forepeak.

This is where things got truly terrifying. I was in the bow of a ship, which was shaped like a bathtub. The rounded bow acted more like a spoon pushing against the force of the water instead of a knife cutting through it. HMS *Rose* would have had canted frames, meaning that the frames were oriented perpendicular to the planking of the hull. The frames in *Rose*, however, were oriented perpendicular to the keel, the centerline of the ship. This orientation put them at an acute angle relative to the planking of the hull. This orientation destabilized the hull up forward, which caused the bow to flex tremendously. As I crouched there in the forepeak, the flexing was happening so much that I could see daylight coming through the seams of the planks. Seeing it in person was terrifying; you should never see light through plank seams.

Gallons and gallons of water rushed into the forepeak through the opening seams every time the bow buried into a wave; it was like standing in a car wash. The pumps were running, but this volume of water was almost more than they could handle. If the pumps went down, we went down.

⚓

By this point, we were near the outer limits of a region known as the "Graveyard of the Atlantic." We were more than three hundred miles offshore, beyond reach of any US Coast Guard land-based air rescue, which likely would have been the USCG MH-60 Jayhawk medium-range recovery helicopter. Even if the Jayhawk could have reached us, they would have been able to rescue only six people at a time. Had this approach been feasible and resources available, it would have required multiple helicopters and rescues over an extended period. Situationally dependent, the Search and Rescue (SAR) controller may have sought additional

Will, after inspecting the forepeak, walking back from the bow,
holding on as a wave breaks over the deck

air resources from the Department of Defense (DOD), in-air refueling capabilities, and helicopters that may have been able to support a scenario that included thirty people. Again, situationally dependent, the Coast Guard also may have tried to seek assistance from large merchant or military vessels using the Automated Mutual-Assistance Vessel Rescue System (AMVER). Rescue by any small-craft pleasure vessels would have been ruled out because of the size of our crew.

There is a long history of boats sinking near the Graveyard of the Atlantic due to the fierce weather that can develop. An estimated five thousand ships have gone down in that region in the past five hundred years. I personally know of two vessels lost there in the years after my passage on *Rose*. The first, in 2007, was a fifty-four-foot sailboat named *Flying Colours*, which was lost at sea. Her last known position was within two hundred miles of where we entered the storm. The captain, Trey Topping, was my friend. He was also Casey's nephew, and he was a good sailor. He and the other three souls on board all disappeared. Nobody knows what happened to them. The search and rescue area was 5,440 square miles.

Then, in 2012, a sister ship to *Rose*, the replica of HMS *Bounty*, sank in Hurricane Sandy. Her last known position was around one hundred miles west of where we entered the storm. Fourteen crew survived after being rescued by the Coast Guard. Deckhand Claudene Christian was recovered but declared dead on arrival, and the ship's captain, Robin Walbridge, was lost at sea.

Abandoning ship is the very last thing anyone should ever do. Even if the ship starts to sink, you need to stay on board for as long as possible. The ship is your island, and you do everything you can to keep it floating. Nevertheless, we counted and prepared survival suits, lights, life jackets, and life rafts.

☸

Around 1030, the starboard side of the fores'l started to come loose. It didn't take more than a few seconds for the sail to begin flailing around like a bedsheet on a clothesline in a tornado. It was evident that if left alone, the sail would shred itself to pieces and possibly cause a dismasting. The wind had eased a bit and was hovering between thirty-five and fifty knots and gusting past sixty knots. We were in between squall lines, which offered us a brief opportunity to contain the sail before the wind picked back up. The only option was to climb aloft and shimmy out to the end of the yard to wrestle the sail into obedience. For some reason, Tony grabbed me and told me to go aloft with him.

I followed Tony forward to the base of the foremast shrouds. The sail was fifty feet up in the air. The waves we were climbing were still topping out at twenty to thirty feet. Falling from where we needed to get to could end up being a drop of seventy to eighty feet. I read somewhere that window cleaners know falling from a height above five stories, or fifty feet, is fatal. As far as I knew, only one person had ever fallen from the rig of *Rose*, and it happened at the dock in New York Harbor. The chief mate, who was on deck, saw it happen and broke her fall by body-checking her into the water before she could hit the deck. She fell from a height of fifty feet and cracked some ribs and a wrist but lived.

Before sailing on *Rose*, any work I performed aloft was always done from a bosun's chair, which is generally how people go up a mast today. A bosun's chair is a seat-like harness that is usually suspended from a halyard for the purpose of doing work aloft in the rig. Modern sailors don't climb aloft to set or strike sail; in fact, most modern boats don't have any means to climb the rig. That is because free-climbing up a mast in the middle of the ocean in the middle of a storm is a horrible idea. It's like climbing to the top of a telephone pole using a rope ladder that gets smaller the higher you go. It gets to be so tight up near the top that you need to twist your feet so they can fit in the slots above the next ratline.

Most of my experience in a bosun's chair was on *Onawa*, and she had a ninety-foot-tall mast. I went up that mast more times than I can count, spending hours aloft repairing metal tracks and making improvements to the rig. All of that work, however, was at the dock and usually done in calm conditions. And for good reason: at the top, even a tiny wave sent the mast oscillating wildly. There was nothing to hold on to up there, so I would wrap my legs and arms around the slippery varnished wood and hold on until the weather settled back down. I was always so scared the person holding me up would let go of the line and I would fall to my death.

Now there I was, on the *Rose* in the middle of a terrible storm, and somehow the idea of free-climbing the rig seemed less terrifying to me than being pulled up a halyard to the top of a varnished mast. At least I felt somewhat in control of my life even if there was no safety line to catch me if I fell while trying to ascend the rig. Clipping in our carabiners could only be done when we got to where we were going, but climbing up or down the rig had to be done freestyle.

We began our ascent by climbing out and around to the windward side of the foremast shrouds. I was now outside of the boat, standing over the water on the ratlines. I knew time was precious and moving slowly would only worsen the situation. Using the foremast as a line of sight, I started climbing while keeping my eyes locked forward on the mast to prevent me from looking down at the frothy waves below. We were not wearing lifejackets, and the likelihood of successfully being rescued from the water after falling from the rig was almost nonexistent.

The thrashing of the ship was causing the shrouds to tighten and slack quickly and randomly. I carefully put one hand over the other as I climbed, making sure to wrap my arms hard around the shrouds when the ship buried itself into a wave. Those moments made the rig shudder like we were slamming into a brick wall. Then the next wave would pick us back up, and we would surge ahead again until we were thrown back into another trough. We were being absolutely pounded.

Experiencing the violence of the storm from the deck was rough, but it was nothing compared to what it was like up in the rigging. The intensity of the wind grew, as did its roar, sounding like an express subway train rushing past a station. I could feel the stinging pellets of rain through my foul-weather gear, hitting me harder and harder the higher I climbed. I felt like a target at an air rifle shooting range. On deck, the ship was rolling from one side to the other. From aloft, we were being thrown sixty to eighty feet across the sky from side to side, every four to five seconds. The random rolling of the ship was like riding a fifty-foot-tall metronome that couldn't keep a rhythm.

Climbing up the shrouds was the easy part. Getting out to the sail was dodgier because I needed to take a small leap of faith off the rigging to get onto the yard and then out to the sail. Waiting for the right moment, I lunged onto the footrope while grabbing hold of the yard and began shimmying out toward the end. I was first out on the yard, a situation I had never been in. Walking along a footrope was like using a long jump rope as a bridge. I held on for dear life, balancing my weight so my movements would be in sync with Tony's when he climbed on behind me. We were standing on the same footrope, and any movement I made was felt by him. Laying on a yard in this kind of weather was the very definition of insanity.

We reached the flogging sail, and I tried to grasp the task before me. Seeing the sail fighting to be released up close was far different from seeing it from the deck. There was no time to get comfortable. The wet sail was filling with rapid bursts of air and thrashing ferociously. It terrified me. My plan was to jump onto the sail as if I was trying to take control of an angry bull at a rodeo. If I did it wrong, I could fall, taking Tony with me. The jerk felt by Tony from my lanyard trying to stop my fall to the deck would make it near impossible for him to maintain his footing. We had our safety harnesses clipped to the back rope with the lanyard, but our harnesses were called "backbreakers" for a reason.

I looked over my left shoulder to see Tony just a few feet inboard of my position. I shouted at the top of my lungs, "How should I do this?"

Tony shouted back, "You need to punch it while jumping on it and wrapping yourself around it!" Then, with a second thought, he added, "Let's go back in and switch so I can jump and you can follow!" We shuffled back toward the mast and switched places.

Tony headed back out as the lead, and I followed. In a blink, he got that violent and disobedient sail into his arms. I came to take the rear, punching the sail with all my might to knock the wind out of it, and helped him gather and secure the sail, all the while shimmying farther out on the yard. Suddenly we were in control, and it felt great. With no time to celebrate, I started securing the sail so nobody would have to come back up until we were through this storm. I worked quickly, and Tony told me to get back down to the deck. He didn't need to tell me twice; the rolling and rocking had gotten worse. I took my time on the descent, bracing myself whenever the bow buried itself into a wave. Tony stayed up a bit longer, making sure everything was good.

Stepping back onto the deck, I was overcome by an immense wave of exhaustion. The ship's motions on deck seemed so much milder than they had before going aloft: being on deck felt easy! I staggered back to midship, near where

Shannon, Carrie, and Russ were waiting. I didn't want to talk to anyone; I was winded and overwhelmed by the moment.

Russ put his arm around my shoulder while shouting how glad he was that I was the one who went up and not him. He said that Jon had filmed the entire event for insurance reasons in case we fell; I wasn't sure if he was kidding. He then slapped my back hard, smiled, and headed below.

Tony made it back to where we were standing a few minutes later and asked Shannon for a boat-check. He was unfazed. Tony was no show-off; he was just doing his job, and he was great at it. She let him know I was on boat-check. Without letting her finish talking, he told her to have someone else do it so I could have some time to recover from going aloft.

I had joked about Planet Tall Ship up to that moment, but being aloft in that storm made me appreciate all I was learning. We were on only day four of our passage, had traveled only one-tenth of the distance to our destination, and I had already seen more than I could have imagined or planned for. There was no off switch, no time-out, no opportunity to stop and take a break. That moment forever changed my understanding of how to handle adversity. The only way out was through.

Chapter 12

ℙROPOSITION

THE DAY WAS LONG as we pounded our way through the storm, becoming more battered, ground down, and soaked to the bone. A-Watch was relieved at 1200, but we had only four hours off before our next watch because the watches were "dogged" that afternoon, meaning B-Watch and C-Watch stood two hour watches instead of the normal four-hour watch. As a result, A-Watch assumed the 4–8 shift instead of the 8–12 shift. The plus was that we would get to see the sunsets and sunrises; the minus was A-Watch got only a four-hour break between two four-hour watches that day.

I was exhausted, having spent most of the day sitting on deck wedged on the weather rail at the base of the mainmast shrouds. For the most part, besides those moments of overwhelming fear when I was aloft with Tony, I enjoyed myself. Fortunately, the mood on deck was jovial. I think most of us acclimated to the rough weather and accepted there was not much we could do about it. The pumps had kept working, the weather was clearly dissipating, and the thoughts of abandoning ship were evaporating from our minds.

There was, however, much to do when it came to getting the ship's interior back in order. At the top of the list was GT's remounting of the dislodged toilet bowl. Once completed, the vacuum system was sealed, and we were spared the putrid stench overtaking our ship's interior.

The bathroom on a boat is called the "head" because the common crew would have done their business off the bow near the ship's figurehead, the decorative carved wooden sculpture, usually embodying the name of the vessel. If lucky, there would have been a fashioned seat to sit on. If not, the headrails would have served as the seat. Dragging in the water below was a tow rag, an old common line shared by all for wiping away any remaining fecal matter. The line would be pulled up, used, and then dropped back into the water until needed again. The captain had his own enclosed head in one of the galleries located in the stern of the ship. In the film *Master and Commander*, there is a brief scene in which you can see a crew member sitting on the headrails, relieving himself.

This position was not without risks. British seaman Aaron Thomas kept a journal of his experience aboard HMS *Lapwing*, a twenty-eight-gun, sixth-rate frigate of the Royal Navy. In an entry dated Tuesday, August 14, 1798, Thomas describes an unfortunate event that occurs to the ship's purser when he relieved himself: "The Purser went into the weather round House, about this time which is fixed in the Galley, on the Ships Bows. While he was on the Seat, a mass of wind was forced by a wave up the Side of the round House; that its violence breaking against the naked *Posterior* of the Purser, it so lacerated his parts & Aunus, that he was oblidged to get medical assistance, as a quantity of wind had forced a passage into his Belly."

The facilities we had were much better than what was described by Aaron Thomas. *Rose* had an enclosed men's and women's head that were used by all crew members, including the officers and Captain Bailey. Our heads were located up forward, near the bow on the gun deck. The heads were spartan but still had private toilet stalls, two sinks for washing up, and a simple shower. When imagining what life was like on a ship two hundred years before my time, I was grateful to benefit from modern innovations like plumbing, hot water, and the vacuum flush toilet system.

With the interior of the ship smelling less foul, and the state of the sea settling down, we were eventually allowed to assess the state of the living compartments. They were a mess. Personal belongings were all over the place. I thought I was walking into the aftermath of a giant hurricane when I first saw the state of B-Compartment. The waves of bilgewater wreaked havoc, making the already squalid living accommodations worse. Nearly anyone with an outboard bunk in the two forward living compartments came back to bedding and personal possessions soaked through with salt water. Little was left untouched, and there wasn't much chance of anything having the opportunity to dry because of the lack of ventilation.

Fortunately for me, the inboard bunks in B-Compartment were spared from most of the carnage, staying dry, and I was on the short list of people in possession of an inboard bunk. Jared, Jon, and Marion had the outboard bunks in our section of B-Compartment, and their bunks got soaked, Marion's in particular.

I was enjoying a few rare moments of a nearly empty compartment, having just brushed my teeth and rummaging through my belongings before heading up to eat dinner and watch. Marion was preoccupied, standing over her bunk. It was quiet, and we weren't talking. I knew what she was doing, and I felt bad for her. She was tough and stoic; there was no complaining from her. You wouldn't know she was sorting through her wet puddle of bedding and personal possessions.

Impulsively, and without even a fully formed thought, I started talking.

"Wow, look at all of your wet stuff," I said, while tossing my things around, trying to appear preoccupied.

"I have an idea: Why don't you sleep in my bunk? That way you could sleep in a dry bunk and we would only have to be in it together for four hours each day because we are on different watch." I was already mentally punching myself in the face for being so bold as to make such a proposition. My eyes darted in her direction, and I quickly donned an overconfident grin, hoping to mask my internal terror of rejection. If it all crashed and burned, I was going to blame my off-the-cuff offer on being seriously overtired.

"Sure," she said, looking over her shoulder at me with not much of an expression, as if it was no big deal. She then turned back to her bunk and continued to sort and reorganize her gear.

I smiled, turned around, and bolted out of the compartment. I did not want to linger and make the mistake of overselling the moment.

As I made my way up onto deck, the overwhelming feelings of excitement were quickly replaced with worries of how this sleeping arrangement would really work. My bunk was small, really small, seventy-eight inches long by thirty inches wide, with only sixteen inches of headroom from the top of my mattress to the bottom of Blythe's bunk above mine. I am six-two and weighed 190 pounds. When I rolled on my side, my shoulder touched the bottom of Blythe's bunk. Marion is five feet, four inches tall and weighed 110 pounds. It was going to be tight with the two of us in there.

I had the bunk to myself while Marion stood watch. I was all nerves during those four hours. I had no idea what to expect. Would she just want to go to sleep? Was I supposed to make small talk? What were her intentions? Did she have a plan?

I was nineteen years old when I met her. She was twenty-two. I had such a crush on her then. Being around her when we sailed on *Nefertiti* left me feeling like a freshman in high school falling hard for the senior prom queen. Her tanned skin, smart laugh, and quiet confidence drew me to her and intimidated me all at the same time. She was worldly, well-traveled, and unflappable.

Whereas I didn't have much of a specific desire to be on a tall ship, she did. Marion had sailed on the tall ship *Gazela* in the spring of 1998 after coming back from a semester abroad in Brazil. The temperature difference between Rio and northern Nova Scotia, she said, was brutal. But the *Gazela* was a cool boat, and she learned a lot. They sailed to Louisbourg, Nova Scotia, to be in the French film *The Widow of St. Pierre*. Rose was there too, sparking her interest.

I felt like I was her polar opposite. My insecurities overwhelmed me as I convinced myself she was out of my league, and it was true. Marion spoke multiple languages and had lived abroad. I was just some kid a year out of high school who had hardly been anywhere. The only other language I knew was American Sign Language because my grandparents were deaf. I was too timid to pursue her when we met.

And here we were, sailing to California. I had already learned more about her in the past four days than I did during that summer of sailing on *Nefertiti* together.

Will on deck, sporting a goatee and enjoying the nice weather

I felt unprepared. I was not popular with the ladies in high school. I had had two girlfriends, both older than me. The first was a college senior who took me home with her one night when I was a high school senior. I don't know what she saw in me, but she was happy to step in and teach me things I wasn't learning in high school. The second was Mrs. Robinson, who also had a few years of experience on me. Our relationship was really one of convenience. I doubt we would have ever hooked up had Jared not been living with her.

There were just those two, plus a few hookups along the way. Being an apprentice at IYRS for two years did not include normal socializing opportunities. My class of ten guys when we started had only seven at graduation. I learned a lot about how to build boats but not much when it came to flirting with girls.

I didn't sleep at all during those four hours, lying in my bunk in the dark, rolling around, feeling inadequate and trying to figure out how we were both going to fit. Jared and Erinn got their wake-up calls, signaling it was time for me to pop an Altoid in my mouth. My anxiety was killing me.

My eyes were wide open when I heard footsteps. I froze, listening, waiting. False alarm, it was only Jon and Blythe. They were quiet and probably tired. It was midnight, and they had just come off watch. In minutes they were in their bunks, and all was quiet again other than the soft creaking of the ship and the accentuated sound of the ocean rushing across the hull as our ship pushed through the water.

Then, like a burglar sneaking into a vault, Marion carefully climbed into my bunk with her back to me, pressing her body against mine. It was like having Raquel Welch climb out of the poster of *One Million Years B.C.* and into bed with me. My heart was pounding through my chest. We just barely fit in the bunk. She didn't say a word. I was doing everything I could not to move, to lie still as if asleep.

I froze there, wanting to explode despite being literally backed into a corner. I bent my elbow, laying my arm over hers. She didn't move, and I breathed a sigh of relief as I relaxed, releasing all my tension. She put her hand in mine.

※

Work-party resumed the following morning, Monday, January 14. A thorough inspection of the ship revealed significant damage sustained up near the bow. The pounding we took in the storm caused a structural failure, allowing the bowsprit to press back against the forward watertight bulkhead, flexing it inward. The fore-aft tension of our rig was dependent on the resistance that could no longer be provided by the bowsprit. The stability of the entire rig was compromised.

The plan was to be in Puerto Rico for three to four nights, giving us two solid working days to fix the problem when we arrived. When I say "we," I mean Todd and me, with some assistance from Jon. Lucky for the ship, I had gotten accustomed to performing intense bursts of hard labor in short periods of time. The undertaking was going to be challenging, requiring a coordinated effort, so Todd and I immediately set to planning the sequencing of the repair. The rest of the crew would deal with the rigging and preparing the ship for the next leg of the passage to Panama.

Much effort was put into creating an intense storm scene in the film *Master and Commander: The Far Side of the World*. In that scene, HMS *Surprise* is pushed to her limit, causing the mizzenmast to break, which results in the death of a crew member. Peter Weir says, "A painting of the British frigate *Prompt* dismasted in a storm became a major inspiration for the storm scenes." To create the scene, Weir's team pooled a number of elements together that were a mix of actual film footage taken at sea and computer-generated imagery (CGI). In an interview for *VFXWorld Magazine*, visual effects supervisor Nathan McGuinness described first shooting test footage from a boat in the ocean. Then, knowing it would work, Fox sent a film crew out on the replica *Endeavour* for a passage around Cape Horn. The footage taken from on board *Endeavour* was then used in combination with the full-scale replica of HMS *Surprise* built in the same tank used for the filming of *Titanic*, various CGI models, and the twenty-five-foot miniature models of *Surprise* and *Acheron*. Richard Taylor, the founder and creative director of Weta Workshop in New Zealand, personally supervised the build and shoot of the museum-grade models. The result was a scene that felt all too real.

We spent the afternoon work-party sitting up on the bow, formulating the repair. We also spent a fair amount of time reflecting on the storm and all we had been through together in the past year. I had not spent much time with Todd since leaving Newport because of our different watch schedules. I didn't understand why Todd even came on this trip with a wedding in his near future. I knew he was nearly forty years old and was under the impression this passage was to be his one last adventure before settling down. Then he told me the engagement was off and he was on board to take a break. The confession took me by surprise.

Todd was an excellent shipwright. He had a Henry Ford–like efficient approach to getting the job done. He was thin and muscular, always looking for surf opportunities when he was not working. He loved his American Spirit cigarettes and giggled with an unusually high-pitched laugh when he got drunk.

Some of our best bonding moments had been on drives to 7-Eleven to pick up cigarettes and lunch when building *Onawa*. Those runs were the few moments of bonding that didn't involve Todd staring at me like I had just shot Lincoln or saying, "Are you fucking stupid?" like it was a statement more than a question.

Todd was a hard mate to work under. He would be cool one minute, then, without warning, suddenly flying off the handle the next. I think Todd felt it was his duty to make sure I was paying my dues just as he had done when he started his sailing career. Our relationship reached a tipping point when 9/11 happened while we were in Sardinia. We were halfway around the world and didn't know what sort of fallout might happen or how that might affect us. That uncertainty pulled us together by pushing aside frustrations. We chose to count on each other more.

Todd had sailed *Rose* across the Atlantic twice back in 1996 with Casey. He told me he had never seen weather as bad as what we had just come through. He praised me and told me I did good, really good, in the storm. I was glad he was sailing with us because I knew I could trust him, and I knew he trusted me. I never could have imagined we would be shipmates again after *Onawa*, yet there we were, in a tough situation, working together to get through it.

It was hard to believe we had been ready to abandon ship only twenty-four hours prior. We were a thousand miles north of Puerto Rico and two hundred miles west of Bermuda. C-Watch was running the deck. The American flag flying off the mizzen gaff, hoisted for the first time five days earlier when we departed from Newport, was shredded. The ends of the red and white stripes looked as if they had been chewed off by a savage animal. The weather continued to improve. The sky was blue, with only a few clouds hovering on the calm horizon. The wind was light coming out of the southeast, and there was a two-to-three-foot swell. Our lower staysails were set, and we steered a course of 180°, due south. The mood on deck was amiable as we took turns poking up on deck to bask in the tranquil light.

Jon broke out his video camera, documenting the moment as we waited for dinner to be served; Hunter was making spaghetti with meat sauce. Rick came up onto deck in a great mood, smiling, and gave me a friendly push.

"Hey, Rick, just because we all live on this thing and it moves doesn't mean it's a mobile home, buddy," Jon said, lighting his tobacco pipe.

Handing me the video camera, Jon was happy to be the star of a mocku-
mentary about surviving life at sea on *Rose*. We took turns recapping the events,
asking obnoxious questions, narrating the scene, and taking jabs at each other.

Marion spent some time sitting next to the main companionway, enjoying a
crossword puzzle. I did my best to avoid looking at her too often or to talking with
her more than I talked to anyone else lounging on deck. I was paranoid because
I felt like I was carrying around a giant secret. Marion acted like she always did,
as if nothing had changed, and really, not much had changed. Blythe sat forward
of us, filing her fingernails. Rich and Russ were mingling, while Alex and Charlie
sat on the deck, laughing and telling stories.

Even Vincent showed up on deck. He sat alone up at the mainmast. It was
the first time I had seen him in two days. He was wearing his heavy foul-weather
jacket, jeans, and sneakers; the rest of us walked around in sandals and shorts. He
had been hiding in his bunk the entire leg, leaving only for meals and bathroom
breaks. At one point Tony ordered Carrie to drag him up on deck if necessary. He
came up wearing only underwear, in the middle of the gale we had sailed through
before crossing the Gulf Stream. He looked terrible, weak and miserable. It was
impossible to not feel sorry for him. The storm didn't just break the ship; it broke
Vincent. He seemed unable to function.

Had he been working on HMS *Surprise*, Vincent may have been punished for
his incapacity under the Articles of War, a set of thirty-six provisions established
for governing the behavior and conduct in the Royal Navy. Article twenty-seven:
"Sleeping, negligence, and forsaking a station. No person in or belonging to the
fleet shall sleep upon his watch, or negligently perform the duty imposed on him,
or forsake his station, upon pain of death, or such other punishment as a court
martial shall think fit to impose, and as the circumstances of the case shall require."
On a ship, the captain was the law. The assignment of punishment was at the
discretion of the captain and, depending on his nature, could be cruel or decent.
Floggings were a common form of punishment, which meant being stretched
out and whipped with a cat-o'-nine-tails, a five-foot-long whip made of nine
knotted tails capable of lacerating the skin. Punishment was a public display, and
up to twelve lashes could be administered without a court martial. In practice,
such was their authority: captains often ordered men to receive twenty-four or
thirty-six lashes, and sometimes more.

O'Brian, being thorough about all aspects of life on a ship, includes refer-
ences to the Articles of War in the majority of the Aubrey-Maturin series. In

The Mauritius Command, Jack Aubrey's former coxswain Bonden, in Cape Town, talks about the cruelness of another captain: "But *Néréide's* short-handed: because why? because the men run whenever they can. There was Joe Lucas, of our mess, as swam three mile, with bladders, off St. Kitts, sharks and all, was brought back, flogged, and swum it again, with his back like a raw steak."

Vincent had talked a big game before we departed Newport and ended up being all foam and no beer. I thought about how callous he was the first time we met. He had rubbed just about every person on board the wrong way, except for Rick. Vincent became Rick's de facto grunt man during the yard period. He ended up being relegated to the dirty jobs that could be done solo. Everyone tried to find a place for him, but nothing ever worked out. He became the perfect example of knowing the difference between talking the talk and walking the walk.

We made a noble effort to include him in our social activities in Newport. I remember the time everyone was trying to rush off the ship to catch the end of a happy hour. Jon and I called for Vincent as we ran through the gun deck. We both worked from aft to forward until we got to the men's head. We opened the door and found him standing in front of the sink, covered in filth with his shirt off, shaving his armpits with a disposable razor.

"What? Shaving my armpits is how I manage my body odor," he explained with an awkward smile.

He looked crazy, like Private Gomer Pyle from *Full Metal Jacket*. For once, Jon and I had nothing to say; we just looked at him, told him everyone was waiting, turned around, and left.

The crew manifesto created before departing from Newport had all crew members listed in order by rank and assignment. Rick Hicks was at the end of the list because he was technically a passenger. Vincent was listed below Rick.

— *Chapter 13* —

LIFTOFF

WE HAD DOGGED OUR WATCHES on the day of the storm, shifting A-Watch to the 4–8 block, and that meant we were responsible for washing the dinner dishes for thirty people. To others, it may have appeared like Planet Tall Ship was rubbing off on me, but in actuality I oddly found comfort from washing dishes.

When I was a junior in high school, my mother found a pack of rolling papers belonging to my friend in my jacket. Honestly, they were not mine! The punishment was severe: I was essentially put on house arrest for three months. I was dropped off and picked up at both school and work, not allowed to walk, ride a bike, or get a ride from a friend. Everything was off the table. I was not allowed to leave the house or see friends. After the first month, I was granted the privilege of driving my sister Kate to her 5:00 a.m. hockey practice before school.

The only other reprieve I got was being allowed to continue working my part-time job at Romano's Macaroni Grill as a busboy and barback. One day, the manager asked me if I would do him a huge favor by hopping into the kitchen to wash the dishes. He offered any meal on the menu as a bonus. After that, I started getting calls a couple of times a week asking if I could fill in washing dishes. Willing to do anything to get out of the house, I found doing dishes was both freeing and meditative.

For me, washing dishes on *Rose* reminded me of those odd moments of feeling free as a teenager. Like the back of that restaurant, the galley on *Rose* was a pleasant shake-up from my work regimen on the ship. The workspace in Hunter's galley was small, there was a limited amount of water allotted for washing, and we needed to separate organic matter into the slop bucket to pour overboard for feeding the fish. The galley was the only place on the ship where anyone was allowed to listen to music without headphones. Hunter had a boom box and a curated selection of music we could choose from so long as we were careful to not scratch any of his CDs.

Hunter in the galley

Hunter was a spot-on doppelgänger for Hunter S. Thompson, in both looks and personality. Like Thompson, his personality was strong, and his mood could flip without warning. He had a voracious appetite for his alcohol and Dunhill cigarettes, and for some unknown reason, probably based on tradition, Captain Bailey made him the gatekeeper of all our booze. Our ship was a dry ship when underway, meaning alcohol was not allowed to be consumed, requiring us to give Hunter any alcohol we were in possession of for safekeeping.

For centuries, sailors in the Royal Navy were issued a daily ration of alcohol. Though deemed a right, the captain could restrict the ration, usually as a form of punishment or because of age, such as in the case of the younger ship's boys. The ration began in the form of one gallon of beer, or one pint of wine, or a half pint of brandy, arrack, or rum, all depending on where the vessel would provision. Rum became an option after the English captured Jamaica from the Spanish in the seventeenth century, and it soon became the preferred form of alcohol served to the crew. In 1740, concerned about alcoholism, Vice Admiral Edward Vernon ordered the daily ration of rum be cut 1:4 rum to water and to be divided into halves so it could be served twice daily. This concoction became known as "grog" after Vernon, who was nicknamed "Old Grog" because he wore coats made of grogram fabric.

The cook was responsible for the daily preparation and distribution of the alcohol. He prepared the grog visibly on deck, and for his service, he was given an extra ration. Janet Macdonald describes popular concoctions developed on board in her book *Feeding Nelson's Navy*: "Rum, water, sugar and nutmeg was known as 'Bumbo'; rum or brandy mixed with beer and sugar and heated with a hot iron was known as 'Flip'; and in the officers' wardroom similar mixtures with lemon juice and hot water were made into punch." The crew did not have to take the daily ration and in that case would be paid instead. It was not uncommon for the crew to exchange rations among one another to pay off debt or as an exchange of service. The tradition of serving a daily ration of alcohol in the Royal Navy remained in place until July 31, 1970.

O'Brian regularly shows the reader how important the ration of grog is to the men and the dangerous effects caused by the ritualistic consumption of alcohol, including injuries from falls, fights, and alcoholism. Irony is not lost through the series, as Stephen expresses his concerns for the long-term effects of alcohol on the men despite the reoccurring appearances of his own addictions and his belief upon discovery that coca leaves will help to free him of his desire for laudanum. O'Brian's sense of humor in regards to the consumption of alcohol shines through in *HMS Surprise*, when Stephen brings his new pet sloth onto the ship. Much to Jack's dismay, the sloth does not like him until one evening when Jack feeds the sloth a bit of cake soaked in grog. After that, the sloth visits Jack to receive its own bowl of spirits, all unbeknownst to Stephen until one day "Stephen looked sharply round, saw the decanter, smelt to the sloth, and cried, 'Jack, you have debauched my sloth.'"

Hunter had been on *Rose* since 1990, after coming from the *Tole Mour*. At the time, the *Tole Mour* acted as a medical support ship for the Marshall Islands in the Pacific. When first hired, Captain Bailey introduced Hunter to the wholesaler Sysco and gave him a copy of the last invoice to use as a baseline for provisioning the ship. The bulk of the ship's nonperishables and frozen food went through Sysco, making it more manageable when planning menus. Hunter needed to procure only items such as milk and produce via local grocery stores when in port.

Rose had ample storage space for dry and canned food provisions scattered around the ship. The first and largest space was the dry-stores compartment located on the starboard side of the lower deck just aft of C-Compartment. The shelves were configured to maximize storage of the large size #10 cans (three quarts). The space was able to store enough dry provisions to feed the entire thirty-person crew for three months. The next most important spaces were the interiors of the benches for the three tables immediately forward of the galley. That location was convenient for immediate access. In addition to the storage spaces for the dry and canned food provisions, there was a large chest freezer located aft of the women's head and a second chest freezer located immediately aft of the mainmast, both on the gun deck. Produce and perishable food were kept in the two industrial-size refrigerators in the galley.

The job of the cook had to be one of the toughest on the ship. Hunter had to put out three hot meals a day for thirty people in all conditions. There actually are laws in place governing the amount of food to be fed to merchant seamen. Under Title 46. U.S. Code 10303, "(a) A seaman shall be served at least 3 meals a day totaling at least 3,100 calories, including adequate water and adequate protein, vitamins, and minerals in accordance with the United States Recommended Daily Allowances." Though *Rose* was not involved in trading goods, the code was observed by the ship. Jon got some good footage of Hunter cooking during the big storm. Working like a circus performer, he timed the rolling of the ship with the tossing of the cheese onto the ham and cheese sandwiches he was grilling. In all the chaos, he stuck to seeing his job through and made sure we were all well fed with warm and tasty comfort food.

I liked Hunter. I got him, and we never had a dispute. However, Hunter could come off as harsh, "could" being the operative word. He had no patience; he had a boat full of people to feed, and if you didn't like what he served, step aside. If you put it on your plate, you ate it, otherwise you wouldn't be eating at the next meal. Vincent left a big glob of maple syrup on his plate once, and Hunter banned him from having maple syrup for a week. You didn't want to cross Hunter. I read between the lines, observed the mistakes others made, and never assumed anything around him. I kept my distance and stayed out of the galley unless invited in.

Hunter's dry stores could feed our crew of thirty for three months, and he also benefitted from the easy access to provisions in just about any port. It was different on HMS *Surprise*. The world was much less developed, and they could have been underway for months at a time. Fresh water, meat, and produce were not always available. Diet had to fall back on provisions that could be stored for long periods in less than ideal conditions. Preservation techniques of food were limited mostly to salting and/or drying. Whenever possible, diet was supplemented with fresh produce and livestock kept on board, such as sheep, goats, pigs, and fowl. If fresh produce and livestock were not available, then the crew could count on receiving one pound of hardtack every day; two pounds of beef two days a week; one pound of pork two days a week; a half pound of pease (peas) four days a week; one pound of oatmeal three days a week; two ounces of butter three days a week; and four ounces of cheese three days a week.

The captain ate at his own table and at his discretion, extended invitations to those he favored to join him. Upon commission, the captain was provided a cask of oxtongues and an allowance called table money for supplementing his meals and entertaining. In *The Mauritius Command*, O'Brian provides an example of the benefits a captain could have when it came to supplementing food. After taking an enemy ship, Stephen briefs Jack about captured provisions: "I have also seen to it that Monsieur Brettonière's wine and comforts have been transferred: to these I thought fit to add his late captain's stores; foie gras in jars, truffles in goose-grease, pieces of goose in goose-grease, a large variety of dried sausages, Bayonne hams, potted anchovies; and among the rest of the wine, twenty-one dozens of Margaux of '88, with the long cork, together with an almost equal quantity of Château Lafite." The officers formed their own mess tables in the gun room and often pooled money to purchase additional wine and food to supplement their daily rations, which were the same as the crew's. The crew formed messes—dining areas—where they slept on the lower deck. Some used their own tableware made from pewter while others used square wooden plates (think of the expression "square meal"), either made by the owner or purchased from the purser.

HMS *Surprise* had a large hold that provided the capacity needed for storing enough provisions to feed the two-hundred-man crew for three months. Items were stored in tiers, with water being the heaviest and taking up the most volume. HMS *Surprise* had the capacity to carry 10,368 gallons of water stored in containers of various sizes: butts, 108 gallons; puncheons, 72 gallons; hogsheads, 54 gallons; and barrels, 36 gallons. The ship's rum was stored in a separate, locked spirit room with a capacity of eighteen barrels, or 648 gallons. In addition to the water, the hold was where the cook stored ingredients such as salted meat, beef and pork, and butter and cheese; and dry ingredients such as flour, oatmeal, peas, and the ship's biscuits, also called hardtack.

There was a limited understanding of the science behind nutrition at that time. We know now that a deficiency of vitamin C (ascorbic acid) can result in the onset of scurvy. Without vitamin C, the body cannot synthesize collagen, a vital element needed to produce connective tissue, an important component of bone, cartilage, muscles, skin, and tendons. Symptoms of scurvy can include anemia, pain in the limbs, swelling, ulcerations in the gums, loss of teeth, and even spontaneous bleeding.

In 1753, a Scottish doctor named James Lind, credited with performing the first recorded clinical trial in history, published *A Treatise of the Scurvy*, in which he details the results of a controlled experiment he conducted in 1747 on the ship *Salisbury*. Lind served in the Royal Navy for nine years, starting out as a surgeon's mate and eventually becoming ship's surgeon. For the experiment, twelve sailors with the symptoms of scurvy were divided into six groups of two. Each group receiving a different theorized treatment for scurvy daily. The prescribed treatments were daily doses of cider; drops of vitriol; seawater; a laxative paste; vinegar; and oranges and lemons.

Only the pair of men who received the oranges and lemons recovered, whereas the others did not. Conclusions drawn by Lind in *A Treatise of the Scurvy* were not entirely clear, and the use of citrus juice as a means for preventing scurvy was not officially implemented by the Royal Navy until 1795.

⚓

We observed a spectacular sunset on Tuesday, January 15. We were about nine hundred miles out from Puerto Rico, and I noticed a growing influx of off-watch crew lingering on the weather deck at the risk of being assigned to extra work. The main excuse of more idle hands on deck was the rising interior temperature. Our engine room generated an obscene amount of radiant heat due to the constantly running machinery. That heat benefited us when we were in colder waters but became a hinderance in the warm water of the tropics, driving up the ambient temperature of the ship's interior.

When on boat-check, I needed to go down into the engine room, or, as I liked to call it, "the pit of despair," to visually inspect the engines and generators. Going down into that inferno always made me feel like I was sitting over a pig roast. The average ambient temperature usually hovered around 120° Fahrenheit (48.9° Celsius). GT spent hours at a time down there, and I don't know how he did it. Added to the unbearable heat was the eardrum-bursting decibels. Before entering, I had to put on a pair of hearing-protection earmuffs that hung on the outside of the engine room door next to a clipboard with a paper sheet log we filled in every hour, recording our observations.

I knew what to look for, and did it as fast as possible: engines running Yes/No, generators running Yes/No, internal temperature recording Yes/No, water flooding Yes/No, fires Yes/No. I would make my observations and get back up to the gun deck as soon as possible. The only good thing about going into the engine room was that after a minute in its oppressive heat, the gun deck felt cool and comfortable.

☸

The deck eventually cleared that evening, not too long after the sunset. There were few clouds, and the sky was particularly dark as the new moon had begun the night before. The stars in the sky were our only source of light other than the ship's running lights. Running lights are a universally accepted configuration of colored lights projected from a boat and used for the purpose of indicating the relative position of one boat to another. We were hundreds of miles from land, beyond the reach of light pollution and smog. Looking up, I saw a nighttime sky that was the darkest shade of black I had ever seen, making me feel as if I was sitting in a theater in the middle of the universe.

I stood on deck, gazing up, taking in the Milky Way as it exploded in a fragmented band of light wrapping across the sky. Until then, I had only seen a sky like that in books or at a planetarium. Orion, Dorado, and Ursa Major were drowned out by the thousands of stars I could then see, showing off their twinkle. The star cluster Pleiades dominated the sky like a band onstage at the center of a large stadium. I searched the sky for the Southern Cross. Tony said I had not yet seen it because the Southern Cross could be seen only south of latitude 25°N, or just north of Key West, Florida.

I was staring up at the sky when a bright streak of light shot up from the horizon high above the ship, continuing across the sky, traveling faster than any jet I had ever seen. It was too large to be a shooting star or comet, and it left a trail of light stretching halfway across the sky. What I saw was the launching of a Titan IV-B, America's largest rocket at the time, from Cape Canaveral on the eastern coast of Florida, over nine hundred miles to the west of our position.

The cargo on the rocket was the Lockheed Martin Milstar 5 (military strategic and tactical relay satellite), the final of five satellites completing the "Golden Ring," a series of government satellites originating from the Cold War era, to provide government leaders with secure and uninterrupted transmissions anywhere on the globe.

Rockets shooting across the sky seemed to be the only explosions happening in my life. Marion had slept in my bunk for two nights, and if I was at a casino, I would say I was breaking even. There had been no passionate exchanges, but she had not moved back to her bunk. I was going bonkers trying to figure out where this was going.

I didn't waste time getting below deck that night. I was exhausted, and the two to three hours of sleep I had been getting for the past three nights were catching up to me. I climbed into my bunk and took out my book, hoping it would help me fall asleep quickly. I didn't even open it before I started to doze off. I lay in bed in a half-awake dream state, enjoying the rocking motion of the ship, thinking of white beaches and imagining what it would feel like to walk along the sandy shores of Puerto Rico.

That night, I dreamed I was back in Europe, in Saint-Tropez, at Le Club 55, the famous beach club frequented by the rich and famous. I had sailed there on *Rose* and could see her anchored off the shore where we had once anchored *Onawa*. The whole crew from *Rose* was there, as well as Casey. I was standing in the middle of the restaurant. People were drinking wine and eating elaborate arrangements of food. I saw Jon, Jared, and Blythe sitting at a table with Casey and Todd, laughing and telling stories.

Jared handed me a champagne flute, asking me where I had been. Speechless, I shook my head from side to side; I didn't know. I looked out toward the beach and saw Marion, who was laughing and speaking in French. I understood every word, even though I didn't speak French.

She glanced over at me, grabbed a bottle of Champagne, and walked toward the beach, motioning for me to follow. We rendezvoused on the edge of the sand, and she filled my glass with the Champagne. I took a refreshing swig of the delicious cold, bubbly beverage.

Then, a rocket launched up into the sky. It was the very same rocket I had just seen on watch. All eyes were on the rocket; everyone there was pointing at it as if we were all witnessing the best fireworks show ever. I stood there with Marion, her back pressed against my chest as we watched the rocket fly high up

into the sky. Marion's hair smelled like the ocean, and her tanned skin was ever
so soft. I stood there wanting to kiss her, but I froze, unable to move.

I suddenly woke up. Marion was already in my bunk, and my arm was wrapped
around her. I blinked my eyes, looking around, wondering what time it was.

She turned toward me; I could see her eyes. We kissed. All at once, my mind
went blank. I was exactly where I wanted to be. My feelings of insecurity and
apprehension vanished, suddenly replaced by feelings of comfort, and sanctuary. I
breathed deeply, relaxing, as I embraced the moment. Her warm, soft skin pressed
against mine. That moment felt more powerful than all the energy used to send
the Titan rocket into space.

Chapter 14

𝒫UERTO RICO

WE SIGHTED PUERTO RICO at 0630 on Friday, January 18, our ninth day at sea. The green, mountainous coastline was an intoxicating contrast to the endlessly flat horizon I had spent days searching. A-Watch had the deck. We were busy adjusting our course as we weaved the ship through a gauntlet of small rain squalls before we could make our final approach for the island. At one point, I got hit by a gust of wind that carried with it the smell of land. I did not know land could be smelled. It was overwhelming, many times more potent than a lush garden, with nutrient-rich soil and blooming flowers after a heavy downpour of rain. It was overpowering, drowning out the smells of salt air and our tar-covered rigging.

After breakfast, with Puerto Rico only ten miles off our port beam, all hands were called to deck to begin taking and furling our sails, meaning to put them away. To strike sail on most boats means to lower the sail to the deck by releasing the halyard. The different nature of the sails we had set meant they were "taken," not "struck," because none were actually lowered to deck. Taking a staysail was easy because one simply needed to release the halyard to lower the triangular staysails. Taking the square sails was different. A square sail hangs from a yard, and to take a square sail means to first ease the halyard to lower the yard—only the topsails and t'gans'ls—and then haul the square sail up to the yard using the clewlines and reef tackles.

To furl a sail means to pack and put the sail away. Depending on the circumstances, there were two methods for furling the sails on *Rose*. The sea-stow method was used at sea when speed was more important to secure the sail, not caring how pleasing the furl looked. We were approaching our destination, and the conditions were favorable, so we would instead be harbor furling the sails. The harbor furl requires more time and finesse than a sea stow, resulting in a more tightly packed sail that looks clean and orderly. It is like buttoning the top button of your shirt and straightening your tie before stepping onstage.

When setting sails, only a few hands were needed aloft. For furling sails, most hands were needed aloft. The sails on *Rose* were large, awkward, and very heavy. The fores'l was fifty-six feet wide and thirty-five feet tall and weighed between three hundred and four hundred pounds. Fifteen of us swung out and climbed aloft while the remaining hands stayed on deck to prepare the sheets, clewlines, reef tackles, buntlines, braces, and halyards.

With hands on the clewlines, reef tackles, and buntlines, Dwight called for hands to the braces. The yards were then squared, meaning they were braced round until perpendicular to the ship's centerline.

Dwight then shouted, "Clew up the fores'l!" And with that, the sheets were cast free while the hands on the clewlines and reef tackles hauled away, pulling the clews of the sail up toward the center of the yard. At the same time, the reef tackles pulled the sail straight up to the yard, from where their gear was connected to the reef points on the leech of the sail. The clewlines and reef tackles were made fast to their pins when they were two-blocked, a term meaning "reached the limit." Dwight then shouted, "Bunt up the fores'l!" The buntlines were hauled, pulling the main body of the sail directly up to the yard until two-blocked; the buntlines were then made fast to their pins. The sail was loose and, in its gear, ready to be furled.

Hands aloft furling the fores'l

With our crew of fifteen spread out evenly along the length of the yard, we began furling the fores'l. Alex was the AB in charge. He told me to stay closest to the mast opposite him because that was where the muscle power was needed since the bulk of the sail hung near the slings, the part of the yard that connected to the mast. First, we released the gaskets so they would be ready when needed for securing the sail to the yard.

I let go of the jackstay, leaned forward while balancing all my weight on my abdomen, reached down as far as possible, grabbed a handful of sail, and pulled it up to the yard. Then, holding that first fold of sail between my abdomen and the top of the yard, I repeated the process until the entire sail had been pulled up in nice folds like ribbon candy, called flakes. The effort needed to be carefully coordinated and done in unison. We made one final reach over the gathered sail for the bottom edge of the last fold and pulled it up and around, swaddling the other folds tightly inside. With a big heave, we then rolled the sail up onto the top of the yard. The harbor furl was completed by wrapping the gaskets tightly around the yard and sail before tying them off. It took over an hour to furl all the sails. It might have gone quicker if so many of us were not gazing at the captivating scenery of the approaching island. Eventually, I made my way back down to the deck to help prepare the ship for docking.

⚙

We docked in Algarrobos, a rural barrio in the municipality of Mayagüez on Puerto Rico's western coast. The name derives from an edible fruit–producing tree, distinguished by its shiny leaves and white flowers. Mayagüez had been a favorite port for smugglers because of its distance from Castillo San Felipe del Morro, a citadel built to defend San Juan Bay from naval assaults. In 1836, the local government built a dock and a longhouse to facilitate the loading and unloading of cargo. The same dock and longhouse are the original installments of today's Mayagüez Shipping Terminal. In 1959, the terminal became the property of the Puerto Rico Ports Authority and primarily serves as a ferry port for service from Puerto Rico to the Dominican Republic.

My excitement from sailing through an ocean to a land new to me fell off a cliff when I realized our destination. The beautiful tropical coastline that greeted us on the horizon had quickly transformed into a sprawl of outdated time-share condos and decaying warehouses that looked like an abandoned set from the movie *Mad Max*. Asphalt, concrete, and rust dominated the miserable landscape

Rose docked in Mayagüez, Puerto Rico

lining the harbor. The air was humid, and there was little breeze because of the mountains blocking the natural cooling effect of the trade winds.

Instead of being secured to a floating dock like we were in New England, we were tied up to a concrete ferry terminal, similar to a quay. This arrangement meant our dock lines would need to be constantly monitored and adjusted due to changing tides and swells. We needed to quickly set up fender boards—planks of wood horizontally hung via two lines, between the fenders and the dock—to act as the sacrificial element, grinding against the piling or dock instead of the rubber fenders.

We next jumped on setting up the rat guards. Barren places like the terminal we were docked at are filled with rats, and a ship like *Rose* was a treasure trove of food. Every dock line had a thirty-inch-diameter round piece of plywood threaded on it, halfway over the water between the ship and the terminal. Imagine a Frisbee oriented on its side with the dock line running through a hole cut in its center. The idea is to create an impassable wall. If a rat attempts to crawl out on the line, it either falls into the water trying to climb over the guard or retreats back to shore.

The terminal in Mayagüez seemed abandoned, aside from the young female port officer who came to greet us after we had settled in. Unexpectedly, as soon as the gangway was set, Jackal, Captain Bailey's dog, bolted off the ship. This caught everyone off guard, as he spent his whole life living and sailing on *Rose*. Maybe the storm had been too much for him. Some customs agents later returned Jackal, but seeing him run away made me envy his ability to jump ship.

As it turned out, Jackal was not the only member of our crew to jump ship. Scott was ready to leave, but with some tender persuasion, Andy convinced him to stay. Aaron, the AB of B-Watch, needed to leave immediately due to a family emergency. The officers had already lined up a replacement who was on a plane to Puerto Rico. I felt bad for Aaron, knowing his departure would be a loss. He had spent most of the big storm in the bowels of the ship, ensuring the bilge pumps never stopped working. Yes, he was from Planet Tall Ship, but he never made me feel obliged to his methodology. His quiet nature and passive approach to teaching only made me try harder to pay extra attention to anything he had to say. Aaron had no ego and gladly shared his knowledge with us newbies, doing anything he could to help us become better sailors. Then there was Vincent. Vincent was basically ordered off the ship.

We rolled into an all-hands muster at the capstan before lunch. Tony and Rick had lots of ground to cover, making the muster run unusually long. I already had a sense of what they were going to say. We had just completed a nine-day sail to Puerto Rico, sustained a considerable amount of damage along the way, and, as a result, had a long worklist that needed to be completed for the next leg of the journey.

Tony's approach to leading the muster was like a football coach during half-time. He said he knew we were all tired, but there was no beating around because we had a massive worklist to complete and not enough time to get it all done. We were not on vacation, so we couldn't just tie the ship to the dock and kick back with some cold ones. He paused while looking around at us all. Captain Bailey and Rick stood there silently on either side of him. Then, with an unexpected smirk, Tony said he would love nothing more than to be at a karaoke bar with everyone watching Jon and Will sing the Divinyls song "I Touch Myself."

Tony's joke was perfectly timed, breaking the building tension on deck. The grinding glints of anger and frustration suddenly turned to smiles, followed by a few random chuckles and elbow jabs. I smiled. I was happy to be the punch line of Tony's joke. After all, it made everyone laugh.

Tony stepped back in to prevent us from losing focus on the agenda of the muster. He told us to remember how lucky we were to be sailing to California to make a movie and that we all needed to keep our mission in perspective. He said we would be broken up into two groups: Shore-Party-A and Shore-Party-B. I was assigned to Shore-Party-A. This was good and bad, as I quickly realized not everyone would have the opportunity to celebrate our arrival together. Despite my frustration with Planet Tall Ship, I appreciated that we got here together and would have liked the opportunity to share a drink with all my shipmates. The consolation for me was that I enjoyed the company of everyone assigned to Shore-Party-A.

Then came the unexpected. We had been working almost nonstop and without a day off since before New Year's Eve. We started standing watch the day before departing. That meant most of us had worked around the clock for a minimum of eighteen days straight. I knew there was a long worklist, and I must have looked like a deer in headlights when we were told we would be given only a half-day off while in Puerto Rico. There was no reaction from any of the crew.

Rick chimed in, and his accent sounded thicker than ever as he told us that the powers that be were going to cover the cost of having all our laundry washed so we could have a bit more fun, considering the tight work schedule. But there were few cheers. The gift of the paid laundry service was received chiefly with silence. I would have preferred a $50 bonus or, at the very least, a few cases of beer to drink while taking turns washing our laundry in the ship's washer and dryer ourselves.

Tony then went over the extensive worklist. I was to devote all my time to working with Todd to rebuild the bowsprit heel tenon with some assistance from Jon. The rest of the deckhands were to mainly focus on slacking the rig for our bowsprit repair, then rigging up the t'gallant yards and hoisting them up the rig. The t'gallants were the highest yards on the foremast and mainmasts. They had not been set for the first leg because we ran short on time when trying to leave Newport. We wanted their additional sail area for added speed on the next leg. Though I was being relieved from the typical deckhand responsibilities, I still had to stand watch at night.

The muster ended with Shore-Party-A being excused from working for the second half of the day. We gathered our filthy, smelly, wet laundry, ate lunch, and organized how we would share the cost of renting a minivan. Eager to savor every second of our single night off, we loaded into the van like a bunch of circus clowns piling into a Volkswagen Beetle. I sat on a cooler in the front row between Todd and Alex; Marion sat on the floor in the middle row with Jared, Jon, and Marshall; Scott, GT, Tom, and Carrie sat in the third row. Our first stop was to get beer and check emails at an internet café—the best option before smartphones and Wi-Fi.

Ever the surfer, Todd pleaded for us to head to the famous surf point called Rincón, and since nobody had a better plan in mind, we all were happy to go along with it. I was open to anything as long as it meant having lots of fun. The mood in the van was jovial. Most of us enjoyed the cold cervezas, and we happily passed the time, staring out the windows and listening to a smattering of Puerto Rican radio stations. Finding Rincón became the real adventure. Our strategy was to drive close to the coast, but that didn't work, requiring us to stop at a rural roadside stand to ask for directions. With the help of Marion's language skills, a local old man was more than happy to offer assistance.

✿

When we finally arrived, the boys and girls split up into two parties with a plan to rendezvous somewhere on the beach. Looking like a bunch of redneck vacationers who showed up too early for spring break, we descended onto Rincón. If I had been sitting on the beach seeing our motley crew, I'd have steered clear. The beach was a welcome exotic contrast to the industrial wasteland where our ship was docked. Tall palm trees ran endlessly down the coast, and the sand was soft and light in color. Unfortunately for Todd, the water was flat, but that didn't stop him from paddling his board out so he could brag about the time he surfed Rincón.

The rest of us boys roamed the shore, drinking beers and cracking jokes. Jon recorded our shenanigans while adding explicit commentary. At some point, I thought I could climb one of the coconut trees. I got two-thirds up before gravity said no more. I'd worn myself out trying to get to the top and had nothing left to ease myself back down. My only choice was to relax my thighs and enjoy the bumpy crotch ride back down to the sand.

Lounging and hanging on the beach was terrific. It was the absolute opposite of the daily grind I had grown accustomed to. On *Rose*, if caught doing nothing, I knew I would undoubtedly be put to work doing something. With the sun setting and bellies rumbling, we found the girls and departed the beach to find dinner.

Some hours later, I found myself sitting up front in our minivan with Def Leppard blasting on the radio and no idea where I was exactly. There still were eleven sailors in the van, and most of us passengers were drunk as skunks. It was 10:00 p.m., and we had been driving in circles for over two hours trying to find our ship.

Our ambitions for our only night off were overzealous. Somehow dinner came down to Chinese or Taco Bell. I don't know how that happened, but there wasn't much else to choose from at the time. We opted for Chinese because the restaurant was next to a bar with a band playing live music. The idea of grabbing a drink for the road made perfect sense at the time. The pumping bar exploded with energy as the band played the No Doubt song "Just a Girl" in Spanish. Our impromptu dinner choice filled my stomach but left me wondering what I had missed by not sampling the local cuisine.

After hours of driving around in a minivan, our buzz and gusto drained away and we finally found our ship. I am sure we looked well licked and probably should have gone straight to bed, but that didn't happen. Stumbling onto our ship, we found a handful of our shipmates lounging on deck. Russ was lit up and playing his harmonica, while Erinn, standing watch, was sitting nearby with Blythe and Jason.

I noticed a new accessory on deck, an oversize inflatable Heineken Beer chair lying on its back. Scott claimed it, sinking into it like a king on a magnificent throne. Marion appeared on deck with her guitar in hand and joined Russ in his musical revelries. They started with "Don't Think Twice, It's All Right," then began taking requests and, much to my delight, played "The Girl from Ipanema." The scene was magical.

It may be said that music came before words, for as long as there have been humans, music has existed in one form or another. Prior to the invention of the phonograph in 1877, recorded music could not be played back. That meant the only way to hear music would be through live performance. Making music can be a way of telling a story and can emotionally bind people in ways that language cannot. Music has always had a place on boats. On or off watch, sailors have always sung and enjoyed music-making activities. When thinking about sailors, many people today often correlate the word "shanty" to the age of sail. In fact, the term "sea shanty" is not very old, tracing only as far back as the mid-nineteenth century.

It felt fitting that music was being made on a ship soon to be O'Brian's HMS *Surprise*, as music was clearly important to O'Brian. The Aubrey-Maturin series begins with the first meeting of Jack and Stephen at a concert in *Master and Commander*. As the plot develops, we learn that Jack, the big lug, plays the tiny fiddle while Stephen, the small, wiry man, plays the large cello. The moments of playing music are used as a mechanism for establishing the mood of a scene and characters. O'Brian uses the shared appreciation of music to build relationships, such as in *The Fortune of War*, when Stephen is inconvenienced because he must have dinner with the captain of the ship he is a passenger on. Stephen's armor of irritability melts away when he sees Captain Yorke's personal possessions upon entering the cabin: "row after row of books, and low down, built in among the quartos, the sheet-music, and the incongruous nine-pounder gun, a small square piano: Jack had said that Captain Yorke was a musician: and evidently he was a reader too."

Jack, being the great captain he is, also knows his stuff when it comes to playing music. Near the end of the series, as a demonstration of his love for Stephen, it is revealed that he has been holding back his capability as a musician so as to not outplay Stephen. This is one of many great examples of the platonic love both men share for each other.

Even during the filming of *Master and Commander: The Far Side of the World*, there were instances when Peter Weir played music from a boom box on set. When asked, Weir said, "The presence was important. I use music to keep me 'inside' the film. To keep me focused. To close out the world. I do this at all stages of the script—shoot—cutting. I wasn't only playing pieces mentioned in the books—Pink Floyd was in my ears as often as sea shanties. As for having Jack and Stephen as amateur musicians, it was a brilliant touch of O'Brian's and key to their unlikely friendship."

Our night wore on as we roped more hands into our gathering on deck, even as our third mate, Christina, joined in on the party. Grabbing a splat line, Jared ran a few steps before leaping off the deck to swing like Tarzan out over the water. Halfway through his swing, he let go of the line, probably because he had less muscle control than he thought due to all the rum he had drunk since returning to the ship. He fell into the water, laughing hard and splashing around like a toddler in arm floats. After a few failed attempts to pull himself out of the water, Christina launched and took command of one of our ship's inflatable dinghies to rescue the water- (and rum-) soaked Jared. With all eyes focused on the rescue at sea, I made eye contact with Marion and we snuck away for some much-needed alone time in an empty B-Compartment.

The officers were scrambling the following morning, reassigning hands to different work-parties based on immediate needs. It was like a giant game of hot potato as we rushed to get our ship back in order. Ron, the new AB, arrived and was promptly thrown into the chaos of work needing to be done. He knew his stuff and loved Planet Tall Ship, but right off the bat he made my skin crawl because of the way he managed the hands under his command. Some leaders are graceful and are good at motivating their team. He struck me as one of those Planet Tall Ship sailors who believed in hard work first, then smart work. I was glad not to be working with him, let alone under him.

With some assistance from Jon, Todd and I jumped headfirst into pulling off one hell of a quick fix for the bowsprit, meant to hold us over till reaching Panama. The bowsprit was held in place by a configuration of structural components known as the upright bits. The bowsprit was stepped to an athwart side-to-side timber called the bowsprit heel tenon. The heel tenon, horizontally positioned, was reinforced by two parallel stout upright bits running vertically from the top of the inner keel up through the weather deck. The three components locked into place with the heel of the bowsprit stepped to the heel tenon. This configuration provided the resistance needed to tension the rig's fore-aft standing rigging against the loads transferred to the bowsprit. The port upright bit fractured, so the heel bit tenon could no longer support the loads of the bowsprit. Completing our task was difficult for many reasons.

Nearly all of the fore-aft tension of the ship's standing rigging relied on the bowsprit, and none of the rigging was designed for an easy disconnect. That

BOWSPRIT REPAIR

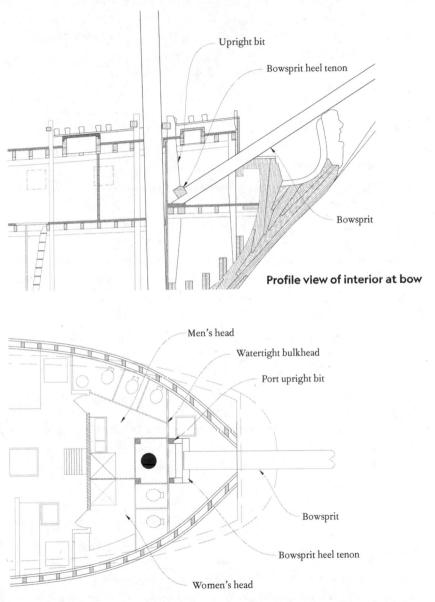

Upright bit

Bowsprit heel tenon

Bowsprit

Profile view of interior at bow

Men's head

Watertight bulkhead

Port upright bit

Bowsprit

Bowsprit heel tenon

Women's head

Plan view of interior at bow

created an immense amount of technical rigging work that needed to be done to slack the standing rigging in order for the bowsprit to be pushed out. Additionally, the force of gravity was working against us when trying to push the four-ton bowsprit uphill because it was oriented at a thirty-degree up angle; it was like trying to push an elephant up a slide. Adding more complication to the repair was the need to improvise our fix because of the limited material resources. We had to make the best of what we had.

My experience as a shipwright on *Rose* had been a mixed bag and mostly educational. Thanks to IYRS, I had a specialized skill set, one of the reasons I had been offered this job. But most of what I trained for did not apply to our situation. I had brought aboard all my handmade planes and perfectly sharpened chisels, only to learn chippy work on *Rose* required a whole other arsenal of both tools and techniques.

To start, we needed to break down the watertight bulkhead separating the men's and women's heads from the forepeak. That delicate task required using a very specialized tool—a chain saw—to cut through the double-planked bulkhead. We could have done it with hand tools but were motivated when Captain Bailey checked in to see the progress of the repair. He looked at us, and the work being done, and furrowed his brow. "Get this job done as soon as possible!" he demanded.

After removing the bulkhead, we were able to ascertain the true extent of the damage. It looked like the decades of rusty water running down the inside of the steel bowsprit was the source of the rot resulting in the failure. After a few hours of clearing the debris, we were able to position three strategic pieces of steel angle bar to serve as a temporary heel bit tenon. We then set up two hydraulic rams between the heel of the bowsprit and the steel angle bars. Lubrication in the form of tallow was applied to any areas on the bowsprit where we believed friction might occur. The lubing process was of course riddled with endless amounts of dirty jokes.

We paused to evaluate our work, taking an extremely long thirty-minute cigarette break to ensure everything was in place and the rig was slacked so the bowsprit could slide forward. We began the fix by loading up the rams, standing clear to avoid any unexpected explosions from the thousands of pounds of load we were cranking into them. Nothing moved. This caused some head-scratching and prompted another thirty-minute cigarette break.

We walked up onto the deck and then back down, trying to figure out why nothing was moving. We then came up with a new plan that involved using the

Un-Fuck-It Tool (UFIT), commonly known as a sledgehammer. As a rule of thumb, I had learned that the UFIT is usually a bad approach, but when nothing else works, you do what you need to do to get the job done.

Our new plan was simple: load up both rams, then, while standing aft of the bowsprit, swing the UFIT like Babe Ruth and strike the bowsprit's heel with full force, hoping to shock it enough to get it moving forward and out of the ship. As our designated pinch hitter, I swung once, and boy, did that hurt. Hitting a four-ton rusty steel tube with a metal-handled sledgehammer had to be the worst feeling my hands and wrists had ever felt. I stopped to search for Captain Bailey to borrow the padded leather winter gloves I had given him for hauling on our

Shannon laying on the main t'gallant yard with Puerto Rico
in the background

fishing line. I figured the gloves might cushion my hands, protecting them from the shock of the blows. Wearing the gloves, I lined up again and swung hard while timing a pump of the rams by Todd. Presto! The combination nudged the spar. We were in business. After five more whacks, the bowsprit began moving with ease.

Once far enough out, we unloaded the rams and started installing temporary shoring in place of the heel tenon. Pickings were slim when it came to material available for the shoring. We used the steel angle bars in combination with some chunks of Douglas fir Rick purchased from the local Home Depot. The bowsprit was then brought back into position, and we rebuilt the bulkheads between the forepeak and the heads. Then, like flies on shit, the rigging work-party went to town tensioning and tuning the rig. The fix looked like a kindergarten art project, but we did the best we could with the two days we had to complete our *MacGyver* repair.

While we were busy completing the temporary repair, Rick worked on lining up a chunk of purpleheart wood that would be waiting for us in Panama City. Purpleheart, also known as amaranth, is a very dense tropical hardwood that is naturally purple in color and ideal for structural applications. The plan was to break down the bulkheads again and swap out the temporary shoring with a proper replacement. Hopefully, the repair would hold.

Chapter 15

T'GALLANTS

IT WAS 0555 ON TUESDAY, January 22, and Tom, our handsome former soccer star, was nowhere to be found. Everyone else was on board. The engines had been running for an hour, and we had been scheduled to depart Mayagüez at 0530. Our dock lines were singled up. We were ready; there was nothing more for us to do. Hunter had made breakfast. I was already on my third cup of coffee.

The only conversations involved outrageous theories about Tom's whereabouts. I could see the officers were not happy. We couldn't just leave him behind, but how long were we supposed to wait? The last person to see Tom had been Mandrew. They had been out with the beautiful customs agent who greeted us when we arrived. They went to a beach with her and a friend, where things got hot for Tom, leaving Mandrew and the friend to kill time without a spark. They parted ways; Mandrew returned to the ship, Tom stayed out.

Then, Jared pointed, and we all saw Tom running fast across the terminal toward the ship as if he were Pelé sprinting down the field toward a breakaway pass. He was breathing hard, mouth wide open, sweat pouring down his face, and he was not looking back. Tom hit the brakes at the bottom of the gangway, putting his hands over his head to help him catch his breath. "I'm sorry, I'm sorry, I'm here! What can I do?" It was hard to understand him because of his frantic breathing.

Tom had spent the night with the female port agent, forgot to set an alarm, woke up late, and realized he might be fucked, that we might be on our way to Panama short one deckhand. Tom woke his date's entire household, and her brother rushed him back to the ship on the back of a motorcycle. He made it, and with a good story.

The weather was in our favor when we departed Puerto Rico. C-Watch took the deck at 0800, the wind was moderate at five to ten knots, coming from the northeast. The sky was mostly overcast, and the air a summery 80° Fahrenheit (26.7° Celsius). I realized I understood the procedures for getting underway, which were very different than our departure from Newport.

We then got to work setting the sails. First, we set the fore and main topsails, then the fores'l, mainsail, and the mizzen staysail. Then we set the t'gallants, the topsails, the fores'l, and lastly the main and mizzen staysails. It was exciting setting the t'gallants; it was our first time setting such high square sails. Setting the t'gallants was a near-identical process to setting the topsails.

The t'gallants were smaller than the topsails and didn't require reef tackle and bowlines. They were also much lighter in weight, their loads much less, requiring fewer hands to set. The main topsail was approximately 1,628 square feet, whereas the main t'gallant was only 782 square feet. Hoisting the halyard for each t'gallant required only three to four hands, whereas the topsails needed almost every hand on the deck. The sails themselves didn't weigh more than a couple of hundred pounds each, but we were not just pulling a sail up when hauling away on the halyard. We were pulling up the sail, the yard, and the metal hardware and rigging associated with the sail. Factoring in the combination of elements meant pulling up between 1,500 and 2,000 pounds of weight for the main topsail and around 500 pounds for the main t'gallant.

GT and Mandrew sitting at the break of the quarterdeck.
The wave behind them is more than fifteen feet high.

We were on our second day out from Puerto Rico and blasting through the Caribbean Sea. Life was good. Our course to Panama had put us in a perfect position to see the ship open up and get pushed along by the prevailing trade winds. We were steering a course of 227°, the wind was east by south at twenty-five to thirty knots, and the seas were four to seven feet. We were making 9.1 knots SOG (speed over ground). SOG is the term used when describing speed relative to traveling on the earth's surface. The speed of a vessel through water can be different than SOG because of factors like the current. If a vessel is making five knots of speed through water but against two knots of current, the vessel is only achieving three knots SOG. A knot is equal to one nautical mile per hour. A nautical mile is equal to 1.15 imperial or statute miles (1.85 kilometers), or one minute of latitude, the horizontal lines drawn around the earth parallel to the equator at the earth's equator.

The term "knot" originates from the common log or chip log, a device developed in the sixteenth century to measure boat speed. A common log was a coil of line with a series of knots spaced at equal intervals on the line with a triangular wedge of wood secured to the end of the line. The wedge would be dropped in the water, and the coil of line would be allowed to run free, dragging behind the vessel for an established period of time. The number of knots that paid out during the period was equal to the vessel's speed.

We had fallen into our watch routines. We were flying the main and fore t'gallants, main and fore topsails, the fores'l, foretop staysail, and the main staysail. We had the mizzen staysail set but struck it to help ease the load on the helm. We crossed a time zone, and A-Watch split the extra hour with C-Watch. Our ship was taking on a fair amount of water. A new issue was the more than average amount of seawater coming into the engine room, requiring regular pump-outs. The ship's barometer broke, the gangway came loose, and it was clear we would need to do a lot more shoring and reinforcing to the bow in Panama.

Dwight and Ron had become a little full of themselves after leading the charge of the intense rigging work in Puerto Rico. A strong dichotomy had formed among our crew. There were those with skills and those without. Unspoken, we mostly knew about the division before our departure from Newport, but the assignment of preferential jobs without rotation began building tension between Planet Tall Ship and the rebels. Rich, Russ, Mandrew, Tom, Jared, Peggy, and Charlie were usually assigned grimy jobs like tallowing the spars, tarring the rig, or scraping and painting hard-to-reach places. Everyone else was mostly assigned jobs like repairing sails, splicing line, or inspecting gear in the rig.

I observed protests in the form of Jared and Charlie acting like the bad kids in class, often deflecting a good amount of Dwight's and Ron's focus. Still despite Jared's attempts, most of our crew was content with keeping busy. The situation was not unique to our ship. In *The Last Grain Race*, a book published in 1956, travel author Eric Newby writes, "The more favoured of the crew, slung in bosuns' chairs, were painting shrouds, an exciting job in such a wind; others of whom I was one, chipped rust from the decking amidships above the living accommodations."

Captain Bailey's woodworking assignments kept me busy most of the time. There were a few moments of me being tasked to help Dwight or Ron. I observed that when assigned to help them, Dwight and Ron told me to do only menial, laborious work, as if as some sort of punishment for mostly being beyond their reach. I felt their division of labor unfairly enhanced the development of seamanship skills for the crew members they preferred.

There were some moments of free time, which many of us used for taking naps on deck or enjoying conversations with fellow shipmates. The mates were able to spend much more time teaching us how and why the various elements of the ship worked. Much of the first leg of our passage had required a substantial amount of reactionary action, leaving little time for learning the theology about the mechanics of how we sailed *Rose*. Our experience at sea had made us more versed in the elements of our ship, and the mechanics of sailing *Rose* became clearer.

Enjoying a rare moment of mellowness, I climbed aloft after my watch ended to take some photographs from the top of the fore t'gallant mast. Climbing up and then out onto the yard was never an easy task. I was over a hundred feet up in the air, and there were only a few ratlines up at the very top of the rig, forcing me to be creative with my weight when laying out onto the yard.

Standing at the top of our ship in the middle of the ocean, with the wind whistling through the rigging, I inhaled the rushing air deeply and breathed it out completely. I relaxed and felt my body become limber, moving in sync with the ship. I let my feet swing with the footrope fore and aft, enjoying the ship's motion rolling from one wave to the next. I looked down, gazing at the towering stack of three square sails beneath me, one on top of the other. I heard the sounds of the wind racing through the rigging and the distant roar of the white-water waves being carved into the ocean by the bow of our ship as we pushed ahead.

Looking down from the fore t'gallant yard with all squares set

There was nobody to talk to, or nobody talking to me. I had time to linger, I could stay up there for as long as I wanted and cherish the moment. I let go emotionally. I was doing exactly what I loved to preach. I was in the moment and drank it all in.

✹

As we sailed deeper into the tropics, the air on board got hotter. *Rose's* hull, predominantly black painted, was far better at absorbing heat than reflecting it. Avoiding the sun was not possible. The air was humid, and the temperature of the ship's interior was near 90° Fahrenheit (32.2° Celsius) during the middle of the day. There were no mechanical means for ventilating the interior. Gunports and hatches had to be kept closed to keep the ship as watertight as possible. The only form of ventilation came from the main companionway; the doors were lashed open.

To combat the never-ending grime and smells generated by twenty-nine dirty sailors at sea, we all took turns cleaning the shared living spaces and heads during the work-party assignment called soles and bowls. The gun deck would be mopped and all surfaces wiped down. The heads were thoroughly scrubbed to combat the foul smells (mostly coming from the men's head). With twenty-two men relieving themselves in the small, unventilated space each day, and in the heat, it quickly became wretched. The men cleaned the men's head, the women the women's head.

Marion had mostly moved back to her own bunk, despite our budding romance. The living compartments were even more uncomfortable in the sweltering heat. Trying to sleep was impossible for me. Lying still in my bunk, I could feel the heat from my oily, sweat-caked skin radiating out in all directions. Minimal fresh water on board meant bathing opportunities while underway had to be limited. I began praying for rain, but there was none in the forecast. In the classic book *Two Years Before the Mast*, the author, Richard Henry Dana, signs on to a ship as a deckhand and sails from Boston to California. He describes how together the crew used the fresh water from a rainstorm to wash themselves and their clothes: "This day it rained nearly all day, and being Sunday, and nothing to do, we stopped up the scuppers and filled the decks with rain water, and bringing all our clothes on deck, had a grand wash, fore and aft. When this was through, we stripped to our drawers, and taking pieces of soap and strips of canvas for towels, we turned-to and soaped, washed, and scrubbed one another down . . . It was surprising to see how much soap and fresh water did for the complexions of many of us; how much of what we supposed to be tan and sea-blacking, we got rid of."

I had no desire to bathe on deck with any of my shipmates, but I would gladly have tolerated it had it guaranteed even the smelliest ones would be washed clean. Planet Tall Ship appeared to be either resistant or ignorant to the modern practices of hygiene I had come to love. Our bodies became sweaty, stinky collections of filth. We couldn't wash any clothing, and if you couldn't see or hear someone coming, you could easily smell them. The whole ship stank.

Not being able to wash quickly became a real problem for me in the form of an acne breakout all over my body. My skin had become irritated to any touch, and the extreme exposure to the sun was compounding the problem. I felt the breakouts were destined to get worse as we sailed farther south. I spoke to Tony, and he permitted me a ten-second shower once a day. My first shower was glorious. I never thought the highlight of my day while sailing through the middle of the Caribbean Sea would be taking a ten-second cold shower. I would wait for everyone to settle down from the watch change and then run into the head to brush my teeth. I stripped down and jumped into the shower before turning on the water. I embraced the shock of the cold water hitting my crispy and overheated skin while counting to ten before shutting off the water. Then I quickly donned some gym shorts and hurried back down to my bunk.

I did not dry off. My reasoning was if I stayed wet when I got into my bunk, and leaving my curtain open, I might feel some sort of cooling air running over me from the fan hanging in the aisle between our bunks.

Chapter 16

EPOXY AND SAWDUST

IT WAS THURSDAY, JANUARY 24, and we were two days out from Puerto Rico in the middle of the Caribbean Sea with Colombia two hundred miles south of our port beam. I got off watch at 1600. It was a beautiful afternoon near identical to the day before. We were ripping through the ocean, heavily canvased with the main and fore t'gallants, main and fore topsails, main and foretop staysails, and the jib, set. The wind was east by south at twenty-five to thirty knots, and the rolling seas were ten to twelve feet high, pushing us along. The ship was in a groove, and we were having one of the best sails of the trip as we steered for Panama. I lingered on deck for an hour before heading below for dinner; I was ravenous.

I was standing just forward of the galley when it happened. We started to roll hard after racing down the back of a pretty big wave. I lost my footing and fell over. At that exact moment, there was a loud, shattering CRACK and a shudder ran through the ship, followed by shouts and then the thuds of rapid footsteps pounding the deck above.

I heard Tony shouting, "ALL HANDS ON DECK!" at the top of his lungs, meaning every person onboard needed to get up to the weather deck immediately. The throbbing ache of hunger suddenly vanished. Adrenaline kicked in, and instinct took over as I quickly sprinted to get up to the weather deck. When I got there, I saw a sight no sailor wants to see, ever, let alone in the middle of the ocean. Looking up, I saw a mess of torn sails and shattered spars hanging in a chaotic tangle of wire and line. We had just dismasted under full sail.

I could not believe what I was seeing. The main t'gallant mast was gone, having snapped at the crosstrees, the point where it was connected to the topmast. As a result, the main t'gallant mast and yard, along with the t'gallant sail, had fallen over forward of the main topsail, and I could see silhouettes of the dangling spars and sail through the set topsail. Looking forward, the fore t'gallant yard had snapped in half and was flailing along with the remains of the fore t'gallant square sail.

Looking up the mainmast from the deck. The main t'gallant mast snapped at the crosstrees. The silhouette of the fallen yard and spar can be seen through the main topsail.

It was nearly sunset, so we didn't have much time to ascertain the situation and determine the best course of action for securing and containing the damage. We needed to get through the night safely without incurring more catastrophic damage.

I saw that Captain Bailey had taken control of the helm, and Andy was already aloft near the upper doubling of the main topmast, right below where the main t'gallant mast used to be. My eyes had focused on Andy when Tony grabbed my arm, taking me with him as he marched forward.

"Will, get up there with Andy and Christina," he said as he let go of me at the base of the mainmast shrouds.

He continued walking forward without missing a beat. He already had a safety belt in hand and was buckling it on as he made his way to the foremast shrouds and started climbing up. I did what he told me and did it without questioning his order. I grabbed a belt off the bar, quickly strapped it on, swung out onto the port rail, and began climbing up the mainmast shrouds. I could see Christina was already ahead of me at the fighting top and swinging out to make her way up to Andy.

Everything was happening so fast. The first thought that flashed into my mind was *Why me?* There were twenty-eight other crew members on the ship, and at least half of them had a lot more experience than me. The only people aloft were the mates, the boatswain, our most experienced AB, and me; everyone else had to remain on deck and wait for orders. Looking down, I could see the rest of my shipmates staring back up, watching and waiting.

We had not struck any sail, which seemed odd to me. Typically, the protocol in a situation like this would be to reduce the loads on the rig by taking down sails. What was stopping the rest of the rig from toppling over the side? I was looking all around, wondering where I should jump if the rig suddenly did start to go over. Could I survive jumping off the rig from over a hundred feet up in the air? Could I manage a water landing, and even if I did, would the ship crush me as the ocean drove her on top of me? Falling from so far up would mean certain death unless I could ricochet off one of the sails below like it were a slide. If I did use my safety harness to clip in, I would be tethered to the tens of thousands of pounds of falling spars, sails, and rigging. I would have no time to think of how to free myself. I chose one risk over the other and decided to not clip in for the time being. I paused and took it all in: shattered spars, torn sails, dangling rigging, less than an hour of sunlight left, and nobody coming to help, so yeah . . . fuck.

Once aloft, I informed Andy and Christina that Tony had sent me up to help them. They were discussing their assessment of the situation. There was significant damage to the top of the main topmast at the upper doubling. The extent of the damage meant we could not strike the main topsail because that would mean loading the lifts (the lines used to support the yard from the mast when the halyard has been released) of the main topsail yard, potentially causing further catastrophic failure. When the topsail halyard was eased, the lift blocks secured to the top of the doubling took on the weight of the yard and sail. For the time being, the load was on the halyard, which appeared to be stable, the lesser of two evils.

Andy determined the best course of action would be to leave the sails set as they were through the night to avoid the risk of another failure in the rig caused by changing loads. He believed it would be best to wait until dawn to continue to evaluate the extent of the damage. With good reason, Andy's plan called for doing the minimum to get us through the night safely.

Christina and I positioned ourselves to provide Andy the support he would need as our surgeon in this situation. He decided which lines were to be cut and when. We worked as a team, helping Andy with our muscles and by relaying information down to the deck. At that point, Jared was aloft on the mizzen topsail yard to offer support from a distance as items were being cut free and lowered. His position helped control a leader line being used to provide an extra leg of control for items lowed via the gantline, a service line run through a block in the rig.

While up there, I saw something that has been branded into my head. Looking forward toward the foremast, I saw the silhouette of Tony standing, holding nothing but a knife in his hand. He did not waver while he stood on a broken yard ten stories up in the air with our ship rolling down twelve-foot waves. I saw an actual, genuine moment of heroism, the kind Hollywood strives to re-create.

Tony standing on the footrope of the broken fore t'gallant yard just
after the dismasting

It was during that moment that I witnessed true outstanding leadership. I can only hope to carry on the straightforward lessons he taught me. Treat people well, never talk down to anyone, know when to be hard, know when to be kind, and know when to be funny. Even that night, with everything so seemingly screwed, he shouted down to the deck, "Send us up a gallon of epoxy and some sawdust. We can fix it."

A joke like that coming from Tony while standing a hundred feet up was exactly what everyone on deck needed to relax a bit and know that we were going to be okay. We had an all-hands muster at 2000 to go over the plan for the night and celebrate the outstanding leadership of the mates and the fact that not a single person was hurt.

Andy made an entry in the ship's logbook after we stabilized the ship. The entry dated Thursday, January 24, at 1715, reads, "*Main topgallant mast carries away when hit by combination of being a bit off course/onto a beam reach, breezes puffing up temporarily, and a deep roll on the face of a rogue wave. The force of the main topgallant falling forward onto the fore topgallant braces causes that yard to carry away. All hands called to stabilize, secure, and salvage. CC to SWxW.*"

A rogue wave is defined as an unpredictable and unusually large wave that can be more than double the average height of 33 percent of the largest waves during a specified period. There is little understanding of their origin and formation. One theory proposes they result from the energy of smaller waves merging to form a more significant wave. When asked, none of my shipmates could explain exactly what had happened at the moment of the dismasting. When the event occurred, B-Watch had the deck. I was below deck, eagerly waiting to eat dinner, Blythe was eating dinner, and Jared was sleeping in his bunk. Jon doesn't remember where he was. Marion was aloft on the foremast just above the fighting top, sewing the main top staysail. Todd remembered sitting on deck looking aft and having the crest of a wave break over the deck and splashing him.

We made it through the night, sailing without any more failures in the rig. Before midnight, C-Watch struck the fore topsail because the wind was gusting up to and past thirty-three knots. The sail was left loose and in its gear, because it was deemed too dangerous to send hands aloft to furl it. By dawn, the wind was east by south at thirty to thirty-five knots, gusting higher at times. We still had a large ten-to-twelve-foot following sea and were steering a course of 240°. We were on a port tack with the outer jib, fores'l, and the main topsail.

At 0620, Captain Bailey took command of the standing watch so Andy could go aloft to better determine the actual state of our situation. At 0800, all hands were called to deck to lower the broken spars. By 0930, we had successfully lowered to deck the broken main t'gallant mast, main t'gallant yard, and the broken fore t'gallant yard. Due to the damage to the upper doubling of the main topmast, Tony, Andy, and Dwight fabricated temporary lifts for the main topsail yard so the main topsail could be struck. Upon further inspection, it was discovered the main topmast had also suffered a failure at the lower doubling.

Broken spars being lowered to deck the morning after the dismasting

⚙

When I was hired, Tony listed some of the potential highlights of our passage, and sailing to the Galápagos Islands was one of them. Before departing Newport, the officers told us of our planned route, which did not include the volcanic archipelago. Still, Captain Bailey occasionally teased of his hope for stopping there. I had been holding on to a thin thread of hope our itinerary would change and we would sail to the Galápagos. The discovery of the broken topmast signaled to me that would never happen.

Two years later, when seeing the film *Master and Commander: The Far Side of the World*, I truly sympathized and understood the sadness and disappointment Stephen felt when being denied his visit to the Galápagos Islands. There is a tense moment in the great cabin when Jack sharply reminds Stephen of the objective of their mission and for that, duty overruled all else: "Subject to the requirements for the service. I cannot in all conscience delay for the sake of an iguana or giant

peccary, fascinating no doubt." The emotion of the situation explodes when
Jack bursts out, "We do not have time for your damned hobbies, sir!" Much like
Stephen, I wanted to see the Galápagos Islands, but my job came first, and that
meant getting to San Diego.

At the time of the dismasting, Captain Bailey's theory for the failure of the
main topmast included factors from a modification to the ship's rig in 1987. Under
the direction of an English rigger, capstays were added to the top of each doubling, possibly creating unequal tension. Also, the square portion of the topmast
doubling was reduced so as to be inscribed relative to the diameter of the spar
at the doubling, when it should have been circumscribed, meaning the spar was
potentially undersized at the doubling.

Months later, during the filming of *Master and Commander*, a film extra called
to Captain Bailey's attention a crack at the base of the steel tube portion of the
foremast just above the deck. Captain Bailey told me, "It was a pretty phenom-
enal crack . . . Two-thirds around opening and closing about a quarter-inch as
we gently rolled in small swells. I could see it was rusty on the inside when it
opened." Upon inspection, it was discovered that the mast was cracked all the
way through, meaning the shrouds were not only holding the mast in place, but
preventing it from falling over, potentially taking the rest of the rig down with it.
Captain Bailey's comment about seeing rust on the inside suggests the crack had
been there for some time. He told me he thought the mast likely cracked either
in the storm we encountered during the first leg of our journey to Puerto Rico
or during our dismasting in the Caribbean Sea.

Chapter 17

*T*HERE ARE NO SECRETS

I REMEMBER BEING A KID, riding in the back seat of my grandmother's blue Honda Civic for a long weekend on Cape Cod. Door to door, we could get there in under three hours if traffic cooperated. My grandmother would take I-84 East to the Mass Pike, then 495, which became Route 25. She would then transfer to Route 6, driving farther than needed so we could cross the Cape Cod Canal using the Sagamore Bridge before continuing on to Hyannis because she preferred that bridge over the Bourne Bridge. Cape Cod is technically a man-made island; it is no longer connected to the mainland due to the construction of the Cape Cod Canal, completed in 1914, the same year as the Panama Canal.

The increasing number of vessels we encountered when I first spotted the Bahía Limón breakwater on Saturday, January 26, reminded me of the traffic jams we would experience when attempting to cross the Sagamore Bridge. I was assigned to bow-watch on *Rose* as we approached Colón, the Atlantic Ocean seaport city of Panama just outside the Panama Canal entrance. There was a seemingly endless number of BMFs coming and going from inside the breakwater, making it near impossible to report my observations to Tony as we made our approach. BMF, short for big motherfucker, was an acronym we used to distinguish larger vessels from smaller vessels.

The BMF category was broad, as it applied to oil tankers, cargo ships, military vessels, cruise ships, etc. By that point of our journey, we averaged something like three BMF sightings every twenty-four hours underway, but I must have seen somewhere around thirty just during my one-hour shift on bow-watch. Sighting a BMF was important because a collision with one of them would have destroyed *Rose*. In 1864, Abraham Lincoln signed the Rules to Prevent Collisions at Sea Act. This contained a number of internationally adopted guidelines and provisions by

COMPASS ROSE

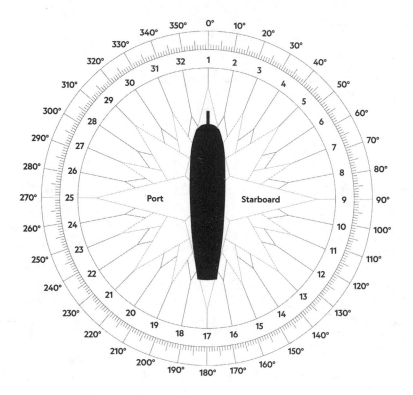

1	Ahead	17	Astern
2	One point on starboard bow	18	One point on port quarter
3	Two points on starboard bow	19	Two points on port quarter
4	Three points on starboard bow	20	Three points on port quarter
5	Broad on starboard bow	21	Broad off port quarter
6	Three points forward starboard beam	22	Three points abaft port beam
7	Two points forward starboard beam	23	Two points abaft port beam
8	One point forward starboard beam	24	One point abaft port beam
9	Abeam	25	Abeam
10	One point abaft starboard beam	26	One point forward port beam
11	Two points abaft starboard beam	27	Two points forward port beam
12	Three points abaft starboard beam	28	Three points forward port beam
13	Broad off starboard quarter	29	Broad on port bow
14	Three points on starboard quarter	30	Three points on port bow
15	Two points on starboard quarter	31	Two points on port bow
16	One point on starboard quarter	32	One point on port bow

over thirty nations to reduce collisions of vessels underway. Today, these guidelines are simply referred to as the Rules of the Road. The Rules do not distinguish between recreational and commercial as a signifier for the right of way, nor do they use the term "right of way" in the rules—they use "give way and stand on." The rules specifically do not use the term "right of way" because at the end of the day, nobody has any privilege over another if a collision is otherwise unavoidable. As we operated, a BMF was assumed to be a vessel restricted in ability to maneuver, or RAM, due to the nature of their work.

Our standing orders were to immediately report any sightings to the officer on watch. If I even thought I might have observed another vessel or something out of the ordinary, I was to quickly run aft to the quarterdeck and inform the officer on watch as to what I saw relative to our ship's position. Observations from *Rose*, when underway, were reported using the point system, a reference method based on the traditional "compass rose." The traditional mariner's compass is divided into thirty-two equal units instead of the 360° unit system used today. The characters depicted in the Aubrey-Maturin series (like the historical sailors the books depict) use the point system when describing wind direction, observations, and sail trim. In *Master and Commander*, O'Brian writes, "Mowett appeared, like a spirit a little late for its cue, and said, 'I beg your pardon, sir, for interrupting you, but there's a ship topsails up three points on the starboard bow.'" Mowett is reporting he has sighted a vessel three points, or 33.75°, to starboard, or the right-hand side of HMS *Sophie*.

My first sighting of Panama was less dramatic than Puerto Rico. A thick smog lingered over a thin sliver of low-level coastline densely covered with tropical vegetation. The evidence of civilization soon followed as we were greeted by the growing smells of engine exhaust and garbage. The approaching landscape quickly transformed into an industrial smattering of cranes and city buildings. It was almost 1600 when I saw the entrance to Bahía Limón, a natural harbor in Panama at the Atlantic entrance of the canal. The low angle of the sunlight spread a dull platinum glow through the hot haze rising off the land. Outside the harbor, the wind was blowing between twenty and thirty knots, with six-to-ten-foot swells smashing against the breakwater, each one shooting plumes of white spray high into the air. Once inside the breakwater of Bahía Limón, though, it was as if an off switch had been flipped. The harbor—the waiting area for ships about to enter the canal—was calm; only a moderate breeze ruffled the water. We were in the lee of the land.

We struck the fores'l and dropped our hook (anchor) by 1627 in Foxtrot Anchorage, a shallow part of the anchorage also called "the Flats." We had to anchor because Panamanian protocol requires a local pilot to be on board for the docking of any large vessel, and *Rose* qualified. A pilot is a local expert ship handler who possesses immense knowledge of water depth, tidal currents, and hazards. Having a local pilot on board is an age-old custom going back centuries. Once on board, the pilot would direct Captain Bailey in safely navigating the ship to our shoreside berth in Cristóbal, a port town in the province of Colón, Panama.

Blythe checking range marks to verify our anchor was not dragging

Shortly after anchoring, the pilot came to board our ship but was not satisfied with the condition of the boarding steps on the side of the ship's hull and our Jacob's ladder, a rope ladder with wooden rungs. I found the name ironic because, in biblical reference, Jacob's ladder refers to a ladder leading up to heaven, and our ship seemed more like Hades. The pilot refused to board the ship until three of the rungs on the ladder were replaced with new rungs. This was frustrating to everyone on board, as it was in fine condition, and it meant we would not be able to get off the ship that evening. We had no choice but to do what was asked. Being the official chippy, Todd was put to work building and installing the new rungs. As chippy number two, I was free to retire for the evening.

I was happy to go to bed when the excitement had died down from our anti-climactic arrival in Panama. I also lucked out because I wasn't assigned to stand anchor watch, so I was guaranteed a solid eight hours of potential sleep. In spite of the sweltering climate in B-Compartment, Marion decided to snuggle up in my bunk with me as I had hoped she might. It had been almost a week since our relationship became more intimate in Puerto Rico.

Marion and I stayed quiet about our romantic interactions, careful not to display affection when around others. Jon, Jared, Blythe, and Erinn obviously knew something was happening, but not even Jared made a joke about it. Our little corner of bunks in B-Compartment remained a safe haven for us to sneak a kiss or a short snuggle. Navigating daily life on the ship while trying to conceal my growing lust had become challenging. I realized that in the occasional few moments I did find for myself, I lamented Planet Tall Ship less and spent more time enjoying the excitement of this unexpected romance.

Marion and I were all snuggled up when I heard a scurry of footsteps just outside my bunk. Suddenly, a beam of light was thrust at my eyes. "Wilbur, Todd needs you on deck!" Captain Bailey shouted at the top of his lungs.

I was completely disoriented, thinking, *Oh my god, is the ship sinking? What the fuck!*

Then I heard, "I'll go," as Jon jumped out of his bunk half-naked and equally discombobulated.

"You're not Will. I said Todd needs Will!"

I was half-asleep and flummoxed. There were rules for waking people up, and this alarmist wake-up went against them all. Captain Bailey was already gone when I put a shirt on and grabbed my knife belt.

I sprinted up to find a quiet, dark deck, just as it should have been. There was no emergency. I could see the hands on anchor watch hanging out near the bow and Todd talking with Hunter midship by the starboard rail. Hunter was trying to conceal a bottle of booze and not doing a very good job of it. What did it matter since we were no longer underway? The two of them were smoking cigarettes and talking and didn't notice me. As I thought, we were at anchor, and all was well.

Then a second thought crossed my mind: *Is this some sort of a prank?* It dawned on me that maybe my budding romance with Marion was more common knowledge than I had assumed. There was almost no privacy, and who didn't love a bit of good gossip? I walked up to Todd and Hunter. "What's so important that I had to come up on deck?"

Not looking at me, Todd said, "Can you go get me the power planer?"

That was it, a power planer? Really? Anyone could have gotten it for him. I rolled my eyes, said nothing, and smiled. I thought I could get the best of them by appearing not the least bit irritated about being summoned onto deck in the middle of the night to fetch a tool that anyone could have retrieved.

There is a saying I like. If you don't know who the jerk is, it's probably you. I had to wonder if maybe I was a particular jerk to anyone in general. Maybe my antics with Jon and Jared had caught up to me. I replayed the day in my head, trying to figure it out. Maybe there really was some sort of prank going on. I came back up to deck, planer in hand, and passed it to Todd. He looked at me casually and said, "Thanks."

That was it. Nothing else. Looking around, I figured I should just relax and make the best of the current situation. The ship was hot as hell down below and I was sure Marion had either fallen asleep or climbed into her bunk, so I decided to spend the night up on deck. Lying down on the hard deck wearing only a T-shirt and a pair of shorts was more comfortable than sleeping in a bed in the sweltering compartment. It began to rain shortly after I lay down on deck, but I was so tired it didn't matter. Sleeping in the light rain felt refreshing.

☸

Of the twenty-nine crew members on the ship, eight were women. When we departed from Newport, two of the women were in relationships with fellow shipmates on *Rose*, and another was in a relationship with someone not on our ship, leaving five single women. We had twenty-one so-called men on board, or large boys with facial hair suffering from Peter Pan syndrome, seven in relationships and not technically bachelors. The available-women-to-men ratio was 3:1, giving the women a solid upper hand if interested in choosing a romantic partner. I am aware that there were moments of indiscretion for some of those crew members whose romantic partners were not on board. O'Brian broaches this topic in *Post Captain* when Stephen writes a diary entry that explores Jack's inability to remain celibate while away from his wife. In this entry Stephen cites a famous Lord Nelson line, "Once past Gibraltar, every man is a bachelor," and wonders, "What will tropical warmth, unscrupulous young women, a fixed habit of eating too much, and high animal spirits accomplish?"

Other than the officers, the men of a nineteenth-century frigate may have been rarely allowed off the ship even when in port. For fear of desertion, crew members may have been required to put up bonds for one another to ensure a return to the ship. It also became practice to bring sex workers out to the ship when in port. The below decks would transform into a space filled with music, alcohol, and sex. In *Sons of the Waves: The Common Seaman in the Heroic Age of Sail*, Stephen Taylor writes, "Other gambols took place between the carriages of the guns, and produced illegitimate offspring frequently enough to give rise to the term 'a son of a gun.'"

It would be presumptuous not to consider there would have been both romantic and sexual activities among some of the men on the ship as well. Just like sex with female sex workers/guests on board, romantic and sexual activities between men would have been nearly impossible to conceal because of the communal living arrangements and their lack of privacy. The Articles of War for the Royal Navy stated: "Penalty of committing Buggery or Sodomy. XXIX. If any Person in the Fleet shall commit the unnatural and detestable Sin of Buggery or Sodomy with Man or Beast, he shall be punished with Death by the Sentence of a Court-martial." O'Brian broaches the subject with a tone of humor in *The Mauritius Command* when Jack reads to the Articles of War to the men in a loud, commanding voice: "He had just reached article XXIX, which dealt with sodomy by hanging the sodomite and which always made Spotted Dick and other midshipmen swell purple from suppressed giggling at every monthly repetition, when two ships heaved in sight."

There are records of court-martials for homosexual behavior, but remarkably very few when considering the number of seamen enlisted in the Royal Navy. This might suggest the adoption of a blind-eyed approach to a majority of homosexual acts aboard a ship. In his book *Sodomy and the Pirate Tradition*, B. R. Burg, a professor of history at Arizona State University, suggests the concept of "situational sexuality." Burg explores the idea that in addition to a population of heterosexuals and homosexuals, there is a population of men who engage in sexual activities with both men and women depending on the convenience of the situation, a bisexual situation based on tolerance. Maritime literature is rich in the exploration of sexuality. There are multiple examples of Herman Melville exploring sexuality in *Moby-Dick*, most notably in chapter 94, when Ishmael describes his pleasures of labor and love for his shipmates: "Squeeze! squeeze! squeeze! all the morning long; I squeezed that sperm till I myself almost melted into it; I squeezed that sperm till a strange sort of insanity came over me; and I found myself unwittingly squeezing my co-laborers' hands in it, mistaking their hands for the gentle globules. Such an abounding, affectionate, friendly, loving feeling did this avocation beget . . ."

I had no romantic aspirations when I signed on as crew and was content with the idea of living the life of a bachelor as we sailed to California. Certainly, our communal living situation was less than ideal, but I was not going to let that curb the excitement I felt for Marion. Instead of worrying about what could go wrong, I found myself spending more time thinking about what could go right.

— Chapter 18 —

CRISTÓBAL

WE SPENT MUCH OF THE FOLLOWING DAY on anchor, waiting to dock our ship. Because idle hands are never a good thing, we were kept busy, continuing to break down the rig by lowering the main topsail yard to deck. As the day went on, we were visited by the port agent and the canal measurers. Finally, at 1600, with the pilot on board, we weighed anchor and moved our ship to a cargo transfer pier with direct access to the crane that would help us with down-rigging the broken spars, just south of the Panama Canal Admeasurement Office. The Panama Canal Admeasurement Office is a unique structure jutting out on a man-made key between the harbor breakwater entrance and the Gatun Locks, the Atlantic entrance to the Panama Canal.

We were docked in Cristóbal, a port town in the province of Colón; formally called Aspinwall. Colón was built by the Panama Railroad Company in the 1850s during the California gold rush. Before development, Cristóbal was mostly a large swamp until the French Inter-Oceanic Canal Company created a landfill using soil from their canal excavation. The proximity of Cristóbal to the canal itself made it an essential port of entry and staging point for the efforts to construct the canal, connecting the Atlantic and Pacific Oceans.

In 1904, under the Hay–Bunau-Varilla Treaty, Cristóbal came under US control because it fell within the limits of the Panama Canal Zone, a ten-mile-wide zone of land between the Atlantic and Pacific Oceans, approximately five miles on either side of the canal. The Canal Zone excluded Colón and Panama City. As such, Cristóbal was developed to have hospitals, housing for canal workers, social clubs, police and fire departments, churches, and even a yacht club. Cristóbal remained under US control until 1979, when the US transferred

Crew standing on deck in Bahía Limón

control of the Panama Canal to the Republic of Panama in compliance with the Torrijos-Carter Panama Canal Treaties of 1977. Today, Colón benefits from Zona Libre de Colón (established in 1948), a free trade zone in which billions of dollars of trade occur annually. As such, Colón is one of the largest duty-free ports in the world. Regardless of the amount of commerce and trade, most of the population lives in extreme poverty due to racial and wealth disparity and a lack of educational opportunities.

We quickly learned how oppressively hot and humid Colón could be. The contributing elements of the ocean temperature and the topography of the land make Colón the wettest major city in Central America. The temperature of the seawater was 82° Fahrenheit (27.8° Celsius). The air temperature mostly hovered in the eighties, peaking in the low nineties midday. The relative humidity remained above 80 percent most of the day. The combination of heat and humidity meant we experienced a heat index anywhere from 76° to 125° Fahrenheit (24.4° to 51.7° Celsius). Without air-conditioning on the ship, we were miserable.

The heat below decks was unbelievable. I fantasized Satan himself had designed the living compartments of our ship. Our clothing, bedding, and books were wet or so damp that mold and mildew began growing rampant, adding another layer of discomfort to our shared accommodations. Rick procured several large industrial fans to run around the clock, but they made little difference due to the thickness of the air.

With the ship secured, we had an end-of-the-day all-hands muster led by Captain Bailey. It was Sunday, January 27, and he said the plan was for us to go through the canal on Tuesday evening. Rick had secured a large crane to lift the main topmast off. We would then have to lower the fore t'gallant mast to the deck without assistance from the crane. A purpleheart timber was procured so Todd and I could further reinforce the bowsprit heel bit tenon. Hunter needed to provision, and we needed to take on fuel and water. We would not be stopping in Panama City when reaching the Pacific because all the breakdown work could be done in Cristóbal. As in Puerto Rico, our laundry would be sent out to a service. Again, I found myself feeling frustrated. There was much to do and little time.

We were told everyone would get a bit of time off, but when was yet to be determined. Neither the mood nor the message were good, and there was grumbling. At this point, Rick chimed in to talk about how dangerous it was in Cristóbal. We were instructed to never leave the ship alone and not to walk around Cristóbal alone. He told us he was working on lining up a van with a driver to help assist with running errands and transporting people around as needed. There was a nearby market where we could procure some beer; we should plan on spending our free time on the ship.

Captain Bailey then closed the muster by announcing that Hunter would remain on the ship so the rest of the crew could have an all-expenses-paid dinner that night at the Panama Canal Yacht Club (PCYC). Some of my shipmates were not shy about expressing their feelings and grumbled about looking for another job. Others who accepted the circumstances changed the topic by talking about ordering a steak dinner and enjoying an air-conditioned dining room. The club, at just over a half mile away from our ship, provided an excellent opportunity for us to walk while taking in Cristóbal. We left the ship around 1800, heading toward town, the best route to the PCYC. Walking in numbers helped take the edge off what felt like a dodgy situation.

After a quarter mile, we ended up on what seemed like a main roadway. There were occasional cars, but nobody else was walking. Someone was telling a joke when suddenly there was the loud thundering sound of an electrical transformer exploding and a bright blue flash that momentarily lit up the entire sky before the city went black. Then, out of nowhere, we heard terrifying screaming and shrieking coming from a building just across the street from where we were walking past. We all agreed that it must have been some sort of women's prison. It had been dark before the blackout because of the intermittent streetlights. Now the only light we had was the nearly full moon rising in the sky, accentuating the previously unnoticed silhouettes of giant rats scurrying down the sides of the street.

We walked the rest of the way in the dark until we reached the PCYC, which looked like it was well overdue for a makeover. The blown transformer meant the club was running on a generator. We enjoyed our meal under ambient backup lighting intermixed with candles, but with no air-conditioning. The limited menu now featured whatever the kitchen decided would spoil the fastest. The food did not live up to the hype. However, even in a blackout, the opportunity to eat at a restaurant on land with a bar and pool table reminded me how nice being on land could feel.

Disappointed as we were, not a single person in our party complained. We all loaded up on drinks at the bar and started shooting pool. There was a pay phone, and the line was still working, so a number of us took turns calling home to touch base with our families and reassure them we were fine despite the dismasting.

⚙

A Liebherr 400 mobile harbor crane, the biggest crane I had ever seen outside of New York City, arrived the next day. Todd and I slaved below in the sweltering sauna of the ship's head, working on the shoring of the bowsprit. We had the necessary spars pulled and secured on deck by the afternoon. Despite our foremast being the tallest mast, *Rose* still could have been called a fully rigged ship, as we had square sails on all three masts. We were all grateful for the crane as it saved an immense amount of time and energy. It would have taken all hands plus the capstan to lower the main topmast to deck.

It was different for the crew of HMS *Surprise*. They had to be able to completely assemble and disassemble an entire rig, let alone repair and maintain their ship, without any shoreside help. They could not rely on the ability to access a dockyard or foreign base depending on where they were in the world. Before there were British overseas bases, the Royal Navy had to rely on foreign post facilities, for example Lisbon, when going to the Mediterranean. Otherwise, vessels of the Royal Navy would need to return to England for repairs and maintenance, as well as for the restocking of food, ammunition, and medical supplies.

The Liebherr crane lifting the topmast off *Rose*

Foreign bases allowed ships to stay stationed away from England for longer periods of time. A problem was that constructing a new base was expensive and could require a large labor force. When possible, the Royal Navy contracted with local tradesmen, but in some instances they used enslaved workers, and if necessary, captains would assign their crews to participate in the construction. The Admiralty also established contracts to use the foreign facilities of merchants such as the East India Trading Company, a privately owned English trading corporation with numerous ports established throughout Southeast Asia. By the end of the eighteenth century, the Royal Navy had dockyards established in Antigua, Barbados, Bermuda, Bombay, Cape of Good Hope, Gibraltar, Halifax, Jamaica, Madras, Malta, Quebec, and Rio de Janeiro.

Dockyards and their stores are a frequent concern for Captain Aubrey in O'Brian's novels. In *Master and Commander*, when Jack is first given command, a Mr. Brown, the officer in charge of the dockyard, tells Jack, "You just listen to me, young man . . . Your *good* captain never wants anything from a dockyard. He makes do with what he has. He takes great care of the King's stores: nothing is ever wasted: he pays his bottom with his own slush: he worms his cables deep with twice-laid stuff and serves and parcels them so there is never any fretting in the hawse *anywhere*: he cares for his sails far more than for his own skin, and he never sets his royals—nasty, unnecessary, flash, gimcrack things. And the result is promotion, Mr. Aubrey." Jack's aggressive handling of his ships throughout the series shows what he thought of that advice.

☸

That night, with the power up and running, some of the crew revisited the Panama Canal Yacht Club, though most of us stayed on the ship. There was a rumor that a couple of our shipmates had decided to explore Cristóbal in search of a massage parlor. I watched *Animal House* on the ship's TV on the gun deck while enjoying a few cold beers with my mates. Jon broke out his video camera to document the low-key evening, Mandrew ate a bowl of rum raisin ice cream, and Marion hung out with Shannon. After the sudden wake-up two nights before, I realized my romantic interactions with Marion were common knowledge. I felt like every eye hoped to catch us in a moment of intimacy. Maybe nobody cared. Alex and Carrie appeared to be sharing a spark, which seemed to be ignored. It was common knowledge that Jon and Blythe began hooking up in Newport, and again, nobody seemed to care.

The next day was filled with hustle as we tried to tie up loose ends before our transit through the canal that evening. After lunch, there was an all-hands muster in which we were told there was a mix-up and we would only be given two and a half hours to take care of personal business in town. The pilot was scheduled to board *Rose* at 1600, and we would be off the dock shortly thereafter. That didn't leave time for moaning, so I grabbed my money and we all packed into the crowded van to set out and see Cristóbal. We drove only four blocks before stopping at an internet café. Along the way, I saw a poor city, one filled with people just trying to make it to the next day. The roads were dirty, and buildings were run-down, with windows covered in metal bars and fences topped with barbed wire. The police I spotted looked like commandos, wearing bulletproof vests. We unloaded from the van, allowing another load of crew members to be picked up for the next cycle. The internet café did not have enough computers for everyone, so some got back in the van and continued on to see the canal. After checking my email,

I walked around with Jon and Jared before being picked back up to return to our ship. Two and a half hours was all the time I needed in Cristóbal.

⚙

In 1513, in search of gold, Vasco Núñez de Balboa along with two hundred men stood at the top of a hill in awe. Overcome by emotion, he got down on his knees to thank God. Unknowingly, they had crossed the isthmus of Panama, and the new body of water they saw was the Pacific Ocean. Shortly thereafter, Panama City was founded on the Pacific in 1519, and later Porto Bello—twenty-two miles northeast of Cristóbal—on the Atlantic in 1597. The region flourished for nearly three centuries under Spanish rule as precious metals mined in Peru were transferred across land from Panama City to Porto Bello to be sent back to Spain. The Spanish American Wars changed the political landscape, as the Spanish Colonies declared their independence. Soon trade languished and transporting cargo around Cape Horn became the preferred route.

The 1848 California gold rush drove a resurgence of interest to the isthmus of Panama. William H. Aspinwall launched a route of steamships, having secured a federal contract for the transport of mail from the eastern United States to the newly acquired territory of California. Aspinwall's route went from New York to Panama via steamship, then over the isthmus and then up to California via a Pacific steamship. This route of passage became known as the Panama Route. In 1850, construction of the Panama Railroad—the first transcontinental railroad—began and was completed in 1855. Passage through Panama was much faster than rounding Cape Horn, and with increased demand came increased competition, spurring a series of steamship companies vying for business. Competitor Cornelius Vanderbilt had developed an alternate route in Nicaragua that required use of a river, crossing a lake, and then trekking over land. This route came to be called Vanderbilt Road.

Soon the idea of constructing a waterway between the Atlantic and Pacific was revisited. The earliest recorded consideration of a waterway had been in 1538, when Charles V, the Holy Roman Emperor, had the region surveyed. The concept was abandoned because it was thought impossible. Ideas of a canal continued to surface over the next three centuries, but nothing took until 1876, when two engineers from the French navy conducted a study exploring several potential routes through Panama. In 1878, a treaty was signed between the French and Colombian governments (Panama was a province of Colombia at the time) to build an interoceanic canal through Panama.

The French company Compagnie Universelle du Canal Interocéanique de Panama (Universal Interoceanic Canal Company of Panama) initially began the canal's construction in 1881. Having successfully completed the massive undertaking of the Suez Canal, the French approached the project with the goal of constructing a sea-level canal. Soon engineering complications and overwhelming waves of malaria and yellow fever killed thousands of workers and depleted the funds raised for the effort, ultimately forcing them into bankruptcy in 1889. A restructured French effort began in 1894 but with a much smaller workforce and the hope of selling the project. Quietly, the design of the canal was evaluated and changed to a more pragmatic lock-and-lake canal similar to what would eventually be built by the United States. While the French were developing a new plan for the canal, the United States was exploring the option of building a transisthmian canal in Nicaragua. Instead, French manager Philippe Bunau-Varilla successfully lobbied for the United States to purchase all French equipment for $40 million through the Spooner Act of 1902, also known as the Panama Canal Act.

In 1904, the United States took control of the project, completing it in 1914. Lessons learned from past efforts were used to accomplish the undertaking. They prioritized combatting disease and improving the infrastructure needed to support the workforce and machinery. The design was still an issue, but in 1907, a plan for a lock system canal was adopted. In the same year, US army major George Washington Goethals was appointed chief engineer of the Panama Canal Project. Goethals, a civil engineer who came with canal digging experience, divided the excavation into three divisions and saw the project through to completion in 1914. At the time, the Panama Canal was the largest engineering project ever achieved.

✹

The compass heading from the Atlantic to the Pacific is southeast, and traveling from the Pacific to the Atlantic is northwest. This may seem counterintuitive until studying a map.

The Panama Canal is about fifty-one miles in length from start to finish. There are locks at each end of the canal. The center of the canal is the man-made Gatun Lake. Implementing the man-made lake helped reduce the excavation that would have been needed to connect the oceans at sea level. There are two sizes of locks. The original locks are 110 feet (33.53 meters) wide and 1,050 feet (320 meters) long. Modern ship design and construction employs the term "Panamax" to define the maximum allowable dimensions a ship can be designed to use the

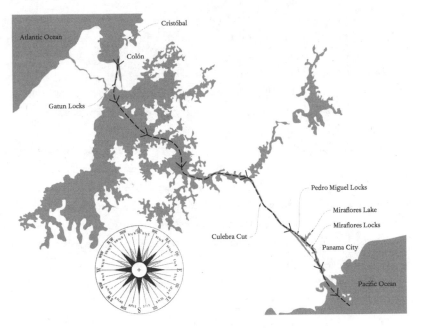

Map of the Panama Canal

Panama Canal. In 2016, a new lock system was built to allow larger ships (New-Panamax) through the canal. The New-Panamax dimensions are 168.1 feet (51.24 meters) wide and 1,200 feet (365.8 meters) long.

We had an extended crew muster in the late afternoon of Tuesday, January 29, to run through the process of going through the canal. The passage would take around eight hours from start to finish. We reviewed the procedures of entering the Gatún Locks, then the transit through Gatún Lake, the passage through Culebra Cut, and finally exiting from the Miraflores Locks. We would have the required pilot on board for the duration of the transit. In addition, we were obliged to hire professional line handlers for each set of locks. The line handlers would board the ship shortly before entering the locks and would be offloaded once through the locks.

We planned to be underway at 1600, but our departure was delayed because the pilot, Eduardo, did not arrive until 1630. There was a reasonable amount of excitement onboard, and why not? We were about to traverse from the Atlantic Ocean to the Pacific Ocean through the Panama Canal! C-Watch was assigned to first watch off the dock. That freed me up to enjoy the approach to the canal as a passenger while sitting up on the foremast fighting top with Marion, Jon, Blythe, Mandrew, Shannon, and Peggy.

Rules were eased because of the unusual circumstances, and anyone not on watch was free to climb the rig and enjoy the process of entering the locks without fear of being assigned to extra work. Typically, we were only supposed to be aloft for a reason relating to ship handling.

It was fun hanging out on the fighting top, taking in the sights around us. There was an impressive amount of inbound and outbound traffic as we approached the Puente Atlántico. As we got closer to the Gatún Locks, we could see the lineup of entrants was forming. Because we were under two hundred feet, *Rose* was assigned to transit the canal along with the 490-foot container ship *Reefer Prince*, homeport Nassau, Bahamas. Of course, we could not resist cracking jokes about her name.

At 1815, the line handlers boarded our ship via a sizable industrial powerboat. They all had on white hard hats and wore light blue collared shirts and dark pants. Once on board, they settled in at their appointed stations, manning the stern, bow, and midship bits, ready to catch the heaving lines connected to the steel cables tethered to the shoreside "mules" (electric trains) on either side of the ship.

Looking forward in the Gatún Locks at *Reefer Prince*

The mules run along a set of tracks parallel to the lock. The tracks are upwardly inclined, as we were to be raised in the lock chambers to the water level of Gatún Lake. For large ships, the mules pull the vessels through the locks. In the case of *Rose*, we used our engines to move through the locks, with the mules keeping *Rose* centered in the locks. The process of catching the lines and securing them to our ship went relatively quickly, and by 1850 we were ready to enter the Gatún Locks.

There are three chambers used to raise the vessels in the locks up eighty-five feet from the Atlantic Ocean sea level to the level of Gatún Lake. Flooding a lock takes ten minutes, and it takes two minutes to open the gates. At 2000, A-Watch relieved C-Watch, and we exited the Gatún Locks at 2005. The steel cables connecting *Rose* to the mules were released, and a small boat came alongside to pick up the line handlers. Under the full moon's light, we spent the next three and a half hours transiting Gatún Lake and through Gaillard Cut, an excavated gorge that runs across the continental divide. Crossing the divide was a moment of celebration when the natural drainage flow of water changes from one ocean to the other. We were now on the Pacific side.

At 2335, as we approached the single-chamber Pedro Miguel Locks, we picked up new line handlers. At 0010, we were secured and began the process of being lowered to the Miraflores Lake water level. At 0030, the steel cables connecting our ship to the mules were released, and we motored under our own power to the Miraflores Locks, the final lock system in the canal. At 0100, we were secure in the first lock chamber. At 0140, the gates of the second lock chamber opened, and *Rose* was officially in the Pacific Ocean! At 0155, the steel cables connecting *Rose* to the mules were released, and the line handlers were picked up. It had taken us just over seven hours to complete transiting the locks. After unloading Eduardo, the pilot, near Isla Naos, *Rose* set a course for Isla Taboga at 0220.

Chapter 19

*I*SLA TABOGA

ISLA TABOGA, A PANAMANIAN ISLAND, was discovered in 1513 by Spanish explorer Vasco Núñez de Balboa. The island was originally named Aboga, meaning *an abundance of fish* in the Indigenous language. In 1515, the Spanish attacked and overcame the Indigenous residents, and in 1524, the town of San Pedro was founded by Father Hernando de Luque. The island's church, Iglesia de San Pedro, is the second-oldest Catholic church in Latin America, built in 1685 and declared a historic monument in 1996.

The island is rich in maritime history. At low tide, its northern end can be connected by a sandbar to the tiny islet, Isla El Morro. Taboga became a destination port for pirates like Henry Morgan and Francis Drake as early as the sixteenth century. In the nineteenth century, the Pacific Steamship Company built out facilities on the island, making it a preferred port due to the deep water around the island. Famous French painter Paul Gauguin briefly lived in a sanatorium on the island after becoming ill as a laborer during the French canal construction effort.

At 0325, in sixty-one feet of water, we dropped anchor south of El Morro. I was so deep asleep in my bunk I was not woken by the violent rattling of the heavy chain falling out of the hawsepipe of our ship, which sounded and felt like the loud clatter in the front car of an old wooden roller coaster during the rattling climb up to the first peak of its track.

Waking up in Taboga was one of the best wakeups of my life. Earlier I touched upon the importance of waking up the next watch, but I have yet to expand on just how important the job was. There were no alarm clocks on the ship because of the tight communal living situation. That meant we all needed to know where each crew member slept so we could wake them up before the start of their watch.

There were exceptions, and common-sense practices usually applied. The worse the weather, the more notice you gave the next watch. Some shipmates would wake up faster than others, and some were prone to falling back asleep. I often was the one to wake people up because I quickly learned how to be good and reliable at the task. On HMS *Surprise*, the crew would have been woken by a loud blast from the bosun's whistle or pipe.

That morning in Taboga, I remember being in such a deep sleep that I did not know where I was. I began hearing some sort of singing. I began to make out the words to the song "You Are My Sunshine." The singing was soft. I realized I was in my bunk, and it was Christina's voice. I then realized Christina was not alone, and others were singing with her. I opened my eyes and saw the compartment lights were on outside my curtain. I was confused because I knew Christina was the watch captain of C-Watch, and my watch relieved her watch. Why was she waking me up? Deckhands wake up the next watch, not the officers.

I pulled open my curtain to get my bearings and, with a puzzled face, looked at Christina. She was wearing a big smile. "Good morning. We are anchored, and you should head up onto deck to see where we are."

I slowly joined the procession of everyone rolling out of their bunks, first grabbing a clean shirt and my knife belt and then heading up, but not before brushing my teeth and grabbing a cup of coffee from the galley.

What I saw when I emerged from the main companionway was a tropical paradise. The bow of our ship was pointed north toward Panama City in the far distance. I scanned the horizon from port to starboard, taking in the beautiful scenery of Taboga. The island was filled with a lush dense forest, tall swaying palm trees, and exotic plants. There was a long sandy beach and the calm harbor was dotted with small boats on moorings lapping quietly. The hillside was decorated with quaint white-painted houses just above the beach. A long pier jutted out into the water. A quarter mile forward of our ship's bow, the beach became a sandbar connecting Taboga to El Morro.

Usually, musters formed quickly, but organizing muster that morning was painfully difficult, like trying to get a resistant child to eat vegetables. Eventually we all fell in as Rick and Captain Bailey announced we were to be granted a day off in appreciation for all our hard work. We would not be broken up into shore parties, we would maintain the watch schedule, but each watch would be divided in half. I would have to stand watch for two hours during the day. A-Watch had the 8–12 assignment, and I got lucky being assigned the first half, which meant I would be able to leave the ship at 1000 and not need to return till the evening. Despite the slow start, muster ended quickly, and we launched our dinghies and, for the first time, our longboat, the *Thorne*. Not wanting to waste time, those not on watch got off the ship as fast as possible and went ashore to explore the island.

Tony ran a low-key watch, like an end-of-school-year detention. I was spacing out, fiddling around up on the bow, when Tony came forward looking as if he was on a scavenger hunt. I was looking over the edge of the rail and admiring the color of the water.

"Boy, that water sure looks nice," he said while avoiding eye contact.

"It sure does," I said, not thinking too much or too hard.

"Yeah, I bet it would be pretty nice to be swimming right now," Tony commented as a big smile grew on his face.

Rose anchored in Taboga

"Yeah," I said, looking out and longing to go have some fun ashore.

"You know, it probably wouldn't be your fault if you fell off the bowsprit right now. I mean, falling in the water is only an accident." He then chuckled as he strolled aft toward the quarterdeck.

Jumping off the bowsprit into the water was strictly forbidden on *Rose*. Captain Bailey had explicitly addressed that in a muster the morning after Jared played Tarzan in Puerto Rico. I realized what Tony was saying and was not going to miss this opportunity, especially considering it was the chief mate who had made the suggestion.

Taking the cue, I promptly took off my knife belt before climbing out to conduct an "inspection" of the bowsprit.

The bowsprit on *Rose* was intimidating in both size and height. Just under sixty feet in length, the outer tip of the jibboom was forty feet above the surface of the water. I had already had some extraordinarily daring moments on the passage, but I thought it might be best if I "fell off" the sprit maybe only halfway out, at the doubling. But then, when I got there, I thought, *What the hell! I've come this far and done worse, so why not head out to the tip?* I took my time climbing out, enjoying the view. I had never really had the opportunity to go out to the end of the bowsprit because of my chippy work assignments.

Being on the tip of the jibboom made me feel as if I were floating, hovering out over the water. I knew I needed to be careful when I jumped. This was not going to be any high dive; I wanted to make sure I hit the water with my feet together. I looked back to make sure nobody on deck was watching. I was sure Tony would be second-guessing his suggestion if he knew I thought jumping off the tip of the jibboom was the best idea. I looked around, looked up, and then jumped to port, swinging my arms in circles as I flew down, taking a deep breath before hitting the water. My point of landing was perfect, my feet together as planned, and my arms created drag as soon as I plunged beneath the surface. Once underwater, I relaxed and enjoyed floating up to the surface.

Looking up at *Rose* from the water made her appear incredibly massive. Swimming around her was like swimming around an island. The copper plating we put on her underbody before departing Newport was still shiny. I swam toward the stern on her port side, rounding her quarter, and then climbed the Jacob's ladder on her starboard side midship. The swim was a refreshing and thrilling way to finish standing watch.

Captain Aubrey is an enthusiastic swimmer in O'Brian's novels. His comfort in the water is put to good use, saving the lives of some two dozen or so crew members over the years who could not swim—including one, "Awkward" Davies, whom he saves twice. But he also swims for pleasure. In *The Mauritius Command*, with his ship *Boadicea* wallowing "with flaccid sails on the stagnant water . . . Jack was obliged to take the jolly-boat a quarter of a mile away for his morning's swim," so surrounded was the boat with their "empty beef-casks, peelings and general rubbish." He has the crew tow their ship, and in reward "after they had pulled her for an hour or two it was the *Boadicea's* custom to lower a sail into the pure, tepid water, buoying its outer corners and thereby making a shallow pool in which those who could not swim—the great majority—might splash about and enjoy themselves, perhaps learning how to stay afloat in the process."

☸

Taboga was everything I needed it to be. Our previous two stops—sketchy, gritty, and industrial—had been letdowns, but this tropical excursion helped boost both my and the ship's overall morale. Being there midweek meant the island was quiet and free of tourists. The lack of people made my exploration feel more intimate. I didn't have much of a plan. Marion, Jon, Jared, and Blythe had left the ship hours earlier, but I was sure I would run into them. I did a bit of hiking and made my way to the top of a trail called El Cruce. The hike was not too bad, and it allowed me to enjoy the tropical wilderness of the island. It was the first time I had been alone in three weeks. It was a weird sensation and even more bizarre knowing I didn't have to be anywhere.

After completing the hike and feeling like I had done something constructive, I walked back into town to see who I could find. Along the way, I ran into Tony and Christina. I next found Jared. We posed for a picture in front of Iglesia de San Pedro. Jared then led me to where the rest of the crew were hanging out at a hotel bar. There was a pool table, and they served piña coladas in coconuts. Captain Bailey had fun feeding his leftover French fries to the wild peacocks that would walk up and take them from his hand. Everyone was in a great mood, and for a brief moment, we celebrated being somewhere far away in the world. As in Puerto Rico, shore party meant a temporary truce between the rebels and Planet Tall Ship; we were there together.

We lingered in the bar until dusk, taking in the beautiful sparkling, distant horizon lit by Panama City. The sea was calm, and the air had cooled, offering a refreshing soft breeze that brought a bit of a chill to my skin. We took turns posing for pictures together as we waited for our turn to be shuttled back out to the ship. That couple of hours all together in that remote hotel bar was the kind of experience I had been yearning for since I'd been hired on *Rose*. It was crazy to think it took that long and that much work to experience paradise.

Jon, Will, Jared, and Scott after a long, fun-filled day on Taboga

Chapter 20

*R*USS

THE FOLLOWING MORNING, Dwight and Ron were charged with managing weighing the anchor. Weighing anchor on *Rose* was absolutely one of the worst forms of manual labor I have ever been part of. Modern boats use a machine called a windlass for this task. There was no windlass on our ship, but there were plenty of bodies.

The fundamentals to understand: *Rose* was a five-hundred-ton ship, and the anchor weighed 1,200 pounds. The anchor was connected to a seven-inch link metal chain, measured in shots. A standard shot of chain is ninety feet long, or fifteen fathoms, and our chain weighed 1,800 pounds per shot. Captain Bailey said he had let out two shots of chain when he dropped anchor. Then there was the hawser; Captain Bailey told me he had no idea how much that weighed. A hawser is a large thick cable that runs through a ship's hawsepipe at the bow of a ship. One end is secured to the anchor chain and the other to the ship.

To weigh anchor meant more than pulling up the 4,800 pounds of chain and anchor, plus whatever the hawser weighed. Picture how a kite flies in the sky, not directly above the handler, but instead at an acute angle and at great distance. Like the kite, an anchor underwater works best when set a considerable distance from the ship. First, we needed to position our ship to be directly above the anchor. When we had anchored in Bahía Limón, weighing anchor there was much easier because Captain Bailey had used our engines to move the ship forward to be directly over the anchor so we could raise the chain and anchor straight up. I don't know why, but he did not use the engines to assist us when weighing the anchor in Taboga. That meant we had to manually pull the weight of our five-hundred-ton ship forward to position *Rose* over the anchor with the added forces of current and wind, before we could pull up the hawser, chain, and anchor.

ANCHOR CABLE PLAN

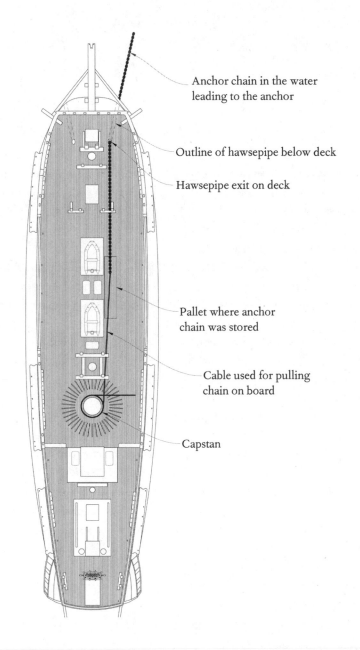

Anchor chain in the water
leading to the anchor

Outline of hawsepipe below deck

Hawsepipe exit on deck

Pallet where anchor
chain was stored

Cable used for pulling
chain on board

Capstan

When not in use, the anchor chain was flaked on deck, meaning it was laid in tight parallel twenty-foot-long fore-aft runs on the starboard side of the main cargo hatches in between the bow and the capstan. To get the chain in place, a line with a shackle on the forward end called the cable was connected to the anchor chain at the hawsepipe opening on deck at the bow. The cable ran from the bow aft, wrapping three times around the capstan and then to a crew member for handling.

I was assigned to man one of the eight capstan bars, wooden poles horizontally inserted into the top of the capstan, used for turning. The capstan was surrounded by a sunburst pattern of wooden staves, each one being one inch by one inch by four feet in length, screwed very firmly to the deck. The staves were there to provide footing when turning the capstan.

The officers stood on the quarterdeck while Dwight stood midship commanding us. Ron stood near the hawsepipe with a large metal hook he was using to guide the chain up and onto deck. A hose connected to a pressurized saltwater spigot was used to wash off any sediment that made it through the hawsepipe.

On Dwight's command, those of us on the capstan dug our feet into the deck and pushed forward as hard as we could, eventually turning the capstan. The loaded cable hovered eighteen inches above the deck, requiring us to take an uncomfortably high step over it every time we completed a revolution.

We had pulled thirty feet of chain up when Dwight shouted out, "Stop and hold!"

Stopped in place, we used all our weight and strength to prevent the capstan from spin-

Mandrew facing the camera while sitting on the flaked anchor chain

ning back while Ron worked to connect a snubber, a short line used to temporarily transfer the loaded portion of the anchor chain. Once connected, Ron shouted, "Snubber secured!"

We then eased off just a bit on the capstan until the load of the cable was completely absorbed by the snubber, which had been secured to the "forward bits."

That gave us a two-minute break to catch our breath and recharge while the cable was run forward and shackled back onto the anchor chain at the hawsepipe. Dwight gave the command for us to grab the capstan bars and to start pushing. We had to repeat this process seven times. A few hands changed out spots, but I stayed on the capstan for the entire process. It was painfully slow, and the amount of effort it took was mind-boggling. I continued to be amazed by the amount of sweat and muscle it took to make *Rose* move.

With the anchor secured and our ship underway, we washed down the deck before setting the mainsail and fores'l. We set the fore topsail at the change of watch at 1200 and at 1300 set the jib, fore top staysail, mizzen top staysail, spanker, and mizzen topsail. At 1350 we began the routine safety drills, beginning with the man overboard. A step in the MOB drill required "heaving to." To heave to means to intentionally trim the sails so as to stall the forward momentum of the vessel. With the ship stalled, we launched the inflatable rescue boat, manned by Todd and Mandrew. Before boarding the rescue boat, Captain Bailey suggested they bring a bucket filled with everyone's cameras to take pictures of *Rose* sailing with her new, unconventional rig. It was a sight to see, and all agreed the configuration was like no other. We settled on calling our ship a "wreckantine," a rigging configuration completely made up on the deck of *Rose* that day.

We completed our drills and set a course of 200° to sail south around the Azuero Peninsula before turning north for San Diego. Getting to San Diego was not going to be easy or fun. We had to cover roughly 3,350 miles, going upwind and against the prevailing north-south current. Our plan was simple: stay close to the shoreline to avoid the strongest winds and currents. Hugging the coast would also set us up for sightseeing opportunities as we sailed past the coasts of Panama, Costa Rica, Nicaragua, Honduras, El Salvador, Guatemala, and Mexico, before finally reaching the coast of the good ol' USA.

Profile of the wreckantine rig, showing the new configuration after the
dismasting and removal of additional spars in Panama

The following day was the first day of February and did not disappoint. We
reached the southernmost point of our route midmorning, just 419 miles north
of the equator. At one point, Captain Bailey slowed the ship to try to catch fish,
but he came up with nothing. It was noticeable that he was getting more and more
frustrated about the failure. We hadn't caught a single fish. Mandrew joked, telling
me if fishing were easy, it would be called catching. Shortly thereafter, Tony was
giving a meteorology lesson to A-Watch when Shannon, pointing, said, "Is that
a waterspout?" The irony was not missed.

Shannon had spotted a well-developed waterspout a half mile off our stern.
I had never seen one. It looked much like the twister that sucked up Dorothy's
home in *The Wizard of Oz*. The formation was fully formed, crisp, and silent. Had
Shannon not noticed it, we never would have known it was there.

There are two types of waterspouts. Fair-weather waterspouts typically occur
in tropical or humid conditions, forming on the surface of the water and working
up to the sky. The other, tornadic waterspouts, are actually tornados on the water

and develop downward from the sky. There was a quick scurry on deck as all hands rushed to strike sails, but the spout dissipated before it could become a threat.

We were eleven nautical miles to the southwest of Cabo Matapalo, a Costa Rican village on the Osa Peninsula, when Russ joined me on bow-watch. He had just completed a sprint up the rigging to try to catch sight of the green flash, an optical phenomenon that occurs the moment the top of the sun dips below the horizon. Hands raced up the ratlines while staring at the horizon in hopes of catching the green flash. The evening wind was west by north at ten knots, and our ship slipped though the gentle seas that were less than one foot. The air temperature was 85° Fahrenheit (29° Celsius), our course was 300°, and we had three headsails set along with the main staysail, mizzen topmast staysail, and the mizzen staysail.

I could never figure out what made Russ tick, and my curiosity only grew the closer we got to our destination. He sounded much like the actor Sam Elliott when he spoke and projected the confidence of a Morgan Freeman character. He was thirty-three years old and had proven himself to be a simple man with few expectations. Coming to the ship with no sailing experience meant he was usually at the top of the list when it came to being assigned to the worst jobs on the ship. He never complained and was always the first person to lend a hand.

Eager to understand, I bluntly asked what made him so content. Smiling as if he had been waiting for me to ask this question, he told me about the moment that changed his life. Russ confessed he had been fired from his last job (he did not say what it was) and decided he should do some soul searching. Without a plan, he ended up hiking on the Appalachian Trail for three months. He began his journey alone, and the solitude gave him the opportunity to enjoy nature while pondering life. One night on the trail he met a woman at a shelter, and they got into a deep conversation that lasted more than five hours. As it turned out, she had done a considerable amount of sailing out of Martha's Vineyard.

It was this conversation over a fire that totally transformed his mindset, and with that, he found a new direction for himself in life. The tales of her experiences mesmerized Russ, inspiring him to try the life of a sailor. Russ called home to say he was not coming back. His new friend told him Newport was a great place to go to find a boat to sail on. She said there were lots of boats that sailed south every year, and it should be pretty easy to find a ride on one. Russ was in Lee, Massachusetts, and conveniently this was the point where the Appalachian Trail crossed the Mass Pike. The next day he walked off the trail and hitchhiked his way to Newport. Arriving alone, and with nowhere to sleep, Russ walked the docks, asking boat after boat for a job. They all turned him down. Russ had spent all his money and was sleeping on park benches when he eventually got up the courage to approach *Rose*. He was hired on the spot. The ship wanted a year of commitment from him. He told me that he knew this was going to be the next adventure in his life. He was looking forward to seeing California for the first time and excited about the possibility of being in a movie.

I liked nearly everything about Russ. Here was this person who always got the worst job assignment but still managed to have one of the most content personalities on the ship. I recognized how happy he was and how he believed everything had a way of working itself out. Where I was a rebel, and Dwight was a Planet Tall Shipper, Russ was a floater. He possessed the capacity to savor the best life had to offer while dispelling all negativity. The worst thing that could happen to him would be seeing a frown on the face of a friend.

Our conversations were well matched, as it seemed we each had something the other wanted. I was young and ambitious, unknowing, always wanting more, whereas Russ was there for the experience. I appreciated how Russ thought life should be experimental and fun. Like Tony, he possessed certain qualities that inspired me. One was a professional sailor who embodied everything I aspired to be, while the other slept on park benches and meandered through life. Yet each of them challenged me to help more. If I saw Russ pulling hard on a line, I jumped in because I knew that he would have done the same.

Russ chuckled. "Hey, you and Marion, that's a special thang you got. I know you know you've got something good." He looked down at his feet before taking a deep drag on his cigarette. "Can I offer you some advice?"

"Sure."

He looked over at me with a big smile. "Keep doing what you are doing. I wish I was where you are now."

I didn't have anything to say. I nodded and with a smile patted him on the back. That was the end of our conversation. We spent the rest of the hour in silence, scanning the horizon and listening to the hypnotic sound of the ship's bow pressing into the water as she pushed forward through the Pacific.

Chapter 21

*T*HE CAPTAIN

WE WERE THREE DAYS OUT from Taboga and more than halfway up the west coast of Costa Rica. Compared to the Atlantic portion of our passage, we had plenty of scenery to observe because of our proximity to the coastline. Now a seasoned crew, we quickly settled into our watch routine. The general sentiment was that the best parts of the passage were behind us, and the remaining miles were going to be a grind. The cooler water of the Pacific Ocean lowered the relative humidity despite the air temperature topping out in the mid-nineties each day. The living compartments were drying out, and my skin was grateful.

Our decapitated ship trudged up the western seaboard, driving against the prevailing winds and currents resisting our progress. Steering a straight line seemed impossible as we dodged both small fishing boats and squalls that would quickly form and dissipate just as fast. The wind was shifty, oscillating from left to right, forcing us to constantly adjust our course and the sails. It was as if Mother Nature was throwing every curveball to prevent us from reaching our destination.

An all-hands muster was organized at 1600 to address a transmission Captain Bailey had received about pirates on high-speed boats with guns.

31.1.2002 at 0745 lt in position 15:41n–098:30w off the coast of mexico. while underway, 8–10 armed men in a fast speedboat doing about 43 knots chased a vessel for about 10 mins from the stern. persons in the speedboat claimed they were from mexican navy. vessel increased speed to maximum, out manouvred the speedboat and did not give her an option to come alongside.

The officers did not take the threat of being attacked lightly. We were an asset of a multibillion-dollar corporation and an easy target. I thought the whole thing was a joke when I heard conversations about setting up cannons and whether we could use them for self-defense if needed. When inventoried, our arsenal resembled a Monty Python prop list. We had two swords, a musket, emergency flares, a saltwater emergency fire hose, and our knives and spikes. We had four cannons on board and a few one-pound cans of black gunpowder with fuses, but no cannonballs. We did have buckets of screws and nails that could be used for ammunition. I overheard Andy talking about arming the cannons. It was the first time he had my undivided attention.

The four six-pound cannons on board were not original, having been purchased by John Millar when he had *Rose* built. Firing a cannon is not so easy. To start, cannons are heavy, and to efficiently arm and fire them requires a gun crew. A cartridge of gunpowder, followed by a wad of cloth, is loaded into the muzzle and packed with a tool called a rammer. Then the cannonball is loaded, followed by another wad of fabric to prevent the ball from rolling out, and then rammed again. The carriage—the wooden cradle with wheels supporting the cannon—is run out. This is when the men pull on the gun tackles to bring the cannon barrel forward through the gun port. Then the gun captain aims the cannon and pulls the lanyard on the cannon lock, a device mounted to the top of the cannon for generating a spark to ignite the cartridge of gunpowder, thus firing the cannon. The cannon is then pulled back, a wet mop is used to swab out any remaining embers from the muzzle, and the process is repeated.

The evolution of loading, firing, and reloading a cannon needed to be quick; the gun crew work was hard. Only a handful of our crew had ever fired a cannon, so the cannons were ruled out. In O'Brian's *The Thirteen-Gun Salute*, practicing firing the cannons is as routine as swabbing the decks: "Far out into the Atlantic, long tack upon long tack, every day having the same steady routine from swabbing the decks at first dawn to lights out, its unchanging succession of bells, its wholly predictable food, nothing in sight from one horizon to another but sea and sky, both growing more agreeable, and the habit of sea-life exerted its usual force; cheerfulness returned to almost its old carefree level and as always there was the violent emotion and enthusiasm of the great-gun practice every evening at quarters—practice carried out with the full deadly charge and the ball directed at a floating target."

In the film *Master and Commander: The Far Side of the World*, the gun crews are able to bring their firing time down from two minutes and one second to one minute and ten seconds, thus earning an extra ration of grog awarded by Captain Aubrey. Learning how to fire the cannons for the film was a choreographed effort. The gun deck constructed for the film had the ability to tilt as the ship would when heeling while underway. Gun crews comprised of seven actors were established, and all practiced learning how to complete an entire evolution of loading, aiming, firing, and clearing the weapon in fifty seconds' time. Other than being lighter, the cannons used in the film were faithful to the cannons that would have been on HMS *Surprise*, even down to naming each cannon.

Piracy continues to be a serious threat worldwide. According to the US Bureau of Transportation, in 2002, there were 383 incidents of international piracy and armed robbery at sea. In a report titled *Modern Piracy: The Impact on Maritime Security*, Lieutenant Commander Charles Mansfield of the United States Navy writes, "In the post 9/11 and USS *Cole* attack period, there has been a resurrection of worldwide piracy incidents that have significant implications on maritime security. The increase of attacks has demanded the attention of global maritime trade and international partners. The possible use of the maritime environment by terrorists poses a real and credible threat to all nations."

I may have felt a bit edgier than some of my shipmates. Not even two months prior, in December 2001, world-famous sailor Sir Peter Blake was shot in the back by pirates when they boarded his sailboat on the northern bank of the Amazon delta near Macapá, Brazil. I had the privilege of meeting Blake four months before he was killed when I was sailing in England. Blake was famous for his successful campaigns in the America's Cup and Whitbread Ocean Race. He was on an environmental expedition for the United Nations when he was killed. The pirates' take amounted to watches, cameras, and some cash.

⎊

Fortunately, we didn't run into pirates and made it to our fourth day at sea, nearly halfway to Acapulco. During the night, we encountered our second gale since departing from Newport, with the wind gusting up to thirty-five knots. Captain Bailey ordered an adjustment to our course so we would be closer to the Nicaraguan coast in anticipation of the building seas resulting from the strong winds. Our ship did suffer yet another casualty in the middle of the gale when the mizzen fife rail broke free from the mizzenmast at 0220, causing chaos. I was not surprised when I learned of the failure. I love the saying "problems are opportunities," and applying that mantra to our situation meant we were all drowning in opportunity. Come morning, the wind had died down, allowing work-party to resume.

I had spent much of the previous day building a gun rack for Captain Bailey's musket but learned that I would be relieved from chippy work for the day at our work-party muster. I assumed my new work assignment had something to do with an altercation I had earlier with Captain Bailey. We had our moments, some sharp, some playful. I could never really tell when he was just messing with me or if it was a serious matter. There were times I had definitely jumped over the line, but I think he liked it when I pushed too far. As a chippy, I spent more time interacting with Captain Bailey than much of the crew.

Captain Bailey was a very private man. His roots came from the sea. He was from Wellfleet, Massachusetts, on Cape Cod. His father had made his living as a commercial fisherman and was lost at sea six weeks before the birth of his only son. Young Bailey was raised by his mother and stepfather and eventually moved to Rhode Island. In time he was legally adopted and became Richard Palmer Jackson Bailey.

Captain Bailey saw *Rose* for the first time when visiting Newport as a young man in the 1970s. *Rose* was already in distress when he first set foot on her. The Bicentennial was over, and the option to operate her as a restaurant had never been seriously considered. Captain Bailey had grown up with portraits of his great-grandfather's trading vessels in his great-aunt's home, vessels such as one of the family's tern schooners and the barque *Freeman*. He had dreamed of large sailing ships as a boy, but he could not believe a ship like *Rose* still existed. She was a museum at the time and had no engines. Captain Bailey became part of her crew, and when the opportunity arose to become her captain, he reached for it.

By 1986, the US Coast Guard had formulated the Sailing School Vessel Regulations, which offered *Rose* an avenue to service at sea. To get *Rose* into working order to become Coast Guard certified, Captain Bailey needed to be more than a captain. He needed to be an entrepreneur and develop a business plan to help *Rose* be profitable and sustainable. The only thing Captain Bailey lacked was the wealth required to execute a plan. So, what did he do? For a few years, he walked away, sailing a passenger schooner in the West Indies and delivering a newly built schooner from Taiwan to New York by way of Hong Kong, Japan, and the Panama Canal. Upon his return, he learned that Connecticut businessman Kaye Williams had purchased the ship. Together, Captain Bailey and Mr. Williams transformed *Rose* from a meager dockside attraction to the preeminent Coast Guard–certified sailing school vessel in America. He had spent three decades of his life giving everything he had to the ship when she was purchased for the film.

Earlier that day, I was below deck working on boat-check, near the galley on the gun deck, talking with Rich and Russ about what team was going to win the Super Bowl, when Captain Bailey injected himself into the conversation. Tony had gotten the crew all stirred up about who would win, and bets were set. The St. Louis Rams were set to play the New England Patriots and their backup quarterback, Tom Brady. I was a diehard Patriots loyalist and was not keen on Captain Bailey's football opinions. I was pretty snappy and clearly crossed a line when suddenly, he started shouting at me, almost screaming at the top of his lungs. "Okay, that's it, Sofrin! Put your hands up." He moved into a Rocky Balboa fighting stance!

I was shocked. The captain of the ship was ready to throw punches at me. Other hands heard the words, and soon there was a circle of crew around us. I thought quickly and looked back at him. "I'm not gonna fight you." I furrowed my brow and looked at all the eyes watching us now.

"What d'you mean you're not gonna fight? Put your hands up." He said this directly, but not in an I'm-gonna-kick-your-ass tone. It's like this fight thing was a game for him, and maybe I might be dumb enough to take the bait. "No, this is

Captain Bailey and Will

not a fair fight," I exclaimed while shaking my head from side to side. My response drew a breath of confusion from Bailey and all the onlookers.

"What? . . . What?" he stuttered back at me, totally confused.

With a big snarky grin, I looked around and then back at him while getting down on my knees. I moved my fists up into a boxer pose and, looking at Bailey, said, "Now it's a fair fight!" Captain Bailey, you see, was a foot shorter than me.

Two things happened the moment those words left my mouth. First, everyone watching exploded into laughter. Second, Captain Bailey's face turned as red as a fire engine as he proceeded to tackle me.

He took me down with some force, and I didn't care. I had just outwitted our captain. I lay there on the ground, playing dead to wave my white flag. The whole scene ended in smiles for all and some head shaking on Captain Bailey's part as he walked away. I think the whole exchange may even have promoted me to the level of "worthy adversary." But I slept with one eye open after that, as I had not known anyone to get the best of Captain Bailey.

My penance for one-upping the captain would be reporting to Dwight for a work-party job assignment. Dwight sent me up the mizzenmast to inspect the iron hardware on the crossjack yard, the lowest yard on the mast used to spread the foot of the mizzen topsail. This job meant crawling around to look for bubbling paint, chip it off, sand the metal, and repaint the exposed areas. The task wasn't challenging, but it was tedious. He directed me to meticulously chip with one hand

Work-party scraping the spars on deck

while catching the flaking paint with my other hand. He told me to show him the paint chips to prove I had done the job.

I wasn't surprised. With Ron by his side, Dwight began doling out nonsensical work-party assignments. If we weren't scrubbing decks, hands were scraping spars or tar varnishing and tallowing. There were some interesting work assignments, such as learning to splice wire and make baggywrinkle, a form of chafe gear on schooners or tall ships. Ron headed up that kind of work, but he tended to mostly pick female crew members and his favorite Planet Tall Shippers, leaving the less skilled, labor-driven jobs for the rebel members of our crew. It quickly became clear to Christina that Ron, the splicing master, was using his position as an opportunity to surround himself with the female deckhands. She found it ironic to be a woman having to tell Ron he needed to adjust the distribution of the work assignments and give the boys an equal opportunity to learn as well.

Andy began making the standby members of his watch repair old sails that would never even be set again. We all knew *Rose* would be completely broken down and rebuilt when we arrived in California.

⚙

Before our dismasting, *Rose* lacked the authenticity Peter Weir was striving for, and plans had already been made for a new rig to be constructed. Weir, much like O'Brian, was striving to achieve a level of indiscernible authenticity. In *Patrick O'Brian: A Life Revealed*, Dean King describes the range and volume of resources O'Brian used for constructing the world of Jack Aubrey: "O'Brian combed logbooks, official letters, memoirs, and period published accounts for details. In addition to Cochrane's memoirs, he studied Admiral Sir James Saumarez's dispatches and reports of Saumarez's famous naval battles at Algeciras . . . consulted with officials at the Public Record Office in London and at the National Maritime Museum in Greenwich and even with the current commanding officer of Nelson's ship HMS *Victory*. He also traveled to Port Mahon, Minorca, a Royal Navy base for the Mediterranean Fleet at the time of his novel, to see for himself that strategic, long, narrow harbor and the island's Spanish fortifications."

The HMS *Surprise* described by O'Brian in his books was an actual ship based on the English-captured French corvette *Unité*. Launched in 1794, her career as a French corvette was short, as she was captured by the thirty-six-gun frigate HMS *Inconstant* on April 20, 1796. Her name was changed to *Surprise*, as the Royal Navy already had a larger *Unité*, another captured French prize. In need of frigates, she was quickly fitted out and joined the Mediterranean fleet. In 1798, she underwent her first and only major refit at an English dockyard in Plymouth, England, under the supervision of master shipwright John Marshall. The survey drawings produced by Marshall are the only surviving architectural records of the ship. HMS *Surprise* remained in service until being sold in 1802 and then most likely broken up.

Weir committed himself to the highest level of historic accuracy, researching historical archives and building a team of some of the best experts on the subject from around the world. To start, Weir needed to decide how he would tell his interpretation of O'Brian. When asked, he says, "*The Far Side of the World* was my choice for the backbone of the movie. Co-writer John Collee and I, in the course of the adaptation, borrowed incidents from other of O'Brian's books. In addition, we invented certain scenes. We were soaked in O'Brian's style and felt we could seamlessly introduce the new material remaining true to his style." Continuing on, Weir says, "I set the story entirely at sea—no carriages, no crinolines, no ball scenes, and no love stories. I wanted the viewer to experience what I had found most singular about the books—life on board a British fighting ship in the age of sail."

When *Rose* left Newport, Leon Poindexter, the master shipwright who helped us prepare for the journey, flew to California to begin working as the technical advisor to the set designers at the Fox Studio arts department. Poindexter had already been working with meshing the plans of *Rose* as built with the John Marshall survey plans of HMS *Surprise* provided by the National Maritime Museum in Greenwich, London. In addition to the major modifications being planned to turn *Rose* into HMS *Surprise*, a full-scale replica was being built on top of a forty-foot gimbal at the Fox Studios tank in Baja, Mexico, the same tank used for the film *Titanic*. Being one for detail, and knowing HMS *Surprise* was originally French-built, Weir instructed Poindexter to ensure the interior sets accurately reflected the French substructure with British appointments. When asked about authenticity, accuracy, and level of detail, Weir says, "Spaces can affect you whether natural or built. Stand in the center of Chartres Cathedral, believer or not, and your senses are raised to awe."

I despised the morale-busting, workhouse-like situation and decided that something had to be said. I planned to talk with Tony while on watch that evening when I was at the helm so that nobody would be around. While I had no problem mocking Dwight and Ron in front of everyone, I felt this issue was best addressed in private. I wish I could say that when the moment came, I was elegant in the way I presented my frustration. In reality, I may have sounded like a brat whining in a candy shop.

Tony stood there and patiently listened. He let me talk for as long as I wanted to and never interrupted. I probably babbled for five minutes, acting like an overly dramatic rookie defense attorney at a murder trial, throwing out arguments to justify my frustration. I eventually wound down, and because Tony was so cool, he just chuckled and asked me if I had a better idea of what I should be doing to contribute to the greater cause. Surprised by his fair rhetorical question, I unexpectedly suggested I be relieved of the standby position on nighttime watch duty to build a large fake wooden fish to prank Captain Bailey. I have no idea how I came up with such an outlandish idea on the spot. I had never put any thought into playing a prank on Captain Bailey.

"We have had a fishing line off the back of the ship for the entire trip and have yet to catch a fish," I said with a smug smile on my face.

"And . . . ?" was the response by Tony, and rightly so.

"I think it would be a great idea to build a fish we could drop off the back of the ship to catch the line, and maybe we could trick Bailey into thinking we caught a fish?"

Pranks were an important part of the onboard culture. We worked hard, and clever humor was encouraged. On the first leg of our journey, A-Watch dropped a fake person out of the rig one night to scare B-Watch when they were having their muster before taking the deck. On the leg to Panama, in the middle of the night, C-Watch woke up A-Watch, saying there was a fierce rainstorm and to don all our foul-weather gear. I remember opening the main companionway doors to edge out on deck and being covered in an intense spray of water. They had the fire hose connected and were blasting water at the door on a cloudless night. Just after leaving Taboga, Charlie put a remote-controlled fart machine in the capstan and sat on the deck near it, pressing his remote control every time Andy tried to speak at a midday muster.

Tony smiled and agreed this was a good idea and well worth the effort. It was decided. At night my job would be to devise and build the most extraordinary fake fish ever. And just like that, I had turned a problem into an opportunity.

— *Chapter 22* —

*T*HE A-TEAM

SUNDAY, FEBRUARY 3, our fourth night at sea, was a calm one as we passed Volcán Cosigüina, a volcano located on the tip of a Costa Rican peninsula projecting out into the Gulf of Fonseca. The large gulf was named for a staunch enemy of Columbus and shares the coastlines of Nicaragua, Honduras, and El Salvador. The following morning presented a cloudless sky, light winds, and intense heat. Having paid my penance for outwitting our captain, I was back on chippy detail working with Todd on a deck repair. The officers were doing everything they could to come up with just about any kind of work to keep everyone busy. Tarps were laid out on deck and hands worked away, scraping the pile of broken spars strapped to our deck.

General irritability began to consume the crew. Where the Atlantic had brought destruction, the Pacific brought boredom. The days began to blend together. Morale was sinking, and like a waning romantic relationship, something needed to change. At around 1500, just south of the border of Guatemala, the officers offered up the opportunity for some whip dunking. This is when a crew member dons a life jacket and sits in a bosun's chair tied to the end of a gantline. The line is hauled lifting the crew member up into the air and out. The line is then eased so the bottom of the bosun's chair is just above the surface of the ocean. Then while the ship moves up and down in the swells, the crew member in the chair enjoys a series of random dunkings, splashings, and occasional draggings. I opted not to go out in the chair and instead volunteered to man the gantline.

The whip dunking did its trick to break the monotony of the day, at least for a little while. The officers were running out of ideas for keeping the crew busy. They initiated lessons on general seamanship and celestial navigation. The added educational sessions did help, but as a crew we all felt we were overworked and

Carrie being whip dunked

we were tired. In the last thirty-five days, I had been granted only two half days and one quarter day off. Had I been working under Jack Aubrey, I might not have had any days off, as sailors on HMS *Surprise* worked every day underway and time off in port was at the discretion of the captain. Through conversations, I knew I wasn't the only one on board who felt taken advantage of. But what were we supposed to do? I had signed on knowing my role as a deckhand meant I was there to do as I was told. Deckhands were at the bottom of the pyramid. We were the mushrooms of our boat, typically kept in the dark and fed a lot of crap.

I understood the mates needed to keep everyone busy, not just for maintaining our ship, but also as a means to help pass time. As the officer of the rig, Dwight may have had one of the hardest jobs on our ship because he had to decide what needed to be done and who would do the job. He was a mid-level boss, sort of like an assistant manager, but he lacked the skill needed to inspire his workforce. Not being a natural leader, Dwight appeared ignorant of the resentment he created by how he treated those beneath him. Yes, Dwight was an officer, and yes, his knowledge and comprehension of the ship's rig qualified him for the position. But we knew he only got the job because the previous boatswain ignored Captain Bailey's order to stay on the ship before we departed from Newport.

As a chippy, I had mostly been able to remove myself from Dwight's clutches, but it was not so easy for others. Shannon said, "Dwight was a real exercise of patience." She would remind herself that he was a crew mate and to not "lose it on him." Mandrew was still licking his wounds from Panama, when Dwight made him climb down into the forepeak to haul every coil of rope up onto deck so Dwight could view the inventory. The task was hard. There was no ventilation in the hot forepeak, and the coils of rope were double their normal weight because of all the salt water they had been soaking up. Mandrew had to climb down the two flights of narrow ladders to the very bottom and either push the coils up above him or drag them up behind him because the hatch openings were too small for him to climb up with a coil.

Mandrew worked for the entire morning when Dwight came up to check on the progress. Mandrew's T-shirt and shorts were soaked through in his own sweat and he was getting tired. Lacking any sense of decency, Dwight set into criticizing Mandrew's technique for hauling the coils of rope to the deck, attributing it Mandrew's lack of muscle, which was rich considering Dwight's own soft and doughy physique. Mandrew was the youngest person on the ship and could have been an obvious target for bullying had he not been such a team player. Mandrew was awesome, and we all looked after him like a little brother. For Dwight, though, he was just an easy target. Eventually Mandrew finished hauling all the coils up onto deck. Dwight glanced at the coils of line for less than a minute before directing Mandrew to return them to the bowels of the forepeak.

As an officer, Dwight appeared untouchable. The situation was tricky. A hand did not have the right to say no to a job assignment. Disputing or disobeying his order would be insubordination, and we all knew that would not be tolerated.

The next morning, Dwight found the keyhole of his padlock on the boatswains' stores locker filled with cured epoxy. The locker contained tools and associated supplies specifically used for rigging work. Until that point, the locker had been unlocked so hands could get the supplies they needed to do their work. Dwight added the lock because he caught Jared cutting line to make a lanyard for his knife. By adding the lock, Dwight created a situation requiring all hands to request access to the contents of the locker. Nothing on the ship was ever locked: not chippy stores, the refrigerator in the galley, or even Captain Bailey's cabin.

The boatswains' stores locker was located in plain sight on the gun deck immediately aft of the women's head. The visibility of the boatswain's locker raised the stakes of this small act of sabotage. Either the culprit was a master of timing and found the rare moment when there was no risk of anyone seeing the crime being committed, or there were a number of individuals who conspired and assisted with the crime.

Had there been an emergency, nobody would have been able to access the locker, and more importantly the epoxy act revealed that at least one member of the crew was at or near their breaking point. A quiet investigation was launched into the matter. It was determined the sabotage occurred during the night, and most likely while C-Watch had the deck. I'm not sure how the officers came to their decision of how to handle the situation, but they did nothing. It was common knowledge that Dwight was not well liked by most, and the trending scuttlebutt was that a number of crew members were already exploring other job opportunities. Would this action inspire others? We were two days out from Acapulco, and punishment might trigger a mass exodus. We weren't in the Royal Navy; any crew member could walk off the ship without consequences when in port, though they'd have to find their own way home.

On HMS *Surprise*, the crew would have faced severe consequences for not following orders or disrespecting an officer. In the Articles of War: "If any officer, mariner, soldier or other person in the fleet, shall strike any of his superior officers, or draw, or offer to draw, or lift up any weapon against him, being in the execution of his office, on any pretence whatsoever, every such person being convicted of any such offense, by the sentence of a court martial, shall suffer death; and if any officer, mariner, soldier or other person in the fleet, shall presume to quarrel with any of his superior officers, being in the execution of his office, or shall disobey any lawful command of any of his superior officers; every such person being convicted of any such offence, by the sentence of a court martial, shall suffer death, or such other punishment, as shall, according to the nature and degree of his offence, be inflicted upon him by the sentence of a court martial."

Jack Aubrey was a reasonable captain so long as there was order on his ship. This was not the case for all captains. While in conversation with an old friend Captain Billy Sutton in *The Far Side of the World*, Jack learns of a punishment handed down to a midshipman for crossing the line by wearing a master's jacket. It started as a bit of a joke but went too far, becoming a very serious matter of disrespect to a superior. Jack assumed the midshipman had simply been kicked out for the service but learned from Billy that the punishment handed down in his court martial was much worse: "'And he is to be employed as the constant scavenger for cleaning the head, until my further orders . . .' 'Good God,' cried Jack, reflecting upon the head of an eighty-gun ship of the line, a common jakes or privy for more than five hundred men."

Fortunately, we didn't have court martials, and corporal punishment was not tolerated on *Rose*, or any tall ship, but the age-old hierarchal system was well in place. In the end, all hands received a stern talking-to and there was no formal charge or punishment. One could conclude Dwight was the only person punished because he was informally humiliated by being denied any sort of vindication. Maybe the lack of serious follow-through by the officers was a way of sending a message to Dwight?

⚓

On Tuesday, February 5, we were two days out from Acapulco. After passing the Guatemala-Mexico border, we had to pull away from the coastline to cross the Gulf of Tehuantepec. Rick had concerns about the best way to cross the gulf because of his rough prior experience when delivering the *Lady Grace* to California, where it portrayed the *Andrea Gail* for the film *The Perfect Storm*. Located within the gulf is the Isthmus of Tehuantepec, the shortest distance that can be traveled over land between the Pacific Ocean and the Gulf of Mexico. During winter months, the isthmus is known for having extreme windstorms known as Tehuantepecers or Tehuanos that blow south through Chivela Pass, a gap in the Sierra Madre Mountains. The wind speeds tend to range from twenty to forty knots and have been known to exceed hurricane force. The two navigational options are to either commit to a straight shot across the three-hundred-mile gulf or to hug the coast. Hugging the coast is a longer and slower route but offers more protection and less fetch if a windstorm comes up. The straight-shot route is shorter but means full exposure to the wind and rough seas should a windstorm develop. Captain Bailey chose the straight-shot route.

Commissioned Mexican naval vessel P103 *Mariano Escobedo*

We made it across, but not before an unusual encounter one hundred miles into the gulf, when we were approached by a relic of a United States naval ship with a bow number P103. The name of the ship we saw was *Mariano Escobedo*, a Valle Class Mexican naval vessel. The United States had donated the 1942 British-built, Auk-class minesweeper USS *Champion* (AM 314) to Mexico in the 1970s, along with a number of sister ships. They were 225 feet in length and displaced 890 tons. A special trait of the class was that their means of propulsion was a combination of diesel-electric instead of just diesel, because of the needs of their magnetic minesweeping gear.

It was surreal seeing this ship motoring along and coming to observe us. I had only seen old warships tied up to a dock and converted to museums. It was amazing the ship was still under commission and actively patrolling the coastline. They sent out a smaller boat to get a close look at us. What a scene it would have been for an onlooker. Two ancient military vessels from two centuries apart inspecting each other like dogs sniffing each other when meeting for the first time.

Normal business resumed after our naval encounter. We had covered thousands of miles and still had nearly 1,900 more to go. We had sailed through terrible storms and survived a dismasting. The Atlantic Ocean had thrown more at us than we could have anticipated, and A-Watch had delivered. I started thinking we should instead be called the A-Team. We had developed a sacred bond and familial dynamic. I cared immensely for the members of my watch and would have done anything for them. I looked up to Carrie and Shannon for their leadership and willingness to share their knowledge. I respected Rich and Russ for their do-anything work ethic. Mandrew was stoic, and I wondered how he would be able to successfully resume life as a high school student after our journey.

We were an untested team when we departed from Newport, and we had successfully overcome the obstacles that arose before us, working together through action and without contention. It was not until this point of our journey that I realized some of us were doing better than others. Unfortunately, it took a bad situation to reveal how poorly Rich was doing. Our ship came within just a few feet of crushing two men in a small fishing boat because Rich, who was standing bow-watch, failed to report seeing them. Fortunately, someone aft noticed the small fishing vessel and called it out so the helm could be quickly thrown over, averting the near disaster.

Carrie shot forward, sprinting up to the bow, shouting Rich's name. He was zoned out and in some other space. It wasn't until she was a few feet away that he acknowledged her. She recalled he was standing there alone, allowing himself to get pounded by waves breaking over the rail. It was as if he was punishing himself.

The physical challenges of life at sea also challenge the mind. The uncomfortable living compartments, interrupted periods of sleep, and the knowledge that I might be suddenly called to work were some of the greatest contributors to the stress I felt. Fortunately, I had Jon and Jared and my budding relationship with Marion.

By this point I was falling hard for Marion, and we were beginning to have conversations about what we might want to do after we reached California. Not everyone else on board was falling in love. Some tried but failed. Shannon told me how Jason tried to convince her they would be a perfect match. He made numerous attempts, even standing outside of her bunk only to be sadly turned away. One night, Peggy drank some liquid courage and tried to climb into Jon's bunk; it was funny watching her run when she discovered Blythe already in there with him. Jared was trying hard to woo Erinn. It was common knowledge that Carrie and Alex had become a couple.

The incident of almost crushing that fishing boat made me wonder if Rich felt alone. He did come off as a loner. Like Russ, he never complained about anything, was always pleasant to be around, and did whatever was asked of him.

I always assumed he was fine. When he wasn't working, he spent nearly all his time with Russ, Marshall, and Jason. They had formed their own little social pod during the trip. I don't think I would have given Rich much thought had we not been on watch together.

During the last hour of watch that night, I asked Rich what inspired him to join *Rose*. I already knew where he was from and that sailing was not his first career, but I didn't know the reasoning. I learned he used to work at a zoo selling popcorn at a concession stand. On a day off, he went to a waterfront festival, saw a tall ship, and purchased a guidebook with a list of America's tall ships. Rich set his intentions on sailing on *Rose*. Before applying, he volunteered on a ship called the *Niagara* to give his nonexistent résumé a boost. His plan worked, and Tony hired him in August 2001.

He then opened up about his life on *Rose*. I learned Rich had one of the worst bunks on the ship. It was in A-Compartment up near the bow and was always wet because our ship leaked so badly. The leaking got so bad that at one point he slept on a bench on the gun deck for almost a week straight even though there were a few open bunks on our ship. The problem with those open bunks was they were on the port side of B-Compartment in a section that came to be known as "Armpit Alley" due to the overwhelming smell of dirty clothes and mildew mixed with strong body odor. It was so bad that even Rich thought it would be better to sleep on a bench instead of in a dry bunk. I understood his decision and felt terrible for him.

I then invited Rich down to chippy stores to check out the prank fish I was making for Captain Bailey. By that point, everyone knew of the fish except for Captain Bailey, but nobody had seen it other than Jon, who was helping me create it. I thought it would be a nice way to include him on the prank and hopefully stir up some more conversation. The wooden fish was six feet long, with pectoral fins on both sides. I explained how I had a marlin in mind, but it came to resemble a dolphinfish or mahi-mahi. The planned color scheme included painting the fish with reflective metallic paint that emulated scales and other characteristics of a live fish.

To add life to the fish, we drilled a couple of holes near the tail and tied lines through them to a number of fender washers to add turbulence and cause the fish to sway back and forth. Just behind the mouth, we added a comic text bubble, and wrote "You caught a sucker fish. Love Jon & Will." I asked Rich what he thought and told him I planned to launch the prank after Acapulco. He just smiled, but it was a great smile.

— *Chapter 23* —

*R*UM SQUALL

THE ENTIRE CREW WAS GIDDY with excitement as our ship approached la Bahía de Santa Lucía, also known as Acapulco Bay. We were only five miles out from the harbor entrance at 0600 on Thursday, February 7. Nearly everyone was awake and on deck. We were overwhelmed with excitement about breaking free from the shackles of our daily routines as we planned our imminent debauchery at what was at one time the hottest celebrity vacation spot in the world. I only knew of Acapulco from seeing the movie *Blow*, which had hit the theaters in the spring of 2001. The main character, George Jung, played by Johnny Depp, celebrates his newfound success in drug running by purchasing a large mansion at the top of Peninsula de las Playas.

Known now for tourism, Acapulco is located in the southwestern Mexican state of Guerrero. After conquering the Aztecs, the Spanish conquistadors recognized the value of the largest natural deep-water harbor on the Pacific coastline of New Spain, or what we call Mexico today. The local Indigenous population was attacked, and soon the Spanish Manila galleons, multideck square-rigged vessels, used the harbor as their preferred North American Pacific port for sailing west to China and the Philippines with silver and other precious resources harvested from Mexico. The same galleons would then sail east, carrying Chinese silks, porcelain, and spices. After arriving in Acapulco, the eastbound Asian cargo was then transported over land across Mexico and loaded onto ships in the Atlantic to be sailed back to Spain from the Mexican port city Heroica Veracruz, on the Gulf of Mexico.

Acapulco enjoyed the wealth and prosperity that came with being one of the most important global trading ports for almost three hundred years, until the Mexican Revolution of 1810. Mexico achieved independence in 1821, thus putting an end to the Spanish transpacific trading route. As a result, Acapulco's economy collapsed due to the loss of trade revenue with Asia. The port city experienced a period of economic revival in the mid-1800s during the California gold rush, but it did not find continuous prosperity again until the first half of the twentieth century, after the construction of Federal Highway 95—a new and better road between Acapulco and Mexico City.

Following the end of World War II, Acapulco became a famous vacation destination for American celebrities like John and Jackie Kennedy, Howard Hughes, Elizabeth Taylor, and Elvis Presley. With fame came problems, and soon the city was overpopulated and polluted. Its geographic proximity to the United States made it a relatively easy getaway. Celebrities not only loved visiting Acapulco; they also invested in the hotel industry. A group of fifteen male stars, including Errol Flynn, John Wayne, and Cary Grant, dubbed "The Hollywood Gang," became owners of Los Flamingos hotel. They closed the hotel to the public, making it available only for their inner circle.

⚙

The mood on board *Rose* as we approached Acapulco was universally pleasant. The tension seemed to evaporate as we neared the harbor of the famous Mexican city. We had made it that far together, and we all needed to cut one another some slack and blow off some steam. Acapulco would be the first time we had reached a port after a long leg without needing to address some urgent repair on the ship. This time we would be free to enjoy the local culture.

The horizon was a rich reddish-orange streak fading into a deeply saturated yellow, eventually transitioning to a muted light blue above the tops of our heads. The breeze was soft as it blew like a whisper, trying not to wake the inhabitants of the sleeping city nestled inside the protecting peninsulas flanking the crescent-shaped bay. The air smelled like a New England beach on a hot summer day from a distance. There was a thin layer of fluffy mist floating on the surface of the water as it softly lapped the white sandy beaches running the perimeter of the bay. Clusters of mature palm trees decorated the long strip of towering white hotels and apartment buildings lining the waterfront. Beyond them were low rolling hills broken into bluish-gray clusters in the foreground of the Sierra Madre del Sur mountain range.

We docked the ship at the Terminal Maritima, a commercial dock usually occupied by cruise ships. Upon docking, we were solicited by a half dozen shady guys offering food, drugs, and women. Carrie had no problem telling them where to go. The pier's location provided easy and centralized access to Acapulco's famous nightlife. Our stay would be for only two nights, and as in Puerto Rico, the ship's company was again divided up into two shore parties. Along with Jon, Blythe, and Marion, I was assigned to Shore-Party-B, the group that would stand watch on our first night. Jon took charge and immediately booked a room for the four of us at Hotel Tortuga, a hotel he had stayed at during spring break five years prior. We would be guests at the hotel for our second night in Acapulco.

I was excited about Jon's plan to stay ashore for many reasons, mostly because I had been living on the ship for more than three months and I loved the thought of sleeping in a bed and taking a long hot shower. The four of us had adapted to living in our tiny wood coffin-like bunks on our ship. The idea of sleeping in a queen-size bed in a hotel room felt like sleeping in the middle of a football field. We were not the only members of the crew seeking refuge from our prison-like dwellings. Tony and Christina also booked a room, but at a different hotel.

✲

My dock-watch assignment worked out well, because it was late enough at night that I could head out to the bars after work-party. I could have plenty to drink so long as I was sober enough to stand watch in the middle of the night. I knew I wouldn't get much sleep, but I had the following day off. That day, work-party was much like the last day of school. We all had to be there, but some hands were less productive than others. I spent three hours, a remarkably long time, mopping the gun deck. Happy and knowing I would be getting time off, I felt motivated to put in some extra effort making sure every nook and cranny was spotless.

Tony cut the workday short, giving us extra time to shower and freshen up before hitting the town. Shore-Party-A had a head start on us, having been free to explore the city since 1000. Without a plan, Jared, Jon, Blythe, Marion, and I, along with a few others, departed our ship for the long, colorful strip of restaurants and bars lining the northern beaches of the bay. We walked along Avenida Costera Miguel Alemán, a busy road divided by a tree-filled parkway. The cars raced along the road in both directions, honking horns, blasting cantina music, and dodging the Volkswagen Beetle taxis. The harbor side was lined with a myriad of restaurants and bars with giant neon signs to lure tourists. The mountainside was packed tightly with hotels, stores, and shopping stalls.

As the veteran Acapulco patron, Jon became our de facto tour guide. We stopped first at a shady-looking bar to wet our whistles. The decrepit bar was large and empty and looked as if it had been through a hurricane. There weren't many patrons, and the bartenders did not seem eager to serve our crew of gringos. We hastily drank our beers and continued walking along the waterfront, eventually stopping at a bar called Barbarroja, located across the street from the hotel we would be staying at the next night. The pirate-themed bar was a bit cliché, but unlike our first stop, it was full of people and had a DJ playing fun music.

We took over a long section of the bar, ordering a few buckets of cervezas and a round of Dark and Stormys to celebrate being free from our ship. Next to the bar was a tall bungee-jumping tower that looked like a crane used for building skyscrapers in New York City. The tower made for some exciting sightseeing when an occasional jumper lost their mind screaming after jumping from a height of 165 feet.

We made big plans for the following night. Jon told us of the exciting night-clubs he knew and suggested we let Shore-Party-A know about our plans so they could rendezvous with us the following evening. Drunk and happy, a handful of us made it back to the ship sometime near midnight.

Shannon, Christina, and Erinn, ready to take Acapulco by storm

The next morning was business as usual. I was up on deck early, enjoying a cup of coffee before our morning muster at 0800. I felt good, mostly because I made sure to avoid the rum drinks and tequila shots and drank plenty of water when standing dock-watch in the middle of the night. I couldn't say the same for everyone else. Jared had returned sometime early in the morning and set up a hammock on deck. He was still asleep and didn't have to report to work until 1000 because he was in Shore-Party-A. Nobody dared disturb him, knowing Jared was quick to thrust his knife at anyone who tried to wake him up. He did become a bit of a joke lying there in his hammock because he had fallen asleep with his shorts halfway down. We all carried on scrubbing the deck around him, letting him sleep the night off.

At 1000 we were free to leave the ship. We had the entire day to kill, skipped off the ship, and headed to Hotel Tortuga. The eight-story hotel stood in the middle of a break from the white towers that lined the city's waterfront on the mountainside of Playa Condesa. The lobby was simple in appointment, with all surfaces painted white, and was very clean. It was nothing fancy—our room, with cheap-feeling mattresses and a spartan interior, was not any better than a worn-in Motel 6, but it felt like walking into the Ritz-Carlton after living on *Rose*. We had two queen beds, a TV, our own bathroom, a terrace, and, most important, air-conditioning!

We all lay down in our room, Blythe and Marion on one bed and Jon and myself on the other. We had grand plans for the day. I was excited to see the famous Acapulco cliff divers. The divers make money by putting on a big show diving off hundred-foot cliffs. I also hoped to explore the markets and try some taquerias. A short, planned nap turned into an afternoon-long siesta. I was slightly sad to not explore Acapulco more, but the luxury of wasting a day in a clean hotel room was worth it. Come late afternoon, Jon and I left the girls and headed down to the hotel pool to enjoy a few beers before meeting up with the rest of our crew.

What luck having Jon end up on *Rose*. I had not before or since met a personality like his. He brought out a confidence in me that seemed to lack an opportunity before he set the stage. Our minds were often in the same place, and we finished each other's sentences with ease. Along with Jared, we were like the Three Stooges at the start of our trip. But I think Jon pairing up with Blythe and me with Marion, in addition to us both doing woodwork on the ship, created a spinoff act starring Jon and Will. Besides which, Jared was a lone wolf. Case in point, our priority in Acapulco was to enjoy being checked into a hotel with our girlfriends while Jared was still on the hunt for his female companion.

Sitting there at the pool bar with Jon was one of the rare moments we had to hang out alone since departing Newport. On the surface he may have appeared to others like a character straight out of *Animal House*, but in fact, Jon was undoubtedly one of the most intelligent members of our crew. His ability to make off-the-cuff gutter jokes or discuss the roots of classical architecture was the real glue that bonded us.

Later that evening we met the rest of our crew at Barbarroja, the pirate-themed bar we'd enjoyed the night before. For our shipmates, it was a two-mile walk from *Rose*, but for us, it was just across the street from our hotel. The party was in full swing by the time we made it to the bar. Almost our entire crew was there dancing and drinking. Mandrew was hammered and in line to do a bungee jump at the bar next door. The DJ had the music turned up loud, and the dance floor was mostly filled with our crew. Even Rick, Hunter, and Captain Bailey were there. Tom had Mandrew's video camera in hand, filming the debauched evening as it unfolded. They had just come from seeing the cliff divers. We stayed for a while, drinking, dancing, and enjoying the company of our friends. After a few hours of revelry, some people made plans to find a famous club in the hills called Palladium. I looked at Marion, and, thinking about our hotel room, we said farewell.

✸

We woke up early the next morning to be on the ship by 0700 on Saturday, February 9. We showed up to a ship that reeked of rum and sweat. Half the crew was still drunk from the night before and would easily fail a Breathalyzer test. Our ship's departure from Acapulco was not pretty. C-Watch was running the deck. Tony was in a terrible mood, the worst I had ever seen him in. He was barking orders and had a vein bulging on his forehead. Fortunately for me, I was in good shape. I am sure that without Marion, I would have stayed up the whole night, pounding tequila and trying to convince anyone to stay up and watch the sunrise.

There are a fair share of moments in O'Brian's books that nod to the shore-side activities of the ship's crew. In *Master and Commander*, success at sea impacts Captain Aubrey's men onshore. A post captain says to Jack at a party, "But your Sophies used to be a quiet, decent set of men ashore. And now they have two pennies to rub together they kick up bob's a-dying like—well, I don't know. Like a set of mad baboons."

There was much scuttlebutt going around *Rose* about the night before. I don't think anyone made it to Palladium, but there was much talk of a foam bar. The gimmick of the bar was to fill the mingling space with foamy suds up to the shoulders of the patrons. Yes, I may have missed a big night with our crew, but I felt good about my decision to make the most of my hotel room. Watching Charlie, who was clearly still very drunk, try to coil a dock line was more entertaining than hearing the story of two female crew members making out at the foam bar the previous night.

Tony must have felt like he was herding blind kittens, and even the titans from Planet Tall Ship were far from tiptop shape. Captain Bailey was in rare form, sharing his own story of not quite making it back to the ship: "I drank a lot, and I tried to go home. I got in a taxi, and he drops me at the head of the pier. I don't really remember. I do a face-plant in the grass and go to sleep. A couple of hours later, somebody is kicking me in the foot. I go, 'You son of a bitch, you kick me again, and I'm gonna get up and kick your ass.'" Captain Bailey looked up and realized he was not sleeping in his cabin but instead had passed out in a park. He looked at the two soldiers who kicked him, got up, and staggered back down the pier to the ship.

⚓

We executed Operation Fake Fish on our second day out from Acapulco. Just after lunch, the conditions were perfect. It was warm, with not much breeze, flat seas, and we were motoring. That set the stage for a perfect afternoon nap. Once it was confirmed that Captain Bailey was asleep in the great cabin, I grabbed the fish. The day before, we measured the size of the lead weight at the end of the trolling line and secured to the mouth of the fish a carabiner with a smaller inner diameter than the lead weight.

With Captain Bailey asleep, I brought the fish up on deck, hooked the carabiner to the trolling line, and released the prize. As planned, the fish slid back through the water to the trailing end of the trolling line, stopping at the lead weight. This caused the snubber, a bungee cord secured to the taffrail, the railing at the stern of the quarterdeck, to stretch out and double in length, signaling there was a fish on the hook. With no fish, the trolling line creates a minimal amount of drag, leaving the bungee in a static state; a taut bungee means there is a fish on the line. When a fish bites the hook, it fights but eventually runs out of energy and cannot keep up with the ship and will begin to slow down, adding drag to the line, thus stretching the bungee out.

Hopefully during this process, a crew member will notice the stretched bungee cord and shout out, "Fish on!" This opportunity can be missed, in which case the fish might break free because of a torn lip. In our case, the carabiner stopped at the lead weight at the end of the trolling line near the hook, and the bungee stretched. All on board knew this was in the works, so there was an unusual number of people who just happened to be lingering on deck.

"FISH ON!" came the call from Tony, who was the officer on watch when the bungee stretched out.

Jon was on deck, video camera in hand, waiting for the moment. Captain Bailey came running up, leaving almost no room as he skidded to a stop at the binnacle. He looked like a kid rushing to be the first in line at an ice cream parlor. Just under the binnacle was a small storage compartment that contained various items, including the pair of cheap faux-leather gloves that I had given him after we crossed the Gulf Stream. Captain Bailey donned the gloves for pulling in the fish. Under load, the trolling line could act like a razor slicing through the hands of anyone trying to pull it in.

Stable and with his footing in place, Captain Bailey pulled the engines back and put them into a full-throttle reverse. The abrupt change in velocity of water passing through the ship's propellers from aft to forward violently shook the five-hundred-ton hull as we suddenly skidded to a near stop in the water. Satisfied, Captain Bailey donned the gloves and headed aft to where the trolling line was tied on the quarter rail. At least half the crew was standing in a semicircle on the quarterdeck like a bunch of farm animals watching the trough being filled. All silently stared, enjoying the rare moment the trick was on the captain and not on the crew. Captain Bailey pulled hard on the line. Initially, I could see a lot of tension on the line, but then the line seemed to go slack.

"This seems like a trick," Captain Bailey uttered.

"It must be," I said. "Maybe the fish broke free?"

I was in complete disbelief as the prank began to flounder. As he pulled, I watched and felt so defeated. All the effort and planning to make this fish had vanished in just seconds following a perfect setup. We had all hoped this would be our moment. Smiling, Captain Bailey pulled the line in with ease, knowing he had been pranked.

Then, surprisingly, the line fought back. Pulling the fish in became a struggle, and suddenly and out of nowhere, Captain Bailey had to dig into the deck. I don't know what happened. It looked like there was tension on the line. He started heaving and pulling, and boom, it jumped out of the water and back under. For a moment, I must have looked like a kid seeing Santa for the first time. The prank was working!

Tony hollered, "Do we have any cheap gin left?" An easy way to kill a fish is to pour high-proof alcohol into the gills. The fish dies instantly.

"Doesn't feel like a fish," Captain Bailey retorted.

"Where's Jackal?" Jon joked.

Then a fin popped out of the water, prompting comments from everyone watching.

"What kind of fish is that?" asked Jon with an underlying chuckle.

"It's a mahi, a dorado!" shouted Captain Bailey.

With all of us as witnesses, a big smile came across his face, etching the moment into stone: Captain Bailey had been pranked. He continued pulling the line up to the deck so all could see the wondrous wooden fish that successfully disrupted a monotonous midafternoon watch.

Captain Bailey, the fish, Jon, and Will

"Looks like you caught a suckerfish!" Jon said, making his final jab.

Standing there on deck laughing, I was surrounded by all my shipmates. Dwight had the biggest smile and congratulated me for pulling off the prank. I looked at Ron, who clearly shared the same sentiment. We all had gotten that far together, and for me, I was accepting that our differences didn't matter.

— *Chapter 24* —

LAND'S END

THE EIGHT-HUNDRED-MILE LEG from Acapulco to Cabo San Lucas was far from boring. Though we mainly had blue skies with air temperatures peaking in the mid-eighties during the day, head seas began building late in the afternoon of our second day out from Acapulco. We had to slow the ship down because swells started breaking over the weather deck, and water was penetrating the deck near the foremast. Bow-watch was moved back to the mainmast, and measures were taken to prevent electrical arcing on the gun deck. The headrails began to bend as the bowsprit shoring continued to deteriorate. The foresail was struck to reduce the load. Todd and I added reinforcements from the interior while Dwight and a few hands worked on lashing a series of lines between the buckling headrails and forward bits on either side of the bowsprit.

On Monday, February 11, our third day at sea, we entered the Sea of Cortez, also known as the Gulf of California. Famous for its abundant sea life, this seven-hundred-mile basin of water is located between the Mexican mainland and the Baja California Peninsula. Jared reported an unusual sighting when aloft during the night. Looking down midship, he saw giant tubes of light surging through the water. They were moving faster than us and swaying from side to side. The tubes shot forward of the ship and disappeared, leaving a wake of dissolving light. Captain Bailey suggested the tubes of light were made by whales crossing through layers of bioluminescent dinoflagellates.

Various course adjustments had to be made through the night to dodge a series of squalls and pockets of heat lightning. At 0800 the next morning, we saw three waterspouts develop at once. We had seen that single waterspout shortly after departing from Taboga, but the sight of three well-formed spouts in front of us was jaw-dropping. Everyone on deck was in awe. The spouts lasted for fifteen minutes before dissolving. The sky soon cleared, and land was sighted at 1045. The air was notably cooler than the day before. We had entered the cold water of the California Current, a southbound cold-water Pacific Ocean current. The ambient water temperature had dropped by nearly ten degrees in a twenty-four-hour period.

Three waterspouts in a row

A-Watch took the deck at 1200. We had the main and mizzen staysails set and dropped the RPMs on the engines as we approached the southern tip of the Baja Peninsula. Believing the Baja California Peninsula to be an island, the Spanish explorers called their new discovery California after a mythical island described in the 1508 Spanish romance novel *Las Sergas de Esplandían*. The Pericú, an Indigenous tribe, had inhabited the region for thousands of years by the time Hernán Cortés arrived in 1534 with the hope of colonizing the peninsula. Nearly 150 years later, after attacking and bringing under control the Pericú, Spanish Jesuit missionaries began establishing missions, some still standing today, such as Misión Estero de las Palmas de San José del Cabo Añuití, founded in 1730. Cabo San Lucas remained a small undeveloped village until 1919, when a US fishing company began fishing for tuna and built a cannery, turning the village into an important fishing port. In 1974, the Transpeninsular Highway was opened, increasing accessibility and paving the way for Cabo to become the tourist destination it is today.

El Arco de Cabo San Lucas

We couldn't enter the small harbor because our berth for the evening would be on the fuel dock, which had no room when we arrived. With our sails furled, we dropped anchor just north of the famous El Arco de Cabo San Lucas, a jagged granite rock formation at the southernmost point of the Baja Peninsula, also known as Land's End. In his book *The Log from the Sea of Cortez*, John Steinbeck participates in a scientific expedition to collect marine life specimens. In chapter 8, he describes his impression of the unusual formation: " The tip of the Cape at San Lucas, with the huge gray Friars standing up on the end, has behind the rocks a little beach which is a small boy's dream of pirates." I certainly felt like a pirate when tourist boats soon came circling around us, as did the topsail schooner *Sunderland*, which made a show of shooting blank cannon fire at us, creating a fun spectacle.

The differences between the Planet Tall Shippers and the rebels had been left behind in Acapulco. Everyone was happy; there were no more groups as we all comingled. Blythe and Jared set up hammocks and read books, some took in the beautiful scenery, while others did crossword puzzles. At 1500, we launched one of our inflatable dinghies so Rick could go into the harbor and see what the holdup was at the dock. After more than two hours, Rick returned; we weighed anchor and entered the harbor, tying up to the Marina Cabo San Lucas fuel dock by 1750. We had a short muster to go over the plan. We would be in port only for the night. Rick would be leaving the ship so he could head back to San Diego to make sure everything was in order for our arrival. There would be no shore parties, but all hands were free to leave the ship for dinner. The schooner we saw sailing when we were on anchor was tied up next to us. They invited our crew over for a beer and a tour. I skipped the tour because we were only going to be in Cabo for the night. My mind was set on taking a quick shower and looking for an internet café.

I was getting ready to leave when Rick pulled me aside to have a private conversation.

"I'm not sure what you are thinking about doing when you get to San Diego, but I want you to stay."

I was surprised by such a direct conversation. I said, "Okay?"

"I want to hire you off the ship to work for me. You would still be working on the ship, but under my umbrella instead of the ship's. I'm working on getting you all off the ship and into condos. You deserve this. I know you work hard, and if you are interested, you're going to make a lot more money than you are making right now. The deal is, you can't say nothing to nobody. I think you are a shoo-in to get a good casting spot in the film."

I did not expect this generous offer from Rick. "Thank you" was all I could say, but I had a big smile.

Rick smiled and gave me a firm pat on the back. "Why don't you think it over on your final leg, and we can talk again in San Diego?"

⚙

There was a general plan for anyone interested to meet up at a restaurant called Cabo Wabo. Stunned by Rick's offer, I washed up and headed off to find an internet café. Casey had emailed me. He had heard about our dismasting and congratulated me on becoming a man. He also offered me the mate's position on *Onawa* for the upcoming season in Newport. He said he could cover the position with fill-in crew if I wanted to stay in California for a while so long as I made it back before Memorial Day weekend.

I was in a rush to get to dinner, not leaving me much time to process the two job offers I had received in less than one hour. I also had Marion to consider. Until Rick's proposal, I was ready to walk off the ship in San Diego. Not because of anger, but just because we had done the real thing. We sailed from the Atlantic to the Pacific, and the experience secured my career decision to continue sailing for a living. I didn't necessarily want to sail on another tall ship, but I really didn't want to make a movie about sailing. But the offer of more money was enticing, and I still didn't know what California would be like.

Casey's offer, on the other hand, was a dream come true for me. I built *Onawa*, sailed her through Europe, and loved working with Casey. However, as a kid, I fantasized about living in California. Now I was only three days away from it. I needed to decide by the time we arrived in San Diego. Did I sell out for the money or focus on sailing? Making the movie would mean almost no sailing and a lot of work with maybe a tiny chance of some sort of break into the film industry. I never aspired to work in Hollywood. The hook was the hint of a lottery shot at making it big.

I wondered where Marion might be regarding her future. She was open to almost anything. Marion was the kind of person who could hop on a bus at a moment's notice to try a new adventure she had only just heard about. When Tony called her about joining *Rose*, she was working on a large wooden sailing yacht in the Caribbean. She walked away from an excellent deckhand job I would love to have had. Yet, despite wanting different things, we were now sharing a bunk and very close to acknowledging we were in a committed relationship.

Suddenly, I felt overwhelmed and frustrated. This was the last night of our incredible journey. The last time we would all be together as a crew. The moment we reached the dock in San Diego, everything would change. Mandrew would fly back home to resume life as a high school sophomore. For weeks others had been looking for new jobs on different boats. Our ship was set to be hauled out in the naval dockyards in San Diego. There would be dozens of new people working on the ship to transform her to HMS *Surprise*. No matter what I decided, life was going to change quickly.

I thought back to my time in Europe on *Onawa* when we were in Saint-Tropez near the end of our racing circuit. I was exhausted and wanted a break to collect myself before figuring out my next steps. In France, I had no opportunities lined up. In Mexico, I was near the end of my journey and had multiple possibilities. Knowing my time in Cabo was limited, I put these thoughts on hold to make the most of the evening with my shipmates.

⚓

We all met up at Cabo Wabo, which had been founded by Sammy Hagar, a former lead singer of Van Halen. The restaurant was mostly empty other than a few tables of American tourists. We all sat at a long table outside. The décor made me feel like I was eating at a Chili's restaurant in America. We ate our food and drank our beer, and the bartender got upset when I tried to pay for a round of drinks in pesos. I looked at Alex and Carrie, and they looked like they were ready to go to bed. Shannon was flirting with a table of guys at a bachelor party. Marion appeared annoyed with me and was not digging the scene, especially after a very drunk woman in the bathroom, randomly and for no reason, looked at her and blurted out, "I have three children." Jared was busy working his magic with Erinn, hoping they might finally ignite that spark. Blythe had just learned her uncle had died while we were in transit from Acapulco to Cabo.

I felt like I was on a different plane than most of my shipmates. This was it, our last big night outside of America. I wanted to do tequila shots and have fun hitting the town, and so did Jon. Looking around and feeling the night wasting away, I stirred the pot with Jon, and we came up with a plan to take Mandrew to a strip club. Marion understandably had no interest in joining us. We recruited Todd and Blythe—Todd needed no convincing. Our ensemble grabbed a cab, and with Jon's broken Spanish, we found a club near the harbor. We had Mandrew wait in the cab, first making sure he could get in. We gave him the nod, and like an excited new contestant on *The Price Is Right*, he came running up the red velvet steps and through the large doors.

The interior was large and dimly lit with black lights. As expected, the DJ played a good mix of popular songs. There was a long stage, a bar, a pool table, and a slide coming down from a second-floor balcony. We had plenty of tables and seats to choose from, as there were not many patrons, maybe a dozen. Mandrew, Jon, and Todd took seats near the stage where a dancer was performing. I sat in the back with Blythe, sharing a round of drinks as we laughed about the setting and reflected on what we were about to accomplish by completing our journey. I didn't care much about the goings-on of where we were. We laughed as we watched Mandrew take in the scene. Todd wandered around before walking up the stairs to the mysterious second floor. Twenty minutes later, he returned to the main space via the slide.

We soon got bored, left, and found half our crew still sitting where we had left them at Cabo Wabo. With a second wind and charged up by the rounds of drinks we had consumed, all were ready to find a new venue. Wandering toward the waterfront, we heard the sound of live music that called us as the Sirens did Ulysses. As luck would have it, we stumbled upon a small piano bar and took it by storm. What started out as a dismal night looking to be a letdown became one filled with revelry as we celebrated our last night in Mexico by dancing and singing aloud. I drank my share and then some. I have no recollection of how I made it back to our ship.

— Chapter 25 —

POINT LOMA

IT WAS THE MORNING OF Wednesday, February 13. We had been in Cabo San Lucas for less than twenty-four hours when we got our wake-up call at 0715 the following morning. Our engines were started at 0825, and we were off the dock by 0900. C·Watch had the deck with Captain Bailey calling the shots as we motored out and around El Arco for San Diego. There was a moderate headwind, the seas were flat, the skies were blue, and the air was warm, peaking out at 88° Fahrenheit (31° Celsius). We departed with only twenty-seven hands on board, with Rick gone and Todd unexpectedly opting to skip the leg and stay at his sister's time-share condo in Cabo.

Todd's departure made me head chippy, and right away Captain Bailey set me to work replacing an eighteen-inch section of deck planking. I knew the section of deck I was working on would be ripped up during the refit when we arrived in San Diego, but that didn't bother me. Instead of feeling frustrated about the mindless work, I enjoyed the peaceful opportunity to quietly sit alone and work on our ship's deck, underway, and on a sunny warm day. Looking around, I saw I was not alone when it came to savoring the moments we had remaining on our passage. The energy of our crew was different; there were only smiles, as it was mostly quiet and calm throughout. Instead of assigning work, Andy kept himself busy creating artwork inspired by an illustration he found in the book *Seamanship in the Age of Sail*, for T-shirts we were going to have made to celebrate the completion of our journey that we all jokingly called "The Voyage of the Damned."

We had left Newport a green crew hurrying to learn the ways of our ship. Mistakes were made, tempers flared, but we figured it out. We were now a seasoned team. Fewer words were needed because we knew what to do, how to do it, and when it should be done. We had learned how to work with one another.

Artwork drawn up by Andy for the celebratory T-shirts made
for marking the completion of the passage

Planet Tall Ship still existed, and I continued to have no interest in becoming a member. However, I came to appreciate it for what it was. I didn't need to agree with the culture of its members. I learned in the worst of it, our differences didn't really matter. My perception of the people I was with had evolved.

Patrick O'Brian once said, "The essence of my books is about human relationships and how people treat one another." To me, his statement rings true when I think about the wild spectrum of personalities that made up our crew. I saw through moments of intense action the traits that separate a leader from a wannabe and how decency and compassion can inspire loyalty. Our journey pushed us to break the shackles of individuality and routine. For many, the loss of routine can feel chaotic, even devastating. But in time, the chaos dissipates, and the establishment of a new routine can be the binding matter needed to create the unity we achieved as a crew.

I stood my last watch on Friday, February 15, from 0000 to 0400. We were fifteen miles to the west of the Mexican coast steering a course of 320°. The air was cool, sky mostly overcast, seas were less than two feet, and the wind was blowing between twelve and fifteen knots from the northwest. I could occasionally see spots of light along the coastline. I wasn't in much of a talking mood. I appreciated being awake and alone in the dark of night so I could think in peace. I thought about how the masts were broken, our headrails were being held in place with lashings of lines, and the steel bowsprit had a crack growing so fast that those on boat-check had to mark its progress with a black marker every hour.

We would be arriving in San Diego later that morning. I thought about my first impressions at Logan Airport after my time in Europe on *Onawa*. The culture shock was something I did not expect. I would be returning again to America, and I wondered how it would feel. I felt anxious about the uncertainty of what lay ahead. Certainty was guaranteed on *Rose*. We got three meals a day, had a bed to sleep in, and would never be alone. In exchange we worked hard, woke up in the middle of the night, and surrendered our freedom to the schedule of our ship. It was all worth it. I wished I could have stopped our ship. I wanted our journey to keep going.

⚓

The air was chilly, and the sky was heavily overcast with a tan, almost smokelike fog, making it hard to distinguish sky from water. The first sighting of a small sailboat marked our arrival, and within minutes the horizon was littered with dozens of sailboats enjoying a Friday afternoon sail in Southern California. Looking out along the horizon, I saw the topography of a coastline that was noticeably different from any of the ports we had approached. The shadows of hills that ran into the shore became more defined as we approached Point Loma Lighthouse, marking the entrance of San Diego Bay. It was Friday, February 15, and we had reached the United States!

In 1542, leading the first European expedition to explore the coastline of North America to the north and west of New Spain, Spanish explorer Juan Rodríguez Cabrillo discovered a new bay he named San Miguel. At the time, the region was populated by a number of Indigenous tribes, including the Luiseño, Cahuilla, Cupeño, Kumeyaay, and the Northern Diegueño. In 1602, while on a surveying expedition of the Pacific Coast, Sebastián Vizcaíno changed the name of the bay to San Diego. Spanish colonization of San Diego did not begin until the second half of the eighteenth century. In 1769, Mission San Diego was established as the first of twenty-one missions along the coastline of what becomes Alta California, a province of New Spain. In 1822, the territory became part of

Mexico after the Mexican War of Independence. Then in 1848, following the Mexican-American War, most of Alta California was transferred to the United States under the Treaty of Guadalupe Hidalgo.

On September 9, 1850, California became the thirty-first state in the Union. Development and urbanization of San Diego continued to flourish through the second half of the nineteenth and into the twentieth century. In 1904, the United States Navy established a coaling station on Point Loma, marking the beginning of a continuous buildup of military presence. Naval repair operations began in 1919, and in 1922, the United States destroyer base San Diego was established. Base operations grew through World War II. The base was redesignated US Naval Repair Base in 1943 and became Naval Station San Diego in 1946. San Diego became the homeport for the US Pacific Fleet in 1994 when the port was again redesignated Naval Base San Diego.

I felt like an alien on an odd-looking spaceship approaching a new planet for the first time. I had changed and grown immensely since we departed Newport. There I stood on the deck of our ship, proudly wearing ragged and tar-stained clothes. My knife and spike had become part of me, as I only noticed them when not wearing my belt. Hard work didn't seem so hard anymore; it was just work. I was back in the United States, and it could not have felt more foreign to me. I left one world for another, and my perceptions of where I was coming from and where I was going had changed along the way.

We motored slowly into the harbor, passing the North Island Naval Station on our starboard beam. Andy brought a signal gun up on deck and began playfully firing away at the yachts passing by as we made our way toward the inner harbor. A signal gun is a miniature cannon made for shooting blank shotgun shells to salute or notify other vessels. Looking around, I saw most of my shipmates smiling and making plans, but some were quiet and kept to themselves. During our morning muster, we had been told that our watch rotations would end. That day would be our last as a crew.

North San Diego Bay was a busy modern metropolis, very different from any port we had visited. The eastern waterfront of the harbor was lined with piers and marinas filled with yachts, commercial vessels, and US Navy ships. Towering over the edge of the harbor was a backdrop of old and new skyscrapers waiting to be joined by a number of new buildings racing to be the tallest. We had to make two stops, the first at the Broadway Street Pier to clear US Customs and Immigration. We were sandwiched between two massive piers where the center of downtown San Diego greeted the harbor. At 1249, we quietly docked our ship before settling in to enjoy a filling lunch of Hunter's fried chicken. While waiting for the customs officials, we kept ourselves busy by organizing and cleaning our living compartments and began planning for the breakdown of the ship to prepare her for the refit that would transform her to HMS *Surprise*.

We cleared customs and got underway at 1613. It took us a half hour to motor the three miles across the bay to Shelter Island. The sky was heavily overcast, and dusk had set in. The harbor was quiet as we solemnly moved through the glassy water that surrounded us with a mesmerizing reflection of the brightly lit urban skyline. Most of our crew stood quietly on deck, staring out at the serene setting. The workers had already left for the day by the time we reached Driscoll's Dockyard. There would be no welcoming party for us, no loved ones excited to celebrate our achievement or to catch our lines. Rick stood there on the dock waiting to welcome us. We had completed our voyage.

Chapter 26

SEVENTEEN YEARS LATER

I WAS IN THE MIDDLE of teaching a course at MIT when my phone rang. I saw the Alaska area code and knew I had to take the call. Excusing myself, I walked into the hall.

"Hello."

"Hi, Will, it's Marion."

It was the first time we'd spoken in nearly two decades. Her voice sounded the same. I had wondered if I would hear back from her after the email I sent. Our relationship had not ended well, and here I was, her ex-boyfriend, reaching out to see if she would be willing to talk to me about another life we had lived together almost two decades before.

I told her about how life had brought me back to California. I didn't know what to expect from her. She was cautious at first, but as time went on, she became a great help through the process of writing this book. We talked for a while, and I learned she had become a public defender and spent two years sailing the Pacific Ocean with her husband. Today, Marion works for an Indian tribe in the Pacific Northwest, where she lives with her husband and cat. They are still sailing.

☸

After arriving in San Diego, Marion and I stayed with the ship for the preproduction refit in the naval shipyards, before delivering the former *Rose*, now *Surprise*, to Ensenada, Mexico, in April 2002 for the filming of *Master and Commander: The Far Side of the World*. We stayed in Mexico for a short while before moving back east. She left first, and I left less than a week later. I took the mate job on *Onawa*, and Marion worked as the mate on the 12-Meter *Weatherly*. Our relationship fizzled out one night in Nantucket at the end of the summer. The last time I saw her was shortly before she sailed south for the Caribbean on a big schooner. Needing a break from sailing, I headed west to try the life of a ski bum in Vail, Colorado.

Much has happened between then and now. I returned to Newport after my winter in Colorado to resume life as a sailor. I was on a schooner sailing to the Caribbean when *Master and Commander: The Far Side of the World* was released in theaters, so I didn't get to see it on the big screen. I continued moving up the ranks and became a licensed captain, working in the boating industry through my twenties before eventually transitioning to a land-based career. Today, I live in Southern California with my wife and young daughter. I started a business that provides architectural consultation services for clients restoring historic homes. I also have a woodshop where I design and build furniture for my clients.

The idea to write this book came shortly after the 2019 New Year's celebration. A friend asked me to tell some stories to a group of people at a party about the time I sailed to California. Later, I thought about how as a teenager I read *Into Thin Air* by Jon Krakauer and *The Perfect Storm* by Sebastian Junger. I was fascinated by the storytelling in those books and how they exposed me to worlds unknown. At the time, my daughter was a toddler, and my career was really taking off. My wife is a pediatrician who had to follow the standard academic route to become the professional she is. The only formal training I had after high school was my two-year apprenticeship at IYRS. I believe in education. However, I do not feel that the traditional academic route is the only way to be successful. I have lived a less-than-conventional life and worked hard to get where I am. Thinking about my daughter, I hope that when she is a teenager, she will read stories of how people chose to live their lives and go on to make her own adventure.

I started by reaching out to Captain Bailey, who, though now retired, was still actively sailing. My timing could not have been better, because he was scheduled to fly out to the West Coast to fill in as skipper on the *Lady Washington*, a replica of an eighteenth-century American privateer. We met in Oxnard, California, and he brought with him *Rose*'s log and helped me photograph it to use as the baseline for the structure of this book. Captain Bailey fielded hundreds of phone calls and reviewed a few versions of the manuscript in the years that followed.

The logbook listed the full ship's company entered the day of our departure, and I used that list to begin searching for my shipmates. Some could not be found, and others chose not to respond.

I spoke with Hunter a few times. He is working as a ship's cook on the *Spirit of South Carolina* and is writing a cookbook. Tony manages a historic hostel located on the California coast. Andy works for the Applied Physics Laboratory at the University of Washington as a captain of their research vessels and periodically as a relief captain on tall ships. Christina retired from sailing to become a journalist, then a teacher, and lives in southern New England with her daughter. Aaron, the AB who had to leave the ship in Puerto Rico, is married with two children and is the waterfront director of the New York Harbor School.

GT is married with two children. He is a port engineer for a US shipping company; he was in Saipan the last time we spoke. Erinn is married, has three children, and works for the Baltimore Fire Department. Tom lives in Newport, is married with one son, and works as professional race crew for high-profile racing yachts. Scott retired from sailing and lives in Milwaukee.

Rick Hicks is still running Big Screen Marine, servicing the film industry. He has since worked on Disney's Pirates of the Caribbean series, *Ozark*, and *Top Gun: Maverick*, to name a few. Alex is married with two children, is a teacher, and lives close to me. We met up with our kids last year at the zoo.

Carrie continued sailing as a tall ship sailor for years, eventually settling down in Maine. She is married—her husband was also a tall ship sailor—and they have two children together. Shannon and Carrie continue to remain great friends. Shannon also lives in Maine, is married, and still works in the industry in the office of a bustling boatyard. Blythe continued to sail, got her captain's license, and went on to become a maritime attorney. She lives in Miami and we have remained great friends.

Todd and I have stayed in touch over the years, mostly through text messages. As a tradition, he calls me every year on 9/11 to catch up and occasionally on Thursday nights in the summer after his golf/drinking league.

Jared is still Jared. We had many more adventures after our time on *Rose*. Our friendship waned until I started writing this book. Now, we talk much more frequently, and last year, we met up for the first time in over ten years. It felt like no time had gone by. He lives in Newport with his captain wife and two dogs. He is an entrepreneur and the captain of a nice sailboat.

Captain Bailey reintroduced me to Mandrew, who had recently moved back to the US from Berlin. Mandrew visited my house a few weeks later and instantly became a part of my family—he spoils my daughter like a wonderful uncle. A year later, when the pandemic began, we bought a sailboat together. It's nothing much, but we love it and race it out of Marina del Rey every week during the summer.

Jon lives in Spain now. He didn't go back to architecture but instead became the captain of a very large sailing yacht based in the Mediterranean. The last time I saw him was at a restaurant in Antigua. We hadn't spoken for nearly a decade when I reached out to him about writing this book. We exchanged a few emails before talking for hours on a call in the middle of the night. He got into some trouble with his wife during that call for waking up one of their daughters because he was laughing so loud.

Shortly after our call, Jon's wife was diagnosed with cancer. There wasn't much I could offer in support other than distracting him by sending an occasional joke or obnoxious text to check in on him. My heart ached for him. Although we had not seen or talked with each other for years, I felt compelled to stay in touch and remain available. My wife, who has never met Jon, spoke with him a few times, offering an informed ear. Jon's wife passed near the end of 2020. We have stayed in touch, and his sense of humor is stronger than ever, helping him get through the hard times.

Then the unthinkable happened when my own wife was diagnosed with cancer. My world was turned upside down. I suddenly found myself where Jon was, a father and husband trying to navigate through the fiercest storm life had just thrown me into. Like the changing of watch, our roles in life shifted. Jon, being the good shipmate he is, now checks in with me to make sure I am okay.

It didn't stop there, and Jon wasn't the only shipmate who stepped up. Word spread, and other shipmates began reaching out offering to help. I didn't tell Tony, but he found out through Christina, and on a call one day, he told me he knew and asked what he could do to help; he offered to come cook dinner. Shannon sends me a text every now and then. Jared checks in on me and always returns my missed calls. Mandrew, being the rock he is, does more than he would ever take credit for. There isn't a thing I couldn't ask of him.

I always knew sailing *Rose* to California was a special, once-in-a-lifetime kind of experience. But it took me two decades to truly understand what I got out of it. We sailed through fierce storms and dismasted in the middle of the ocean, and through it all not a single person died or was hurt. Like being born into a family, I did not get to choose who was on our ship. We lived together, worked together, laughed together, and took care of one another.

I grew up feeling mostly alone, not relating to the majority of the people in my life. I didn't know it then, but signing up to be a deckhand on *Rose* was my opportunity to earn the right to become part of a great family. The *Rose* family goes beyond the shipmates I sailed with; it includes the generations of those who sailed on *Rose* before my time. It has been two decades since we completed *Rose*'s final voyage. I have come to believe life is a series of journeys. Sailing *Rose* to California was only one of them.

$\mathcal{A}$CKNOWLEDGMENTS

First and foremost, I wish to thank my shipmates. You are all so wonderful, and having the opportunity to reminisce about our grand adventure was the best part of writing this book.

For all the other people who helped contribute to this book, it would not be fair to put one name at the top of the long list of those I want to thank for helping me see it through. Some may have contributed more than others, but a recipe is not complete if missing even a pinch of one ingredient. In truth, the list below is probably half of what it should be, but I have chosen to omit the names of some to respect their privacy.

In alphabetical order, I would like to thank: Ray Ashley, Richard Bailey, James Berry, April Blair, Ginny Bliss, Ian Bradley, Harold Burnham, Kent Dresser, Sally Eagle, Tracy Edwards, Iris Engstrand, Skip Erikson, Mark Ewachiw, James Ewing, Casey Fasciano, Paul Fremont-Smith, Susan Ganett, Rodger Hambridge, Kurt Hasselbach, Rick Hicks, Geoff Hunt, Kirsten Johnston, Kate Katin, Bill Kayser, Catherine Keenan, Mark Kelley, Dean King, Jay Koogan, Chris Kouzes, Tina Moore, Tessa Norton, Deirdre O'Regan, Kathryn Pascucci, Philip Russell, Mike Shank, Dan Shotz, Sheli Smith, Carl Steeves, Ruth Taylor, Stephen Taylor, Michele Trout, Kris Von Wald, and Bruce Williams.

At the USCG Motion Picture and Television Office, thanks to CWO Paul Roszkowski, for helping to ensure an accurate representation of the resources of the US Coast Guard, and details about the loss of the replica ship *Bounty* and *Flying Colours*.

Thanks to University of Miami Libraries, Special Collections, senior library assistant Chelsea Jacks for assisting me in regards to my transcription of seaman Aaron Thomas's journal.

At the Maritime Museum of San Diego, thanks to Jim Davis, who provided special access to the living compartments on HMS *Surprise* so I could verify the technical illustrations I developed for this book.

John Hattendorf, thank you for being such a great teacher and resource. Your knowledge is unparalleled.

Peter Weir, I wish to thank you for your kind nature and elegant perspective. You gave more than I asked, and I hope to never forget the thought-provoking impact our conversations left on me. You, sir, are one of a kind.

Tom Rothman, I thank you for the wonderful foreword you wrote. Without your persistence, there would have been no movie, and I would not have had one of the greatest experiences of my life.

Max Sinsheimer, my agent: I thank you for jumping headfirst into taking me on as a client. You are everything I could have hoped for in an agent and more. Thank you for always being available for important questions and fast answers, even at 11:00 p.m. on a Tuesday night.

Jamison Stoltz, you are so much more than an editor. To quantify my gratitude for you is not possible. You are a great teacher. Your expertise, creativity, and patience are unparalleled. You brought dimension and perspective that I had never considered for this book and, like a shepherd, guided me as we weaved the many threads of this story. Huzzah!

Lastly, I would like to thank my wife and daughter. Alicia, from the very first time I told you about my idea to write this book, you never said a discouraging word. Instead, you supported me through the entire process and always prioritized giving me the time I needed. Samantha, thank you for your never-ending suggestions and feedback on our morning drives to school. I am excited to see what adventures you make for yourself!

*B*IBLIOGRAPHY

PUBLISHED WORKS

Bolger, Philip. *30-Odd Boats*. Camden, ME: International Marine Publishing Company, 1982.

Burg, B. R. *Sodomy and the Pirate Tradition: English Sea Rovers in the Seventeenth-Century Caribbean*. New York: New York University Press, 1995.

Cervantes, Fernando. *Conquistadores: A New History of Spanish Discovery and Conquest*. New York: Viking, 2021.

Coad, Jonathan. *Support for the Fleet: Architecture and Engineering of the Royal Navy's Bases 1700–1914*. Swindon, UK: English Heritage, 2013.

Cunningham, A. E., ed. *Patrick O'Brian: Critical Essays and a Bibliography*. London: W. W. Norton & Company, 1994.

Dana, Richard Henry. *Two Years Before the Mast: A Personal Narrative of Life at Sea*. San Bernardino, CA: Seven Treasures Publications, 2008.

Grossman, Anne Chotzinoff, and Lisa Grossman Thomas. *Lobscouse & Spotted Dog*. New York: W. W. Norton & Company, 1997.

Hill, Richard. *The Prizes of War: The Naval Prize System in the Napoleonic Wars, 1793–1815*. Stroud, UK: Sutton Publishing Limited, 1998.

Kemble, John Haskell. *The Panama Route, 1848–1869*. Columbia: University of South Carolina Press, 1990.

King, Dean. *Patrick O'Brian: A Life Revealed*. New York: Henry Holt and Company, 2000.

———, with John B. Hattendorf and J. Worth Estes. *A Sea of Words: A Lexicon and Companion to the Complete Seafaring Tales of Patrick O'Brian*. New York: Holt Paperbacks, 2000.

Lavery, Brian. *The Arming and Fitting of English Ships of War, 1600–1815*. London: Conway Maritime Press, 1987.

———, and Geoff Hunt. *The Frigate* Surprise: *The Complete Story of the Ship Made Famous in the Novels of Patrick O'Brian*. New York, W. W. Norton & Company, 2009.

Lees, James. *The Masting and Rigging of English Ships of War, 1625–1860*. London: Conway Maritime Press, 1984.

Macdonald, Janet. *Feeding Nelson's Navy: The True Story of Food at Sea in the Georgian Era*. South Yorkshire, UK: Frontline Books, 2020.

McGregor, Tom. *The Making of* Master & Commander: The Far Side of the World: *The Official Guide to the Major Motion Picture*. New York: W. W. Norton & Company, 2003.

Melville, Herman. *Moby Dick*. Project Gutenberg, 2013.

Miller, David. *The World of Jack Aubrey: Twelve-Pounders, Frigates, Cutlasses, and Insignia of His Majesty's Royal Navy*. London: Salamander Books, 2003.

Newby, Eric. *The Last Grain Race*. London: William Collins, 2014.

O'Brian, Patrick. *Master and Commander*. Philadelphia: J. B. Lippincott & Company, 1969.

———. *Post Captain*. Philadelphia: J. B. Lippincott & Company, 1972.

———. *HMS Surprise*. Philadelphia: J. B. Lippincott & Company, 1973.

———. *The Mauritius Command*. New York: Stein and Day, 1978.

———. *Desolation Island*. New York: Stein and Day, 1979.

———. *The Fortune of War*. New York: W. W. Norton & Company, 1991 (first published 1979).

———. *The Surgeon's Mate*. New York: W. W. Norton & Company, 1991 (1980).

———. *The Ionian Mission*. New York: W. W. Norton & Company, 1992 (1981).

———. *Treason's Harbour*. New York: W. W. Norton & Company, 1992 (1983).

———. *The Far Side of the World*. New York: W. W. Norton & Company, 1992 (1984).

———. *The Reverse of the Medal*. New York: W. W. Norton & Company, 1992 (1986).

———. *The Letter of Marque*. New York: W. W. Norton & Company, 1991 (1988).

———. *The Thirteen-Gun Salute*. New York: W. W. Norton & Company, 1991 (1989).

———. *The Nutmeg of Consolation*. New York: W. W. Norton & Company, 1991.

———. *The Truelove*. New York: W. W. Norton & Company, 1992.

———. *The Wine-Dark Sea*. New York: W. W. Norton & Company, 1993.

———. *The Commodore*. New York: W. W. Norton & Company, 1995.

———. *The Yellow Admiral*. New York: W. W. Norton & Company, 1996.

———. *The Hundred Days*. New York: W. W. Norton & Company, 1998.

———. *Blue at the Mizzen*. New York: W. W. Norton, & Company, 1999.

———. *21: The Final Unfinished Voyage of Jack Aubrey*. New York: W. W. Norton & Company, 2004.

Sinowitz, Michael Leigh. *Patrick O'Brian's Bodies at Sea: Sex, Drugs and the Physical Form in the Aubrey-Maturin Novels*. Jefferson, NC: McFarland & Company, 2014.

Steel, David. *Steel's Elements of Mastmaking, Sailmaking, and Rigging*. New York: Edward W. Sweetman, 1932.

Steinbeck, John. *The Log from the Sea of Cortez*. New York: Penguin Books, 1995.

Taylor, Stephen. *Sons of the Waves: The Common Seaman in the Heroic Age of Sail*. New Haven, CT: Yale University Press, 2021.

Toss, Brion. *The Complete Rigger's Apprentice: Tools and Techniques for Modern and Traditional Rigging*. 2nd ed. New York: McGraw-Hill Education, 2016.

Tougias, Michael J. *A Storm Too Soon: A Remarkable True Survival Story in 80 Foot Seas*. New York: Square Fish, 2016.

Tougias, Michael J., and Douglas A. Campbell. *Rescue of the Bounty: Disaster and Survival in Superstorm Sandy*. New York: Scribner, 2015.

Wilson, Ben. *Empire of the Deep: The Rise and Fall of the British Navy*. London: Weidenfeld & Nicolson, 2014.

OTHER RESOURCES

Bailey, Richard. *A Manual for Sailing Aboard the American Tall Ship* Rose. Bridgeport, CT, 1994.

Harvey, Ralph. *Man of the Waterfront: The Story of Kaye Williams and Captain's Cove*. Self-published, 2012.

Mansfield, Lieutenant Commander Charles. "Modern Piracy: The Impact on Maritime Security." Master's thesis, USMC Command and Staff College, 2008.

Thomas, Aaron. *The Caribbean Journal of a Royal Seaman, 1798–1799*. Special Collections. Otto G. Richter Library, University of Miami.